Preface

This book is for anyone who wants to understand the economic crisis issues of the 1980s and the conflicting economic ideas and theories being offered to explain them. In this book you will see how these crises and conflicting theories have evolved—as a part of the rapid sweep of historical change—and you will gain insight into the far-reaching, basic changes which the 1980s are sure to bring.

There's quite a lot of economics—principles, and theory—in this book, because there *must* be. You can't understand what has been happening throughout history or what is happening in the 1980s without understanding the *economic forces* at work. So as the book explains the evolution of events and ideas it also explains and integrates the economic principles involved.

Even before you begin this rapid trip through time, you need to understand some basic economics. So the first chapter, "Introduction to Basic Economic Concepts and Principles," explains that to you—and does it in such a way that you will have no difficulty understanding. The writing style in that chapter, as throughout this book, reflects my personal convictions:

- that the easier the reading, the more it will be read and the better it will be understood—that the task at hand is tough enough without compounding it by couching the explanations in language unfamiliar to the student;
- that scholarly prose is not an efficient medium for the transmission of deep, basic thoughts to students—there's no idea so deep, no theory so rigorous that it can't be explained in simple English;
- that one of the reasons students don't see the *flow* of history is that they spend so much time memorizing details and stumbling over scholarly vocabulary and syntax.

In short, I believe that learning can be (and whenever possible *should* be) fun. In this book I have tried my best to make it that.

This book has but one purpose: to explain the economic realities of today—the conditions, problems, and ideas—in historical perspective and thereby to provide better awareness and understanding of the present, and insight into the future. There isn't much *historical detail* in this book. The flow of thought moves rapidly from one period to another and from one developer of ideas to another, touching the highlights, gathering the threads and pulling them all together.

The facts of history, once learned, are easily forgotten. But an awareness of the flow of history, once gained, is never lost. All of us can gain this awareness—can learn to see ourselves and our world as a part of this evolutionary sweep through time. I have tried to design this book to enable the reader to gain this awareness.

I would like to acknowledge the significant debt which this book owes to Robert Heilbroner. My ideas about how to conceptualize and synthesize the history of economics and the economic history of the world have been greatly influenced by his *The Worldly Philosophers* and *The Making of Economic Society.* Also, I acknowledge Alvin Toffler, author of *Future Shock,* whose influence on my thinking about the speed and impact of change is evident at various places throughout the book.

My sincerest appreciation to Professors Maryanna Boynton, Ann N. P. Fisher, Warren L. Fisher, Kanji Haitani, Richard K. Hay, Ricky Kirkpatrick, Kenneth M. Parzych, and Charles Spruill, whose careful criticisms and suggestions have resulted in significant improvements; and to Mary Ann Burgess, Lois G. Eggers, Dinah Lanning, and Laura Page whose secretarial skills and cooperation have made the preparation of this book much more pleasant than I had any right to expect.

Elbert V. Bowden

ECONOMIC EVOLUTION

THROUGH the PRINCIPLES...ISSUES...IDEAS LOOKING GLASS of TIME

Elbert V. Bowden

Professor of Economics
Chair of Banking
Appalachian State University

Published by

H06 **SOUTH-WESTERN PUBLISHING CO.**

CINCINNATI   WEST CHICAGO, ILL.   DALLAS   PELHAM MANOR, N.Y.   PALO ALTO, CALIF.

Contents

Book One

THE EVOLUTION OF IDEAS AND EVENTS
FROM ANCIENT TO MODERN TIMES

Part I: The Slow Evolution of Traditional Economic Life—
Ancient Times Through the Middle Ages

Part II: Emergence of New Economic Conditions, Ideas, and
Theories—The Industrial Revolution

Book Two

THE TROUBLED WORLD AND DISAGREEING ECONOMISTS OF MODERN TIMES

Part V: Recent Developments and Current Controversies in Economic Theory

Book One

THE EVOLUTION OF IDEAS AND EVENTS FROM ANCIENT TO MODERN TIMES

Part I: The Slow Evolution of Traditional Economic Life—Ancient Times Through the Middle Ages

Part II: The Emergence of New Economic Conditions, Ideas, and Theories—The Industrial Revolution

Part III: Rapid Changes in Theory and in Society—The Evolution Becomes Explosive (1850s—1920s)

Part IV: The Great Depression and Keynesian Economics (1930s—1940s)

Introduction

The United States and the world have entered the 1980s in a "near crisis" environment. The problems are not entirely economic, but economics plays the dominant role in most of them—even in such crises as the Iranian hostage situation, the Russian invasion of Afghanastan, the Cuban "Boat Lift," and the Cambodian refugee problem. But these attention-getting international crisis issues are not the only crises issues of the early 1980s.

THE WORLD'S ECONOMIC CRISES OF THE 1980s

At home we are faced with serious inflation and serious unemployment—and with the energy crisis which is playing an important role in both of these. The Chrysler Corporation is near bankruptcy, as are a few major banks, and a few of the large cities. Angry taxpayers are fighting for relief while government spending-cuts threaten the anti-poverty programs. Some people fear that the Social Security program is in danger of being unable to meet its commitments. Many people can't afford to buy homes because of the high interest rates—which also have been creating serious problems in the nation's financial markets, and for many financial institutions.

Productivity in the nation's economy has slowed down. This is contributing to inflation and bringing declining standards of living to many people. Foreign producers are now out-producing American industry in many fields and out-selling American products in many markets, both in this country and worldwide. Environmental destruction continues to be a serious problem, while attempts to contain it add to production costs and result in reduced productivity.

There has been a continual worsening of the competitive position of the United States in the world economy. The high price of imported oil together with the high and increasing volume of imported foreign products have contributed to a series of dollar crises in the international money markets.

Among the less developed countries (LDCs) where the great majority of the world's population lives, many of the non-oil-producing ones are facing a near-hopeless situation. In addition to their chronic problem of historically low levels of production and consumption and the problem of exploding population, they are now facing an impossible balance of payments situation. Their meagre receipts from their exports and from foreign aid and all other available sources cannot possibly pay the high price of the oil required to permit their economic development to proceed.

CONFLICTING ECONOMIC IDEAS

In the midst of all these crisis and near-crisis conditions, you might expect the economists of the United States and the world to have analyzed these situations and to be providing clear guidance for remedial action. But nothing could be further from the truth. Disagreement is so widespread among economists that from the outside looking in it must appear to be a situation of total confusion.

Academic economists are in wide disagreement among themselves, as are government economists, Federal Reserve economists, business economists, labor economists, news media economists, and all the others. There is strong disagreement between the monetarist economists and the Keynesian economists—and the radical economists are taking positions against both of them. But that isn't the end of it. There is conflict and disagreement within each group—within each "school of thought"—and from economists whose ideas don't fit neatly into any of the "schools."

WHAT CAN YOU EXPECT TO GAIN FROM THIS BOOK?

This quick glimpse at the economic conditions and conflicting economic ideas of the early 1980s shows a serious and sobering picture. Please don't hope to get from this book the answers about how we're going to solve all these problems. You know that isn't possible. But a thoughtful reading of this book can help you to understand these problems and these conflicting economic ideas. And I believe this book will enable you to see all this turmoil and apparent confusion more clearly as you view the economic issues and ideas of the modern world in historical perspective—as a part of *this moment* in the continuing sweep of historical change.

A BACKWARD GLIMPSE THROUGH TIME

For more than ten thousand centuries people have been roaming around on various parts of the earth. That's right—more than *ten thousand centuries!* All this time these people have been struggling to make it, trying to choose the best ways of using their limited resources to meet their needs, to satisfy their wants, to achieve their objectives—that is, trying to solve their "basic economic problem."

It is only in the fleeting moments of recent history that people have made progress in improving their economic conditions. This recent change, once touched off, turned out to be *explosive.* And you who are lucky (or unlucky?) enough to be living today were born right into the middle of this blast.

Much that will happen during your lifetime will be incomprehensible to you unless you have some awareness and understanding of this explosive change we're all caught up in. In just your short lifetime you have observed rapid changes in so many things—attitudes toward acquiring wealth, toward the environment, toward minority groups; feelings about authority and freedom, about poverty, marriage, sex, education, music, dancing, purpose in life. And you have seen so many new ways of doing things, new productive processes and technology, the computer revolution—so many, many changes! The world of today is already a very different place from the world into which *you* were born.

I don't know if it's possible for a person who has lived only about one-fifth of a century to fully grasp this explosive rate of change—this tidal wave sweeping us, hurtling us on into our unknown future. But I'm going to try to give you an overview of what's been happening. Many things will make a lot more sense to you if you understand the rapid changes which have been and are occurring—changes caused, to a very large extent, by changes in the economic *conditions* and the economic *behavior* of mankind, and by changes in mankind's *philosophies* about economics.

How Rapidly Time Passes!

How quickly the years (even the centuries!) go by. You have not yet lived long enough to observe the passing of very much time, so it may be difficult for you to develop an awareness of how rapidly time passes —especially historical time.

If you are twenty years old you have lived one-fifth of a century— perhaps one-fourth of your lifetime. During the other three-fourths of your life, time will seem to go by much more rapidly than during the first one-fourth. And after the other three-fourths go by, all your time will have passed. You see, a human lifetime really isn't very long. Historically speaking, one lifetime, or even one century, is a very short time. After all, you have already "lived up" a fourth of a lifetime and a fifth of a century!

If you can realize the speed at which time passes you may be able to feel the explosive rate of change in our world of the 1980s. It was only about *two centuries ago* that the United States was established as a nation. That's less than three complete lifetimes. It was *three centuries before that* when Columbus discovered America. But it was *ten centuries before that* when the Roman Empire collapsed, and some *thirty-five centuries before that* when the early civilizations were emerging in Babylonia and the Nile Valley. And before that, for how long had man already been on the earth? *More than ten thousand centuries!*

Explosive Change Is Being Fueled by Economic Factors

Today's explosion isn't entirely an economic explosion. But economic factors are providing much force to the blast. Without the disruptive influence of adventuresome and acquisitive individuals, breaking free, following the market, struggling to enrich themselves and simultaneously enriching future generations—without all this, the explosive thrust of the modern world wouldn't have developed. So if you are going to understand what is happening to you, to your world, now, in your lifetime—if you are going to be able to see the explosion in which you are caught, hurtling along, mostly out of control—if you are to gain any idea of where all this might be going, and why, and how—then you must be able to see and understand the economic forces at work.

It isn't that understanding the economic forces of change will let you see with any certainty where the world is going. It won't. But at least it will help you to understand that you are caught up in a world of explosive change. You will be able to understand a little better what's happening to all of us, and how, and why, and perhaps you'll gain some insight into where it all *might* be going. If you get all that out of reading this little book, then surely your time and thoughts will have been well spent.

Chapter 1: An Introduction to Basic Economic Concepts and Principles*

Soon, this book will begin back in ancient history. Then it will bring you swiftly forward through the changing economic conditions and ideas from one age to another, up to the major problems of the 1980s. But first, before you begin this rapid journey through time, there are some basic economic concepts and principles you will need to understand. Otherwise you won't get the full meaning from the historical sweep of events and ideas that follow.

As you read through the chapters of this book, many more economic concepts and principles will be introduced. But you will understand those as you go along because each is explained as it comes up. Then by the time you arrive at the issues and problems and conflicting economic ideas of the 1980s you will be able to understand. You will be able to see all this current confusion in historical perspective.

THE ECONOMIC PROBLEM

The economic problem is the problem of *having to decide how to use the available things.* How does an individual or a family unit—or even an entire society—decide which ways to use the things they have? Of course they would like to use the things available so as to come out "best."

Every family and society would like to have enough food and clothing and shelter to take care of its people. Then, after these basic needs are satisfied there are all kinds of other things they would like to have —better food, better clothing, better housing, better transportation, more opportunities for music and the arts and recreation, and lots of other things—including more leisure time to enjoy. The problem of deciding—of choosing among all of these conflicting objectives—that's the "economic problem."

---

*If you have already learned basic economic principles, unless you feel the need for a quick review you may skip this chapter and go immediately to the next.

Scarcity

The "economic problem" of choosing among alternatives is basic to every individual, family, and society. It is forced upon all of us by the natural condition of *scarcity*. Scarcity means that the things available to work with are *limited*. We always have (and probably always will have) less things available to work with than we would like to have.

Throughout history, in most societies there have always been poor and hungry people. This has resulted from the basic fact of scarcity—not as much as we would like to have of resources to work with. It has resulted also from the inefficient, primitive methods with which the available resources were used.

In the modern world, great advances in production technology have made it possible to get a lot more output from our available (scarce) resources. But from ancient times all the way up to recent centuries, production methods remained very primitive. For many centuries there weren't any important technological breakthroughs. But even in the most advanced nations of the modern world, scarcity still exists everywhere. Almost everyone would like to have more and better things and more leisure time to enjoy them.

The Economic Problem Deals with Scarcity

The economic problem is the problem of dealing with scarcity. It's the problem of deciding, given the scarcities of the things we have, exactly how each of the available resources (including natural, human, and capital resources) will be used.

Opportunity Cost

The idea of "opportunity cost" is that "you can't have your cake and eat it too." Opportunity cost results from the basic fact of *scarcity*. It applies to every individual, every family, and every society. The availability of things is always limited. So when you want to use something for one purpose, that means you can't use that same thing for some other purpose.

Each time you choose to use an acre of land to produce wheat, then you give up the opportunity to use that land to produce corn. So the "opportunity cost" of the *wheat* you get, is the *corn* you must give up. When my daughter spends her allowance on candy bars she gives up the opportunity to go to a movie. So to her, the opportunity cost of the candy bars, is the movie. When any society decides to increase its output of one thing (say, military hardware), then it must give up something else which it also wanted (say, better highways, or schools, or social security programs).

The concept of opportunity cost provides a helpful way of looking at and understanding the difficulties involved in making the economic choices.

The Marginal Concept

Economists use the term "marginal" to refer to *small adjustments* which individuals, businesses, and societies make as they are trying to "fine tune" their resource choices, seeking to arrive at their "optimum position" of (for the consumer) maximum satisfaction, or (for the producer) maximum profit, or (for the society) maximum "social good"— however the society may choose to define that.

The idea of a "marginal" adjustment is that a small change is made in the way in which resources are allocated. Then you ask "Is that better than before?" If the answer is yes, then you have moved closer to the "optimum" which you are seeking. Each individual, business, and society is constantly making "marginal adjustments" as they attempt to "optimize."

The marginal concept is very important in economics because it provides a way of describing and analyzing the process by which "optimization" is achieved.

THE THREE BASIC ECONOMIC QUESTIONS

As the society works out its "economic problem" there are three basic questions that must be answered:

1. Which products (and how much of each) will be produced? How much food? clothing? shelter? and which kinds of each? And how much of various other things? transportation? education? arts and recreation? etc.? etc.? This is the *output* question: "What to produce?"
2. Which resources (natural resources, work-time inputs, tools, etc.?) will be used in the production of each product? And how will the production be organized? Much labor on each small piece of land? Or much land for each worker to till? Many tools of the best-known kinds? Or only a few of the most primitive tools? Will the corn rows be planted one foot apart? Or three feet apart? This is the *input* question: "How will the products be produced?"
3. Which members of the society will get a share (and how big a share) of the output? That is, how will the output which is produced, be distributed (shared) among the members of the soci-

ety? Will everyone receive an equal share regardless of age, sex, health, strength, "noble birth," political affiliation, or whatever? Or will more of the output go to the "nobles"?—or perhaps to the ones who "need" more?—or to the ones who *produce* more? This is the *distribution* question: "How do we divide up the output among the people?"

All three of these questions somehow must be answered in every society. This has always been true. It probably always will be true. Certainly it will be true as long as *scarcity* exists—as long as people desire more and better things than they have. So the questions must be answered. But how?

THE THREE WAYS TO ANSWER THE BASIC ECONOMIC QUESTIONS.

There are three ways—and *only* three ways, or "processes" which can be used—to answer the three basic economic questions and thereby solve the "economic problem" for the society. This is true for every society—ancient or modern, primitive or advanced. The three ways or "processes" are:

The "Social Process" of "Tradition"

Tradition can answer all three of the questions. This means that all three questions can be answered in the "traditional" way—all the answers are the same as they always have been in the past. The people produce the same products, use the same kinds of resource inputs and production techniques, and then share the outputs among themselves in the same way that their parents, grandparents, and all their other ancestors did before them for as far back as anyone can remember.

Tradition played the most important role in solving the economic problem in ancient times and, in fact, throughout most of history. It still plays a very important role in some of the less developed countries of the world. Its influence still can be seen even in modern society in such things as the economic relationships among family members, and (sometimes) job discrimination against women.

The "Political Process" of "Command"

The power of *government* can be used to decide the answers to the three basic economic questions. Government can decide which products will be produced, which inputs and production techniques will be used, and how much of the output each person will get.

As you read the following chapters you will see that *command* has played an important role in solving the economic problem in various societies from time to time throughout history. In the modern world there are several major nations in which command plays the most important role. That's true of the USSR, the People's Republic of China, and of several other nations.

Even in the "capitalist" countries such as the United States, the political process makes many of the production and distribution choices. You can see it in the development of highways and education, in the welfare and social security programs, in the armed forces, in urban renewal, and in many other government programs, federal, state, and local.

The "Market Process" and the "Price Mechanism"

The idea of the "market process" and the "price mechanism" is that people produce things, not because that's what their ancestors did and not because the government directs them to do so, but because they think they can *sell* what they produce and *earn income.*

When the market process is in charge of working out the choices, people produce things for "the market." Whatever people are demanding most and are willing to pay the highest prices for, those are the things which producers will produce. That solves the "output" question for the society automatically without anyone having to "decide."

The "input" question is also solved automatically by the market process and the "price mechanism." Every producer will carefully conserve those inputs which are most scarce and therefore most valuable— the ones that have the highest prices. Producers will always try to use the most plentiful, lowest-priced inputs and the lowest-cost production techniques. That's how they can earn the most *income,* or *profit.*

So when the market process is answering the basic questions, each producer responds to *prices* and tries to produce the most demanded (highest priced) things and to produce them using the most plentiful (lowest priced) inputs and the most efficient production techniques.

The third basic question also is answered automatically. The people who produce the most valuable, most demanded things and do it most efficiently will earn the most income. With their income they "claim their share" of the society's output. This is called the "productivity principle of distribution"—the "distributive share" which each person receives is determined by the value of what that person produces. The more valuable the *productive contribution* the greater the income and the greater the "distributive share" of the output received.

The "productivity principle of distribution" didn't have very much influence in the traditional societies of ancient times. Each person's production was meant to be shared with others. The political process of command sometimes used the productivity principle. But mostly governments in those days stimulated people to produce by the threat of punishment—not by the promise of "rewards for productivity."

In the advanced non-Communist economies of the modern world the "productivity principle" plays an important role in determining each person's income and "distributive share" of the society's output. It also plays the important role of stimulating people to be more productive—to try to "work to get ahead." Even the "command" economics these days (the USSR, the People's Republic of China and others) make some use of the productivity principle because they find it to be an effective method for stimulating people to produce more.

THE POWERFUL PRICE MECHANISM

The market process works through the "price mechanism." The price mechanism works automatically, responding to changes in demand and supply. It encourages the production and discourages the consumption of the higher-priced goods, and it discourages the production and encourages the consumption of the lower-priced goods.

When people for whatever reason begin demanding *more* of something, that causes *shortages* in that market and the price is forced up. The higher price stimulates more production of this item and attracts new producers to enter this market. But when people begin demanding *less* of something, *surpluses* develop and the price is forced down. The lower price discourages the production of that item and producers shift into the production of something else—something that brings them more income.

Businesses, and workers too, shift from producing one thing to another, from one place to another, from one kind of production technique to another, all in response to the "signals" of the price mechanism. Why? Because that's how they can increase their incomes and their "distributive shares" of the output.

The price mechanism exerts a powerful, almost irresistible force. And it works automatically, almost like magic. When the price of something goes up very much, if you will wait awhile, you almost always will see more of this item being produced and less of it being consumed. Whenever the price of an item goes down very much, if you wait awhile you almost always will see more of this item being consumed, and less of it being produced. If the price of something goes low enough, eventually none of it will be produced. The price won't cover the cost. If the price goes high enough, none of it will be consumed.

When you get to the chapter on the industrial revolution you'll see the great power and influence of the price mechanism in directing and influencing the economic choices.

FACTORS OF PRODUCTION

The *inputs* which are used to produce outputs, are called "factors of production." There are hundreds of different factors of production, of course. But for convenience and to simplify economic analysis, economists usually group these factors under three different headings: land, labor, and capital.

Land. All natural resources—the "free gifts of nature"—are grouped together and called "land."

Labor. All human effort, whether it be physical effort or mental effort, highly skilled effort or unskilled effort, is grouped together and called "labor."

Capital. All tools, equipment, factories, and everything else which has *already been produced,* and which is to be used *to assist in further production,* are grouped together and called "capital."

Be careful to note that as economists use the term "capital" it does not mean "money." It means the physical things which have been produced and are going to be used in further production. Much of the process of economic growth consists of building more and better *capital.* But economic growth also results from improving the abilities and skills of the society's *labor.* Improving the ability and skills of the labor force is sometimes referred to by economists as "building human capital."

Capitalist. The reason the owners of big businesses are called "capitalists" is because they are the ones who own most of the capital—the buildings and machines and equipment and other things—needed in the production process. And the reason some economic systems are referred to as "capitalist systems" is to emphasize the importance of "the capitalist" in the functioning of these economic systems.

The Entrepreneur. Economists sometimes define the *entrepreneur* as a fourth factor of production, separate from the other three. Ideally, the "entrepreneur" is the enterprising person who sees the opportunity to bring together some capital, labor, and land and produce a product which people will buy. The entrepreneur who succeeds in producing products which are in high demand and who produces the products efficiently (at low cost) will make a lot of profit—and then will reinvest the profit in more capital and generate even more profit. The entrepreneur is responsible for increasing the productivity and growth of the economy.

In a "market-process-oriented" economic system, it is necessary for the "entrepreneurial function" to be performed. Otherwise the economy will not keep going, and growing. In the modern world, this function is performed mostly by big business organizations, not by one individual—an "entrepreneur." But as you will see in the following chapters, during the period of the industrial revolution and the rapid industrialization which occurred between the mid 1700s and the early 1900s, the individual entrepreneur played a vital role.

ECONOMIC SYSTEM

The term "economic system" is used to refer to the kind of arrangement which exists in a society for solving the "economic problem"—for working out the answers to the three basic economic questions: What to produce, What inputs and production techniques to use, and How to distribute (share) the output among the people.

In all economic systems in the world today there is some mixture of all three processes—social, political, and market—for working out the answers to these questions. In all present-day economic systems, some of the economic choices are made in each of the three ways: some by tradition, some by command, and some by the price mechanism. But the *importance* of the role which each of these decision-making processes plays differs greatly from one economic system to another.

In some systems, tradition is most important. We see this in some of the less developed countries. In some other systems, *command* is most important. We see this in the so-called "Communist" countries. And in still other systems—including those of the United States, Canada, Western Europe, Japan, Australia, and several others—we see the *price mechanism* as most important. But in all economic systems, all three processes are at work to some extent. As you read through the following chapters you will find that throughout most of history, the social process of *tradition* has been most important in most places, most of the time.

Capitalism

Capitalism is a form of economic system in which the market process and the price mechanism are left free to work out the answers to the three basic economic questions. "Pure capitalism" would operate with no government interference, and with no restrictions from "tradition."

When the people are free to follow the influences of the price mechanism, to produce whatever they think will be profitable, to produce it in the ways they think will be most efficient, and to earn and keep as much income or profit as they can—that's "capitalism." It is a system of "laissez-faire" (hands-off by government) and competition, where each person has an equal right to get into any market, to produce anything which looks profitable, to out-sell and under-sell the other producers—and "let the devil take the hindmost."

In a system of "pure capitalism" the people who are highly productive get high incomes; the people who do not produce anything do not get any incomes at all. This kind of harsh, dog-eat-dog, unrestricted capitalism doesn't exist anywhere in the world today. But a somewhat modified and tempered version of capitalism does exist in the United States, in the countries of Western Europe and Japan, and in several other places in the world.

MARKET STRUCTURE AND PURE COMPETITION

Pure competition is a kind of "market structure" in which there are many buyers and many sellers of the product. Pure competition means no seller or buyer has any "monopoly power." Because of the large number of buyers and sellers for the product, no buyer or seller can do anything but accept the price as it exists in the market.

In a market structure of pure competition, the only time the price would go up is when many buyers are all trying to buy more, or many sellers are all offering less of the product for sale. Any *one* of the many buyers could buy two or three times as much and it wouldn't influence the price. Any *one* seller could stop producing and selling this product altogether, and it wouldn't influence the price.

In markets of "pure competition" the price is set by the "impersonal forces" of demand and supply. This kind of market structure (or something which results in approximately the same conditions) is necessary for the "pure market forces" to work as they are described in the "pure market model" developed by some of the economists you will be reading about in this book. You will find out that one of the important reasons for disagreement among economists in modern times stems from their basic disagreement about the extent to which modern-world economic systems work the way a market system of "pure competition" would. It's a question of whether or not the monopoly power (the lack of pure competition) which exists in most real-world markets does (or does not) prevent real-world economic systems from working more or less as the "pure competition model" specifies.

ECONOMIC PROGRESS, OR ECONOMIC GROWTH

Economic growth is the process which results in *increasing output* per person. With economic growth, the average worker produces more, so in the end there is *more total output* to be shared among the members of the society. As economic growth proceeds, it softens some of the harshness of "opportunity cost"—the idea that when you get more of one thing, that "costs you" the opportunity of having more of something else.

With economic growth, a society can to some extent lessen the limitations imposed by opportunity cost. Over time, if better techniques of production can be introduced, or if more and better agricultural land can be discovered and/or developed, then that society will be able to have more of some things without having to give up something else. That's the great appeal of "economic progress" or "economic growth."

Economic growth comes about mostly from the discovery of better techniques of production, and the development of more and better tools and machines to work with. With more and better equipment, each worker can produce more output per day, week, or year.

But here's the problem with trying to generate economic growth. When everybody is already busy producing the food needed to keep the people from starving, who has the time to do what's necessary to bring economic growth? Economic growth requires that energies and resources be directed toward developing new techniques, and building tools, clearing land, and doing other things that will increase worker productivity in the future. Who is going to do this?

The Dilemma: Present Consumption? or Future Growth?

The energies and resources which are aimed toward increasing *future production* are not adding any output for *present consumption.* If the society can only produce enough to just barely get by on, what happens when some of its energies and resources are shifted out of food production and directed toward economic growth? You know what happens. The output of food goes down and some of the people starve! That's the opportunity cost of economic growth. But if everything currently produced is aimed toward current consumption, then there is no economic progress—no economic growth.

So the society faces a dilemma. If resources are diverted from consumption and aimed toward increasing *future* output, then some people will go hungry. And in a society where *tradition* locks everyone into their "proper role" in the production-distribution circle, there isn't much chance for anyone to break loose and strike out for economic progress. As you read the following chapters you will be able to understand why so little economic progress occurred for so many, many centuries.

The Definition(s) of Economics

Now that you understand some of the most basic concepts and principles of economics, you know what economics is all about. So now you're ready for a definition. Economics can be defined in various ways. One definition would be: "Economics is the study of how people—individuals, families, businesses, organizations, and societies—work out their economic choices—how they 'solve' their 'economic problem.'" Or economics can be defined as: "How people (and businesses, societies, etc.) choose (decide) about how to use the things they have." Another definition of economics would be: "Economics is concerned with how people (and businesses, societies, etc.) use the things they have to try to get the most of what they want."

You can see that all of these definitions are saying the same thing. Economics is concerned with facing the natural condition of *scarcity,* and choosing which ways to use the available things. It always must deal with the inescapable reality of *opportunity cost.* Every choice to have more of one thing involves the loss of the opportunity to have more of something else. That's *economics.*

Political Economy

The term "political economy" refers to working out the solution to the "economic problem"—deciding the answers to the three basic economic questions—just as does the term "economics." But the term political economy assumes that *government* will be playing an important role in influencing those choices.

If you want to understand how an economic system can work "on its own," through the operation of the market process and the price mechanism, then you study "economics." But if you want to investigate the operation of an economic system in which government policies are playing an important role in influencing the operation of the economy —trying to re-aim and redirect the economic activities and choices of the people—then you study "political economy."

In the late medieval period and in the early years of the industrial revolution, most economic writers wrote books on "political economy."

During that period, government was exerting strong influences on the operation of the economy. A good bit of the emphasis of these early "political economy" books was aimed toward explaining how government policies were interfering with the efficient operation of the economy—holding down production and slowing economic progress in the nation.

Since the late 1800s, most books in the field of economics have been called "economics"—not "political economy." The emphasis of these more recent books has been on explaining how an economic system operates on its own, directed by the forces of the *market process* and the *price mechanism.*

Microeconomics

Microeconomics is that part of the study of economics which is concerned with most of the concepts and principles you have been reading about so far in this chapter. Microeconomics is concerned with how "the economic problem" is solved—with how the three basic economic questions are answered. It is concerned with making *choices* about what to do with the available resources, given the natural condition of *scarcity.*

Microeconomics is concerned with how these questions are answered by the individual, the business, and the total society. Microeconomics is the study of opportunity cost, of substitution, of choosing this or that, of trade-offs, of "deciding (among all of the possible alternatives) which ways to use the available resources." The definitions of *economics* which you read a few minutes ago are really definitions of "microeconomics."

Macroeconomics

Macroeconomics is a term which has come into use since the Great Depression of the 1930s. *Macroeconomics* is that part of economics which is concerned with understanding the *speed,* or *rate* at which the entire economy will run. It is concerned with *totals:* the total level of production, output, employment, consumer spending, investment spending, government spending, national income, etc.

If you are studying *macroeconomics* you are trying to understand what causes the economy to speed up and slow down—what causes recessions or depressions, and inflation. The term "macroeconomics" has arisen in connection with "Keynesian economics" which was introduced by John Maynard Keynes during the depression of the 1930s.

As you will be finding out in this book, Keynes introduced some new ways of looking *directly* at the question: "What determines the rate at which the economy will run?" As this "new approach" became integrated into the study of economics, it became necessary to have terms to distinguish between this kind of economics, and the other economic theories which had traditionally been "economics." So that's why we now talk about "microeconomics" and "macroeconomics." In this book you will find out how these developments occurred.

Part I: The Slow Evolution of Traditional Economic Life— Ancient Times Through the Middle Ages

*After Thousands of Centuries of
Very Little Change, Economic
Forces Suddenly Trigger an
Explosion and Everyone is Caught
in the Force of the Blast*

Chapter 2: From Ancient Times to the Middle Ages

People have been on earth for more than *ten thousand centuries.* But it was only about fifty centuries ago that "civilizations" began to emerge.

THE CRADLES OF CIVILIZATION

Historians talk about the "cradles of civilization": Mesopotamia, Babylonia, the Nile Valley—all places you have heard about many times. In Asia there were still other early civilizations, some even older and perhaps more advanced than those of the Middle East. In all these places, people always faced their economic problem—how to deal with scarcity, how to choose what to do with the limited things they had: What to use? And what to save? What to make? And who will get how much of what?

The Role of "Tradition," and "Command"

Each of the ancient societies had to have some kind of economic system—some way of getting the choices made and the decisions carried out. And what system? Like all economic systems, some mixture of social, political, and market forces or processes. But the choices in the ancient societies were made and carried out mostly by the social force of *tradition,* as influenced and altered in various ways from time to time by the political force of *command.*

Some trade existed, but very little. Trade had almost no influence on the life patterns of the people. Usually, people produced for themselves and shared with their families and leaders. Sometimes the force of command by the ruler—sheik or pharoah or some such—would turn people into slaves and exert a powerful influence on the society's economic choices. (Certainly the pyramids were not built in response to the free wishes of the common people!)

ANCIENT GREECE AND ROME

From the cradles of civilization we can leap forward about twenty-five centuries to the early days of Greece and Rome—at about the time of Confucius and Buddha in Asia, about five centuries before the birth of Christ. And what do we find that was different? Actually, not very much. There had been a good bit of social and political evolution. Specialization and trade were somewhat more developed. People had learned how to do and make a lot more things. But the economic systems were still mostly tradition-bound.

"Tradition" Was in Control

Workers, craftsmen, noblemen, slaves, all followed in the footsteps of their parents—the traditional way. Except when conquerors would come in, take rule, and use the force of command to make changes, the economic choices of production and distribution followed the same traditional patterns, century after century.

Early Civilizations in the Far East

This same pattern of rule by tradition was followed in the early civilizations of India, China and Japan. Ruling families came and went, kingdoms and empires waxed and waned, but customs and traditions controlled most aspects of people's lives. Economic allocations were determined by the customs of society—that is, by the social system. By tradition.

In the twenty-five centuries between the early civilizations and the rise of the Greek and Roman city-states, the economic systems—the ways of solving the basic economic problem, making the economic choices—really didn't change much. Some changes would occur in one place or another from time to time. But the movement was mostly back and forth. There wasn't much continuous progress—no step-by-step evolution of new and better ways of solving the society's economic problem; no cumulative chain reaction of economic progress from one period to the next.

The Role of "Command"

From time to time, political control over the economy would be more powerful in one place or another. But as time passed, the rulers (the "government") would change, government directives would be relaxed, and tradition again would take over. Throughout these many centuries the economic choices generally reflected the traditions of the society, but as modified by the waxing and waning of political controls.

Under the early Greek and Roman civilizations there was some economic (as well as social and political) progress. Some markets were developing and expanding. The market forces of demand, supply, and price were having some influence on the production and distribution choices of the society—but still only very little. Almost all of the choices were either preordained by tradition or ordered by command.

The same was true of the civilizations of the Far East. Societies were essentially agrarian; most people were peasants, earning their subsistence from the land. Many members of the "labor force" were slaves, serving and carrying out the economic choices of their rich and powerful masters; many were soldiers, serving and carrying out the economic choices of those who held the political powers of the state.

EARLY IDEAS ON ECONOMICS

As you know, during the days of ancient Greece and Rome, philosophers were trying to understand and explain things. The most outstanding of them was Aristotle. While Aristotle was becoming "the father" of almost every science—astronomy, chemistry, psychology, biology, medicine, geology, and others—economics did not escape his scrutiny. He expressed some very definite thoughts about economics. Would you believe that Aristotle's ideas about economics set the tenor of Western economic thought for the next *ten centuries?* That's a fact.

Aristotle's Economic Philosophy

Aristotle's economic philosophy was ideal for maintaining stability and harmony and social justice in a tradition-bound society. In such societies, flexibility and change would be disruptive and socially undesirable. But for a society which has broken the bonds of tradition—a society which is responding to the powerful forces of the market—Aristotle's economic teachings would not fit. Yet even today we find fragments of Aristotle's economic thought lingering in the minds of many people in the world. So let's take a minute to look at some of the things he said.

Aristotle considered exchange, and borrowing and lending money to be unproductive activities. Each family should produce what it needs for itself. A person who happens to have a surplus may exchange it or sell it to someone else for a "just" price. But it isn't good for one person to buy something with the idea of selling it to someone else at a profit. The middleman-trader is detrimental to the society because the middleman must be buying for *less* than the "just price" or selling for *more* than the "just price," (or both), otherwise there would be no profit on the deal! So the middleman is a parasite on the society who gains riches at the expense of others. So said Aristotle.

Even worse than the middleman-traders, according to Aristotle, were those who would lend money and charge interest. Interest is *usury* —an unjust charge. Since people can't actually make things with money (as they can with machines and raw materials, etc.) money is not productive. Therefore anyone who lends money should not expect to get back any more than the amount lent.

Early Religious Writings on Economics

Aristotle was not the first to write on economics. There were many before him. Economic thoughts have been included in the writings of most philosophers from the very beginning. The Old Testament and New Testament of the Bible contain much economics, as do the writings of religions other than Christianity. Every religion has been concerned with the issues of the right and wrong economic behavior, and with social choices.

The economic question, "How to do the best for our people with the limited things available," has been an important question for every religion. The Bible, the Talmud, the Koran, and other sacred scriptures and religious writings contain much economic thought. The concepts of right and wrong in economic matters—of sharing, of "just price," of work and leisure—have been discussed by religious and moral philosophers as far back as recorded history can take us (and very likely even before that).

One Person's Gain Is Another's Loss

The basic ideas of Aristotelian economic thought were reflected in the economic philosophies of early Christianity. The most outstanding economic writer among the many medieval Christian philosophers was St. Thomas Aquinas. His writings on economics emphasize the idea of "just price" and go into great detail on the injustices of lending money for interest, and of trading for profit. The concepts of trading, working to get ahead, acquiring material wealth—all the conditions essential for the market process to operate and to stimulate economic growth—were condemned by the medieval Christian writers.

It was not considered moral to acquire things and to try to enrich one's self. Underlying this anti-acquisitive attitude was the idea that there was only so much of wealth and things around. Any person who worked to acquire more would be forcing others to get by with less. That was bad. A good, moral person would practice "personal denial"— would be charitable and give things to others.

There Was No Escape from Poverty

It wasn't that the religious (and other) philosophers wanted everybody to be poor and miserable. Not at all! The hard economic facts of life required that almost all of the people be poor almost all of the time, anyway. So, better to be purposefully poor and feel good about it than to be accidentally poor and be miserable! Also, consider this: Poor people (and poor families and poor tribes) never get murdered for their possessions! And there was a lot of that going on in those days.

The highest form of "economic morality" was to live in poverty, consuming very little and leaving almost everything for others. The idea of economic growth—of people working out ways to become more productive; of each person producing more and thereby achieving personal enrichment and also helping to enrich the society—that idea wouldn't be understood and accepted until many centuries later. In the traditional societies and in some religions it still is not accepted, even in the world of the 1980s.

THE ROMAN EMPIRE

The early civilizations of Greece and Rome began about five centuries before the time of Christ and continued until the Roman Empire took over at about the time of Christ. The Roman Empire continued for about five centuries after Christ. Under the Roman Empire the political force of command took control over many of the economic choices. The government decided about the uses of many resources and about the activities of many people. Many of the social forces of tradition were pushed aside.

Great changes were made in the organization of economic activity and in the choices as to what was to be produced and how it was to be shared among the people. As the Romans spread out over the land, they changed the ways the resources and the energies of the people were used. They redirected and forced increases in productive activities. Using the force of command, they generated increased outputs and held down consumption, created *forced savings* and generated the surpluses needed to support the administrators, the soldiers, and the idle rich, and also to make "investments"—in military equipment, roads, buildings, and whatever else those who held the political power wanted the "savings" to be invested in.

COMMAND GENERATED PROGRESS

Here's an interesting point: Throughout all of ancient and medieval history and until capitalism emerged (only recently), economic progress —savings going into investment and bringing economic growth—rarely occurred except under the impetus of command. In the ancient societies there always seems to have been an elite group running things, living high, and ordering other people around. And always lots of slaves. Most of what we call the advance of civilization—in the arts, in knowledge and philosophy, in buildings, roads, port facilities—all seem to have been brought about by government command, exercised by one or a few forceful rulers.

Traditional systems are designed for survival. Because they seek stability they impede change. So until the force of the market process (only recently) began to wield its influence, progress had to depend on the redirecting influences of powerful political forces. People had to be ordered around. Could it have been otherwise? As long as people follow the social process of tradition, the society is maintained—but that's all. The society remains stationary. All the output is consumed; no economic growth occurs.

Through the force of command the people can be made to produce more and consume less. Surpluses can be generated and economic progress can result. That's the way it happened in the early civilizations, and in the Roman Empire. It is happening that way in several places in the world even today.

Chapter 3: The Medieval Period

During the fifth century A.D., the Roman Empire came to an end. The administrative ties—the communications and controls which held all the outlying units of the empire together—weakened and ultimately dissolved. Each of the outlying regions was left free to go its own way. In some localities Germanic peoples took over control from the Romans. But eventually, in most localities the people were just left alone to go their own way. Without the controls, laws, and productive activities directed (commanded) by the Romans, each little locality slipped back to a traditional, subsistence economic system.

THE EMERGENCE OF FEUDALISM

Little separate, independent socio-economic-political units emerged throughout Europe. As time passed, the ties that held together the larger of the little units dissolved. The result: more and more smaller and smaller units. Different activities and patterns of behavior emerged in different places. In most places there was a general breakdown of law. People had to figure out their own ways of protecting themselves. There was almost no trade or commerce. Throughout most of Western Europe there evolved the economic, social, and political arrangement we call *feudalism.*

You have already heard many times about feudalism. It took a variety of forms. You know that it was a kind of "mutual responsibility" arrangement. The "lord of the manor" was supposed to protect the people from wandering bands of thieves and plunderers. In exchange, the people had to work to support the manor. The serfs worked the land to produce food and made the implements and other things needed to keep the little economy going. Each person had a job to do and each was allowed a meager share of the output.

The serfs were not exactly slaves. But they weren't free to leave, and they were bound to do the bidding of their lord. Still, customs and traditions placed some limits on the lord's power to run the lives of his serfs. For example, serfs weren't usually bought and sold, and usually they were allowed some land rights and some chance to produce things for themselves. The serfs lived much better on some manors than on others, of course. It depended a lot on the attitude and the wisdom of the one who held the political power—the lord of the manor.

This variety of feudalistic economic-social-political arrangements evolved during the centuries after the end of the Roman Empire and continued to exist for about *ten centuries*—up to about the time Columbus discovered America. Each century saw some change, but usually not very much. Most of the changes were just back and forth—not cumulative, progressive changes. For many centuries there was very little trade and commerce. Usually the obstacles were too great. Some of the Italian trading cities—Venice and Genoa especially—and some cities in Flanders (the present-day Belgium-Holland area) and some elsewhere managed to engage in some successful ventures. But these were the exceptions.

Eventually as the centuries passed, little by little, *cumulative, progressive* change did begin to occur. Very slowly at first, then more rapidly, some chain reactions began to get started. And these changes began to set the stage for the destruction of the stable, tradition-bound feudal way of life. But before going into that you need to know more about the economics of medieval times.

What Kind of Economic System Is Feudalism?

Suppose someone asked you what kind of economic system existed in Western Europe during this period of ten centuries—between the time that Rome fell to pieces and the time that Columbus discovered America. What would you say?

First you would admit that there was much diversity from one place to another and from one time to another. Then you would be quite safe in saying that the thousand-year period was characterized by the existence of many small, tradition-bound socio-political-economic units.

As the centuries passed, feudalism became the dominant form of these tradition-bound units. Then as the ten-century period neared its end, feudalism began to crumble. Without knowing it, the world began preparing itself for the emergence of modern times.

Feudalism really isn't an economic system. It's a situation in which there isn't any "nationwide" economic system. There isn't any "nation," really—just a lot of little independent units (little socio-political-economic systems), each operating almost entirely on its own.

All these little political-economic systems were scattered over the face of the British Isles and Western Europe. Some were much larger than others, some much more enslaved by ruthless masters than others, some had more ties with the king, or with surrounding feudal estates than others. Each was an individual unit. This was feudalism. It's interesting to note that in much of Asia, especially Japan, similar patterns of feudalism emerged quite independently of what was going on in the Western World.

The Economics of Feudalism

How were the economic choices made on each feudal manor? Tradition was the controlling force, but command was important, too. Almost all of the production and distribution choices were determined by the rules of the society, but as interpreted, enforced, and sometimes modified by the lord of the manor. People were bound to the manor where they were born. They produced the things they were supposed to produce—usually the things their family was supposed to produce—and they received their traditionally established "just shares" of the food and other things.

Some trading was going on, to be sure. People bought, sold, and traded things, but usually tradition established the just price for each transaction. The market process—the driving force of demand—was a very minor, almost negligible influence on the production and distribution patterns in the society.

During this period the Roman Catholic Church was a unifying and stabilizing influence. The teachings of the Church emphasized the importance of continuity and stability and of following the established social, economic, and political traditions. No one was supposed to try to break loose, to get ahead. Anyone who did this would only be hurting others. This life was to be accepted. Preparing for the next life was what really mattered.

Somehow, as the centuries passed, change began to creep in. The system began to erode. Ultimately the stage was set for the destruction of this stable socio-economic-political arrangement which had lasted for so many centuries. How easily it might have lasted for many more centuries! But it didn't.

Except for the cumulative series of events which burst the dike and brought the tidal wave of change, we might all now be living on little feudal estates. Maybe I would be your lord—or maybe you, mine! But under the pressure of change, feudalism began crumbling—slowly eroding away. Finally it was swept away. What happened? What touched off the chain reaction—the cumulative series of events which were to destroy the feudal way of life and bring the end to this stable, tradition-bound world of Feudalism?

THE SLOW DEATH OF FEUDALISM

Just as feudalism didn't spring up suddenly, it didn't disappear suddenly. The erosive influences were grinding away at it for several centuries. Near the end, the pace of change was quickening. Various forces for change were reenforcing each other. The chain reaction was beginning. Change was in the wind. Here are some highlights of what happened.

The Crusades

One of the earliest and most continual erosive influences was the Crusades. The Crusades—the "holy wars"—started at the end of the eleventh century and continued, off and on, until about the time Columbus discovered America. (That's *four centuries*—twice as long as the United States has existed as a nation!) The Crusades were going on when Genghis Khan and Kublai Khan were dashing about with their armies, conquering most of Asia, and when Marco Polo made his famous 25-year-long trip to China.

The Crusades had an important "how you gonna keep 'em down on the farm after they've seen Paree" effect. Just as some do now, people then found it easy to live at bare subsistence and to follow custom and tradition if they didn't know of any other kind of life. But once people saw and experienced new and different, more and better things, they were no longer satisfied with things as they were.

Aspirations and feudalism didn't mix. Just as today, aspirations and the traditional societies don't mix. I suppose if there is any one key to the end of feudalism it would be aspirations—the desire for more and better things, and perhaps for more freedom—and the awareness that such things may be possible.

Today, some economists refer to "the revolution of rising expectations" among the people in the less-developed countries. Aspirations are bringing the rapid destruction of these stable, tradition-bound (semifeudalistic) societies today, right before our eyes! Even in such advanced nations as the United States, Canada, and those of Western Europe, the urban poor and the people in the depressed rural regions refuse to placidly accept their fate. When people see or hear about better conditions, they *want* better conditions.

Fairs, Traveling Merchants, Growing Cities

The Crusades were not the only window to the outside world. There were fairs and traveling merchants. Even cities were beginning to grow up in several places in the British Isles and on the continent—hundreds of small but slowly growing settlements. The cities grew as centers for specialized production and for trade. Some of the adventuresome people were breaking loose from the feudal manors and were going to the towns or traveling with the merchants. Some went to work on ships as trade between the port cities expanded. More and more people were breaking their feudal ties.

Countries Were Emerging

As the Middle Ages wore on, nation-states (countries, or kingdoms) were growing, becoming more powerful. Most of the feudal manors had been under the jurisdiction of some king all along, but these kingdoms existed in name only. Also, the Byzantine Empire of the Eastern Mediterranean and the Holy Roman Empire of Western Europe had claimed jurisdiction over large areas for many centuries. But so far as the day-to-day matters of living were concerned, these "empires" usually had little or no influence.

In the later centuries of the medieval period, some of the kings began to develop the power to maintain law and protect the people throughout their kingdoms. Travel became safer so trade became easier. Cities could more easily flourish and grow. Business could be conducted more regularly, more dependably, more safely.

Exploration and World Trade

As the nation-states became stronger and travel increased and cities grew, there were more fairs, more traveling merchants, more shipping and trade. Markets were developing here and there. There were many voyages of exploration. Gold and silver were becoming more plentiful and more widely used as money. These new developments were providing more opportunities for people to escape from their feudal bonds, and more and more of them did.

Enclosures of Common Land

While some of the people were trying to sneak away from the feudal manors, others were being pushed off the land. Traditionally, much of the land (especially in Britain) had been available for common use. This common land was important to many serfs for their subsistence. But as the population expanded, more land was enclosed—the land was fenced in by the lords; the common users were fenced off.

The enclosures didn't make the common users happy. Some fences were torn down from time to time, but the enclosures continued. The common land was becoming private property, with fences and "no tres-passing" signs. Remember what it was like in the "Old West" when the homesteaders came and started fencing in the open range? That's the kind of thing that was happening from time to time and from place to place in late medieval Europe.

The enclosure movement began as far back as the twelfth century and continued (sometimes rapidly, sometimes slowly) for more than seven centuries—through the nineteenth century. As the enclosure movement proceeded, those who had previously used the common lands were forced to move elsewhere. Many of them moved to the towns to seek jobs or some other means of staying alive.

The Increasing Use of Money

With the land enclosures pushing on some of the people and the attractions of the growing towns pulling on others, the towns grew. Trade and money became a part of everyday life for more and more people.

Gold and silver had served as money far back into history. But even in the years when England and the other Western European countries were emerging from feudalism, there were many people who had never seen a gold coin. Then, as feudalism continued to erode, more aspects of life began to be related to money. More people began to produce things *for sale.* The market forces of demand, supply, and price were beginning to direct more of the economic choices of the society.

What we are watching is the slow crumbling of the rigid structure of feudalism and the gradually increasing role of market forces in direct-ing the economic life of society. But the ethics of medieval times didn't approve of letting market forces run things. So what happened? Soon that problem got itself worked out, too. Here's how.

The Protestant Ethic

Remember what the Christian philosopher, St. Thomas Aquinas, had said about not being acquisitive, not producing and trading for profit, about "just price," and about not charging interest (usury) and all that? How can the market forces direct the economic choices unless people are trying to *acquire,* to get ahead by producing something that other people want to buy? The market forces can't work unless people are producing and working to earn more money!

That "don't acquire" philosophy of the Church was really a drag. But then it happened that the opposite philosophy burst forth. The Protestant Reformation occurred just in time to justify the emerging market forces. The one person most responsible for this new philosophy was John Calvin. The philosophy was, of course, *Calvinism.* You can find some of the philosophy of Calvinism buried deep in the teachings of most of the Protestant churches.

According to the medieval Catholic Church, anyone who would produce and trade for the purpose of personal enrichment would be doing wrong. But now, suddenly, in the mid-1500s John Calvin offers the world a new economic philosophy—the Protestant Ethic: Work hard. Stay busy. Be thrifty. Save. "The Idle Mind is the Devil's Workshop." Produce a lot and get wealthy. You will produce a lot for yourself, and for your society, too. That will show the world that you are a godly person! (That was quite a switch!)

As Calvin and his followers were spreading the word, the Spanish explorers were over in Mexico and Central and South America relieving the local inhabitants of their gold and silver and bringing it back to Europe—just in case more money might be needed. Somehow the pieces were beginning to fit together. It seems that the market forces of demand, supply, and price are going to get a chance to have their day after all!

THE CUMULATIVE EFFECT OF THE EROSIVE FORCES

The many changes—these erosive forces you have been reading about—were chipping away at the frozen structure of feudal society for more than five centuries. I'm sure that for a long time it wasn't clear to anyone that anything very different was going on. But the worms were in the woodwork. It was just a matter of time.

As the centuries passed, the forces for change began speeding up. By the time of John Calvin and the Spanish Conquistadores, irreparable damage to the old social order had already been done. Many cities had emerged as centers of economic life, with money and trade, and each with its own set of customs and rules—its own ways of doing things.

Life in the emerging cities was distinctly different from the traditional ways of feudal society. City dwellers couldn't be farmers! They had to depend on production and trade for their living.

The slow, steady growth of these urban producing and trading centers resulted in the development of "the city" as a new form of sociopolitical-economic unit—a new kind of little political and economic system. Each city had its own developing customs and traditions. But the newly developing "traditional ways" of the cities were designed *to accept and respond to market forces.* Then, as trade expanded, the cities were ready to play an ever-increasing role in the economic life of the society.

The Pace of Change Speeds Up

In the sixteenth century the pace of change in the Western world was beginning to speed up a little. But in Asia the traditional ways of life continued. No cumulative chain reactions of economic progress were touched off in India, China, or Japan. The peoples of Asia, just as those of Africa and the Americas, were unwittingly waiting to fall under the domination of the progressing, progress-hungry, profit-seeking Westerners.

At first the economic progress of the Western world was slow. Even after America had been discovered, it would be yet another three centuries before the forces of the market process—supply and demand and prices—would really thrust aside the restrictive, rigid forces of tradition and claim control over most of the economic choices of society. Three hundred years still had to pass before the world would be ready for the Industrial Revolution.

During this three-hundred-year interlude between the discovery of America and the beginning of the Industrial Revolution the world was unknowingly preparing itself. Money was becoming more important. The expanding nation-states were trying to increase their national power. They exercised tight controls over economic activities and trade. The economic policies and philosophies which dominated this transitional period are called *mercantilism.* That's what you will be reading about in the next chapter.

Chapter 4: Mercantilism, to the Industrial Revolution

The basic idea of mercantilism was that the government should direct the economy so as to gain more national wealth and power. More national wealth and power was usually thought of as "more gold and silver." Many of the production and distribution choices were made by the political process—by the king and the nobility. The government would (a) stimulate the output of goods which could be exported in exchange for gold, and (b) limit domestic consumption, both of exportable goods and of imported goods. (The people must not be allowed to overeat, or to own many things. Only kings and queens and other nobles should do that!)

Every king knew that if he had enough gold he could hire enough soldiers, buy enough armaments, and build enough ships to be the most powerful king in the world. Then he could send out many explorers and privateers and get back even more gold. Gold was seen as the key to the nation's wealth and power. The economic condition of the average person was not a matter of much concern to those who were making the economic choices for the society under mercantilism.

MERCANTILISM IMPOSED STRICT ECONOMIC CONTROLS

In a word, then, mercantilism was a closely controlled economy, aimed at maximizing exports so as to maximize the inflow of gold. Imports of raw materials were good because these would go into more manufactured goods for export. It was good to import cotton, make shirts and skirts, then export the shirts and skirts to trade for more cotton —and for gold. But imports of consumer goods "for the people to enjoy" (like wheat, to eat) was discouraged. Exporting industries were favored in various ways. Imports were restricted.

The Importance of Gold

Does gold make a nation wealthy? Or powerful? If we're thinking in medieval terms, it does. In the days of the feudal kingdoms, gold was power because with gold you could buy those things necessary to be powerful. But when things are exported in exchange for gold, the people have to make do with less. Obviously. So, from the point of view of the rulers and wealthy merchants of the nation, the nation with the greatest inflow of gold would be gaining the most wealth and power. But in terms of the welfare of the people, the greater the gold inflow, the less "wealthy" the nation would be—the fewer things (food, clothing, etc.) would be available for the people.

Competitive National Self-Enrichment

What was happening? The emerging nations were grabbing at the new opportunities and trying to use them to play the old "national power" game, by the old medieval, feudal rules. The very conditions which were bringing the end to feudalism offered the opportunity for the emerging nations to engage in "competitive mercantilism."

But mercantilism was based on the idea of every nation getting rich and powerful at the expense of every other nation. The ultimate objective was national wealth and power—not of the *people* (of course not!) but of the few who were running things. And wealth and power were judged by the old medieval, feudal criteria: gold, and military might.

Empire-Building

Under mercantilism, each nation should establish colonies to provide guaranteed sources of raw materials. With these raw materials the nations should produce things, then sell the things back to the colonies and to anyone else who will buy and pay with gold. It might be an overstatement to say that the American Revolution came as a result of the mercantilist policies of England during the 1700s. But certainly British mercantilism was an aggravating factor.

When we look back, mercantilism may not seem to make much sense. But if you can picture the tenor of the times, you can understand it. It was partly medieval, partly "modern world." And as with so many things, once the competition began, once everyone else was a mercantilist, no one could afford to be anything else. Various forms and shades of mercantilism persisted for about three centuries. We still hear mercantilist utterings from time to time, even today. And what about all that gold, first dug out of the ground and refined, then traded to the government for dollars, then reburied in the ground at Fort Knox? We still do strange things. (More on that later.)

For almost three centuries—from soon after the discovery of America to the time of the American Revolution—mercantilism was the name of the game. The British, the French, Dutch, Spaniards, Portuguese, Italians, and some others all tried to do whatever they could to increase the "wealth of the nation"—the nation's gold. The rulers and merchants of each nation worked together, playing their own little game, trying to enrich themselves, their nation—both at the expense of all the other nations, and at the expense of their own common people and their colonists as well.

This idea, "There's only so much wealth around, so more for me means less for you," was still accepted as a basic truth. The world was not yet ready to accept the idea that there might be economic growth, with a growing amount of total wealth for everybody.

Mercantilist Ideas Still Influence the Modern World

It is easy to look back at mercantilism and criticize this hangover of medieval psychology. But we can forgive them. Even today we can see several medieval hangovers still alive in the modern world.

Powerful nation-states still wage medieval wars (using modern weapons) and everyone knows that *everyone* will lose. No one can win in such a conflict! Yet wars persist. Nations keep building weapons. And so long as military power is the name of the game, no nation seems to have any choice but to play it that way. This is one of the sad realities of our moment in history. But we are in the midst of an explosion, remember? We should expect to find fragments and chunks from the pre-explosion period hurtling with us through time. And so we do.

A Three-Hundred-Year Transition

All the time mercantilism was controlling things, trying to hold down consumption, control trade, limit imports, and all that, the conditions for the market economy to emerge—or rather *explode*—were getting set. During this three hundred years of mercantilism—of exploration, colonization, urbanization, the increasing use of money, and the emergence of prices as economic incentives—all this time the conditions were being laid for the real explosion.

Quietly, almost without notice and certainly without plan, came the Industrial Revolution. As a small fire in the low grass begins creeping and nobody notices until suddenly it reaches the tall brush and then the trees and then the forest and all is out of control—like that came the Industrial Revolution.

THE INDUSTRIAL REVOLUTION

The Industrial Revolution destroyed the traditional ways of doing things. It destroyed the traditional ways of making the economic choices.

It blasted away the previous way of life and brought a new one which was for some much better, for others much worse. But for everybody it was different. We, today, are still in the midst of the explosion which was touched off by the Industrial Revolution. We are hurtling along at a dizzying pace—and the pace seems to be picking up all the time. No wonder things are confused these days!

Economic Growth Speeds Up

The Industrial Revolution gave the capitalist industrialists the opportunity to hire the displaced peasants. There were many workers looking for jobs. Wages were low. The new machine production was much more efficient than the hand-tool production of the craftsman. Output per worker was higher; businesses made big profits. With the high profits, the capitalist industrialists bought more machinery. They built more factories, produced more goods, and made even more profits, built even more factories. On and on went the process of industrialization. Faster and faster and faster.

The early thrust of the Industrial Revolution was in England, in the textile industry. From there it spread to other places and to other industries. You've heard all the names of the famous inventors and their famous gadgets—from John Kay and his "flying shuttle" (about 1750) to Hargreaves' "spinning jenny" (about 1770) and to Eli Whitney's "cotton gin" (about 1790). By 1800 the output per person had increased greatly in the textile industry. Much more cloth was being made, and the demand for cotton and wool was expanding rapidly. The increased demand and the higher prices made cotton-growing and sheep-raising very profitable.

In the United States, Southern plantation owners got rich, bought more slaves, cleared more land, planted more cotton, and got richer. In England the landlords speeded up their enclosures of land, forced the peasants off, turned the lands into grazing pastures for sheep—and got rich. The peasants went to the cities where jobs in the textile mills were available. More and more of the pieces were fitting together. Labor and land and capital were responding to demand. The automatic market forces of the "price mechanism" were beginning to direct and control society's scarce resources.

Market Forces Begin to Direct Production

With the breakdown of the *traditional* uses for resources—land, labor, and capital—the owners of these "factors of production" began to sell their factors to the highest bidders. For example, before the enclosures, land was just land, available for common use. After the enclosure of a piece of land, that land became a person's private property. The owner would use the land the way it would bring the biggest return. Once the land became enclosed private property, it became a "responsive factor of production," ready to do the bidding of the forces of the market—of changing demand, and prices.

In the case of labor, as long as tradition establishes each person's occupation and station in life, that person is not available to "sell labor" in response to the market's demands. But after a person gets pushed off the land, with no money and no source of food, that person's labor suddenly becomes very responsive to the market forces of demand, and prices.

When you're free and on your own you look for a job anywhere you can get a price (wage or salary) for your labor. Market forces begin to direct your labor. This transition wasn't always pleasant for the person involved. But for the productivity of the economic system, and the growth which was about to happen—growth which would bring freedom from want to so many people in future generations—the long-run benefit of the transition was undeniable.

Back in history, whenever the traditional society was to be induced to do things differently—to get people to produce more things and consume less, or to move from one kind of activity to another—the political process (government command) usually was required to bring about the change. But here, as the Industrial Revolution is getting going, we see *market forces* directing more and more people and things. Desire for reward is replacing fear of punishment as the motive force driving and directing the energies of people.

The Economic Choices Were Shifting

When all this begins to occur, there are major shifts in both the production and distribution choices in the society. And notice this: The political process does not need to be involved at all! In fact, quite the opposite. The unleashed forces of the market are exercising their great power, wresting the economic choice-making functions both from the traditional heritages of the society and from the political control of the kings and nobles. The "natural process of the market" is moving the factors of production (land, labor, capital) into different uses, causing the factors to respond to *prices,* which reflect the *market demands* of the society. And production is expanding in a way that never happened before in the history of the world!

Market Forces Generate Economic Growth

Capitalist industrialists were making big profits. With their profits they bought more machines, built more factories, and caused more and better kinds of capital goods to be produced. More factors of production flowed into making more capital. More and better factories and machines were built. This was the process of economic growth in action. This is what was happening rapidly during the industrial revolution.

This process of rapid growth was going on in the late 1700s and throughout the 1800s and on into the present century. This is the process which built the industrial base for the economically advanced nations. It's because of this economic growth process that most of us in the advanced nations are enjoying so much freedom of choice, so much leisure time, such easy working conditions, and so many products and services—warm houses, fast cars, medical attention, and all that.

WORLD SOCIO-ECONOMIC UPHEAVAL IN THE 1800s

The big thrust of industrial growth in the world didn't really get going until the early 1800s. By that time steel had been developed and the bugs had been worked out of the steam engine. Now better machinery could be built and driven by steam power. Then came the steamboat, the railroads, and the telegraph. By the mid 1800s, not just Great Britain, but all of Europe and the United States were undergoing the violently disruptive impact of rapid industrialization.

During the 1800s, centuries of social tradition were ripped apart. This was the period which rang the death knell on a way of life. It marked the beginning of another way of life—one of continual, explosive change. It was during this time that in the United States, in a few short decades, "the West was won." And it was during this time that in Europe, Friedrich Engels helped a bitter and impoverished Karl Marx as they wrote the *Communist Manifesto* calling for and predicting the end of capitalism. You'll be reading more about that later.

It isn't much of an overstatement to say that during the 1800s the entire society of the industrializing part of the world, restructured itself —physically, geographically, socially, economically. People bred like rabbits. The growing population moved toward the industrial centers— toward the coal and iron deposits—and along the expanding railroads, to the seaports, the transportation and trade centers—and to the United States and Canada. Some poor people got very rich. But most of them just moved somewhere else, got jobs, worked hard, and stayed poor.

Most working people in most places were living under miserable conditions. Were they miserable? Who can say? Perhaps they accepted their fate in the same way that most of the people of the world always have had to accept their fate. Hunger has been the "natural condition" of most of the people in the world, much of the time. In the 150-year period of rapid socio-economic turmoil between 1750 and 1900, many people looked very miserable. Their meager possessions, their lack of opportunity to get ahead, the many hours they had to work just to keep going—these conditions certainly didn't give them much time or cause to be happy.

Traditional Patterns Were Stripped Away

What was happening? Suddenly people were no longer being cared for by the traditional social processes. A person no longer had a "niche" in society as in feudal times. The "social security" of traditional society was gone. Everything was changing. It was a new ball game.

Suddenly people were living in a world in which they had no choice but to take care of themselves. Each person received an income (a "distributive share" of the output) on the basis of what "factors of production" that person owned, and could "sell in the market." People (most people) who did not have any land or capital, had to sell labor. So that's just what they did. As Bob Dylan would say, "the times they were a-changin'." The Industrial Revolution was in progress and the market process—the price mechanism—was taking control of society's economic choices. People and things were being shifted. Yesterday was suddenly thrust into tomorrow.

Who likes to see the former peasants working in the sweat shops from before sunrise until after sunset? And their children too! While the rich factory owners are making millions, building new factories up and down the valley and living off the fat of the land? Nobody. What a miserable, unjust solution to society's economic problem!

To be sure, the peasant is glad to have the job because it's a way of staying alive. But an economic arrangement which distributes so much of the output (income) to the factory owners and so little to the workers? This is capitalism? Yes, this was the capitalism of these disruptive days of the nineteenth-century Industrial Revolution. The market forces of demand and supply and prices were being unleashed. The *market process* was exerting its influence. Overthrowing tradition. Sidestepping command. A new, powerful, explosive force was being set loose in the world.

Rapid Economic Progress Was Being Made

Anyone who wasn't too concerned about the poverty of the people could see that progress was afoot. More product was being made. More factories being built. More people hired. More output per worker. But still, poverty among the masses. Everywhere.

The enclosures continued to spread. More and more people were forced off the common land. They drifted into the cities to seek jobs. Miserable though the jobs were, and miserably low the wages—still, it was a way to survive. In England, the "corn laws" (mercantilist tariffs to limit the import of all kinds of grain) forced high prices for grain and flour and bread and for most other kinds of food eaten by the common people. The high prices limited consumption—so the common people didn't get very much to eat.

People worked for low wages and had to pay high prices for food. But profits were being made. The landowners were doing very well. The capitalist entrepreneurs were making high profits and investing in more factories and better machinery and equipment. They were doing just fine. And as a result of all this, the productivity and output of the economy was growing by leaps and bounds.

The Population Explosion

Population was expanding rapidly. After all the thousands of centuries that people have been on earth, and then over the many centuries from the cradles of civilization to the days of the ancient Greeks and Romans, to the Roman Empire and on into the Middle Ages—up to the time of the first of the Crusades (about 1100 A.D.) the population of the world was still only about *300 million people.* By the time Columbus discovered America (only four centuries later) the population of the world had *increased by about 50 percent*—to about *450 million.* Then from 1492 until the time the United States became a nation (only *three centuries later*) the world's population *doubled*—to about *900 million.* Can you see what's happening? It's a population explosion!

But the figures for world population don't really show the seriousness of the true picture. What was going on in Europe? In the places where all this new activity was underway?

During the 1700s—only *one century*—Europe's population *doubled.* And look at this: During the 1800s, England's population expanded from about nine million to thirty-five million—a *fourfold increase!* By 1900 the world's population stood at 1.5 billion. It was destined to double again (to *3 billion*) by 1960, and perhaps to *double again* (to *6 billion*) before the end of the twentieth century.

Now do you wonder why the world suddenly finds that it has a pollution problem? A problem of ecological imbalance? More on this later.

During the 1700s and 1800s, the rapidly expanding population compounded the human tragedy of poverty—but it supplied labor to support the rapid industrial growth, and markets for the industrial output. There is no question that growth was rapid. Was all this economic growth—this increased industrialization and increased output—the result of the mercantilists' economic controls? Or was some other force at work?

The Challenge to Mercantilism

During the 1700s the mercantilist philosophy of "restrict local consumption, export more goods, get more gold, and make the nation wealthy" was much in evidence. But as the industrial revolution exploded on the scene the voices of others began to be heard—the voices of *the new industrialists.* Many of the industrialists wanted to be free of the government restrictions and regulations of mercantilism. The new industrialists saw the advantages of selling wherever they had the opportunity to sell at the highest price, and of buying inputs or whatever else they wanted from wherever they could find them available at the lowest price—in England, France, Germany, the United States, or wherever.

The industrialists and the mercantilists did not agree. And the humanists who were concerned about the poverty of most of the factory workers in the rapidly expanding cities were not happy with the situation, either. What was going on? Why were conditions as they were? Why was there so much disruption and poverty? What was it all leading to? What should the government be doing? What should anybody be doing? What had gone wrong with the world? Nobody seemed to know.

The "Historical Explosion"

Historical explosion was beginning. But no one could know that. Things just looked confused. Not enough cumulative change could be seen to be able to tell what was happening. To many people it must have looked like chaos. Certainly they never could have dreamed of what really was going on. It wasn't easy to see order or purpose in all that misery and turmoil! Maybe it takes until about now—until the last half of the 20th century—for us to be able to look back and see what really was beginning to happen. We can't see where it's all going, even yet. Of course not. Only time will reveal the answer to that question.

Today we can look back over the broad sweep of history and see the cumulative effect of hundreds of years of little, erosive changes— changes which like worms in the woodwork were eating away at the old, stable, traditional social structure and preparing the world for violent change. We can see how the rate of change started speeding up—leading into, supporting, and then being whisked along by the rapid-fire series of new inventions and innovations. The growing factories and machines, the socio-economic disruption, all this turmoil—this is the period we call the Industrial Revolution. It was really the blast-off on this trip that now we all are taking—this trip of explosive change, hurtling us through time, heading at breakneck speed into an unknown future.

How did it look in the late 1700s to the people who were trying to figure out what was going on? There was a lot of human suffering. People disagreed about what was happening. But there was no question that *new things were going on.*

Various philosophers, scholars, industrialists, commercial dealers, and others were trying to figure out what was going on—many were trying to explain and evaluate the situation. Some were suggesting ways to try to improve things. Mercantilism had both its proponents and its critics as far back as the 1500s. But during the late 1700s the critics of the government's economic controls of mercantilism were becoming more insistent and more effective.

BEHOLD! THE MARKET PROCESS TAKES OVER

You and I can look back and understand some of what was happening. We can see that the market forces were exerting their influences more and more over the economic choices of the society. The great supply of labor was holding down the wage rate, providing markets for products and keeping profits high. The high profits were providing great stimulation—both the money and the incentive—for building capital. So economic growth was proceeding rapidly. But it wasn't easy to look at the rapidly expanding population and all the suffering and confusion and make any long-run sense out of what was going on.

Adam Smith Offers an Explanation

How could they know that the market process—the free market forces of supply and demand—were taking over, automatically directing the economy? They couldn't. Then, in 1776, a new book appeared. It explained the whole thing—all about the automatic operation of the market process, and how it works for the ultimate good of everybody.

The book was written by a professor, a Scotsman with an unlikely name: Adam Smith. Professor Adam Smith was not the first to talk about "free market forces" and how they work. But he was the first to pull it all together. He explained the whole process in his big economics book, titled: *An Inquiry into the Nature and Causes of the Wealth of Nations* (usually referred to as *Wealth of Nations*). That's what Adam Smith did. For that he is called "the father of modern economics."

Adam Smith gave the philosophers and the other thinking people of the world a new way to look at what was going on. He gave them a new explanation of what it all meant, where it was all going, and how. Soon you'll be reading about what Adam Smith had to say. But that discussion, and the discussion of who else said what—the economic ideas of Malthus, Ricardo, Mill, Marshall, Owen, Marx, and others who were trying to make sense out of what was going on in the world—that must wait for the next chapters.

The World "Turned Upside Down"

For now, take a few minutes to think about this broad sweep of history leading up to the Industrial Revolution. Then take a few more minutes and try to picture the turmoil the world had gotten itself into. Explosive, cumulative, accelerating economic change, like a tidal wave, was sweeping away the stable social structures of the past and leaving in its wake masses of people struggling for new ways to survive. A world turned upside down—a real "Poseidon Adventure"!

As the people struggled to survive they followed the pull of the powerful forces of the market—forces which were grasping control, taking over, beginning to direct the economic choices of the society. The answers to the basic production and distribution questions were being made in a new and different, totally unfamiliar way.

Part II: The Emergence of New Economic Conditions, Ideas, and Theories— The Industrial Revolution (1750s - 1850s)

The Classical Economists Tried to Explain the World and the Utopian Socialists Tried to Change It

Chapter 5: The Physiocrats, Adam Smith, and Jeremy Bentham

It was the late 1700s. Hard times were everywhere. What a miserable world! Hungry, cold, sick people. Split up families. Very tedious work. Very long hours. Very low pay. No wonder people were trying to understand the economics of all this. What was going on? Wasn't there some better way? Couldn't something be done? Some new government policies or programs perhaps? Surely life on earth could be made into something better than this! But how? The answers were not easy to find.

The Increasing Challenge to Mercantilism

One thing was dawning on an increasing number of people: Mercantilism did not seem to be the answer. You remember that during the Middle Ages and on back into ancient times, the philosophers, religious writers, and concerned citizens of each day and age were commenting on (frequently criticizing) the economic issues of the day. As you might expect, the critical commenting continued throughout the three-hundred-year period of mercantilism. As time went on, mercantilism came more and more under attack.

During the 1700s the mercantilist philosophy suffered some serious blows. The most devastating came from the perceptive Scotsman, Professor Adam Smith. But during the mid-1700s (a few decades before

Smith's *Wealth of Nations*) some French philosophers were developing a new explanation of what was going on. Before getting into Smith's *Wealth of Nations* you need to know a little bit about these French philosophers—the ones called the "Physiocrats."

THE PHYSIOCRATS

The Physiocrats said that it would be better if the government would just leave people alone. They concentrated on *physical production* and emphasized the economic importance of *agriculture.* Only agricultural production created "new things out of nowhere." Manufacturing and trade were "sterile" activities. Such activities only moved or changed things. Nothing was really "created."

It was their idea that when people produce from the soil, nature and people are working together. This partnership was necessary to produce more physical output—that is, more *real wealth* for the nation. They said that mercantilist controls interfered with this process. The term "laissez-faire" comes from the French Physiocrats. As you know, the term means that the government should let people alone to make their own economic way—to do whatever they want with their time, energy, resources, capital, and with whatever else they have to work with.

The "Tableau Economique"

The French Physiocrats called attention to some of the fallacies of mercantilism. Francois Quesnay (frawn-SWA kay-NAY), a leading Physiocrat, developed the concept that economic activity follows a kind of circular flow. His *Tableau Economique* shows that the people of the society produce, then consume some and save some, then produce again. Using what they have saved, they can produce more. Around and around goes the production-consumption circle. Each time, some is saved. The economy grows. This was Quesnay's explanation of *how the nation gains its wealth.*

The Physiocrats attacked the mercantilists by offering a new, different explanation of both the *form* and *source* of the nation's wealth. To the Physiocrats, the nation's wealth was the *physical output* produced from the soil. Government controls only interfered with the wealth-producing process, so the Physiocrats called for a policy of laissez-faire.

To the mercantilists, wealth was the *gold* acquired by selling things. Government controls were called for, to force the people to produce the "right" products and not to consume too much, and to force trade to flow in the "right" directions.

The Nature and Causes of "Wealth"

The Physiocrats and the mercantilists disagreed about both (a) the *nature* of a nation's wealth and (b) the *causes* of a nation's wealth. Perhaps now you can understand why Adam Smith chose for his book the title: *An Inquiry into the Nature and Causes of the Wealth of Nations.* You know by now that Smith's book is going to say that the mercantilist concept of the *nature* of wealth is wrong, and that the mercantilist explanation of what *causes* a nation to be wealthy is wrong. You probably also know that Smith is going to explain the automatic operation of the market process—how the forces of free markets (demand, supply, price)—work to bring about the wealthiest nation.

Smith's book explains *how* a nation will become wealthiest if it will follow a laissez-faire policy and just let the automatic market process take care of things. That was the real purpose of his book—to make that point. He made the point very well. So well, in fact, that his book had quite an impact on the world and on all future ideas about economics.

ADAM SMITH AND THE WEALTH OF NATIONS

Adam Smith's historic book was published in the historic year 1776. It offered some comprehensive and plausible answers to the question: "What's going on in this confused, miserable world?" His answers were good. Much of what he said is as true today as it was then.

Adam Smith's book contained a lot of economics. It talked about the advantages of specialization and trade. It talked about savings and investment and economic growth. It explained how the market process automatically gets the "right" things to be produced, how it automatically moves the factors of production to the "right" places to do the "right" things, and how it automatically arranges for the "right" amount of the output to be shared by each person. Truly, *Wealth of Nations* was, and is, an outstanding economics book.

Laissez-Faire and Competition

Wealth of Nations explained how the trader, industrialist, landowner, worker, or anyone else, in trying to get ahead, would automatically be tricked (by the free market forces) into serving the best interests of the society—by conserving resources, and by producing the right numbers of the right kinds of goods.

It worked like this: People who used their energies and resources to make what the society *wanted most,* would get paid a lot. The businesses which would produce a much-wanted, highly valued product—while being careful to conserve society's scarce resources—would be doing a great service for society. For this they would be rewarded with big profits. Everyone in the society would have a strong incentive to be productive, so everyone would work hard producing the most valued things. The total product would be great. The nation's wealth would grow more and more. A neat, automatic system!

Wealth of Nations explained how everything would come out best if the government followed a policy of laissez-faire—that is, if it just kept its hands off and did not interfere with what people were producing or consuming, or with prices, or with anything about the operation of the automatic market process. The book emphasized the essential role of competition, to protect the society against monopolistic sellers or buyers, or groups of sellers or buyers. It explained that "laissez-faire" would *not* mean economic chaos, because the natural market forces would keep the economy in control and moving in desirable directions. And it explained even more.

Yes, there is much good economics in Smith's book. Also, there is much anti-mercantilism—much argument for individual freedom and against government interference and controls. While Thomas Jefferson in the *Declaration of Independence* and other philosophers in other writings were offering the world justification for *political freedom,* Adam Smith was offering the world justification for *economic freedom.*

Nineteenth-Century Liberalism

The *Declaration of Independence* (also, as you know, written in 1776) and the *Wealth of Nations* both reflected their times—the emergence of "nineteenth-century liberalism"—the idea of freedom of the individual, the "inalienable rights" of every person. The United States, a new nation created in the midst of this newly emerging philosophy, still carries a deep commitment to democracy, and to laissez-faire. You can see it in the U.S. political system and economic system. This anti-government philosophy was really strong at the time the United States Constitution was written. Perhaps this helps to explain why the U.S. government for so many years showed such great reluctance to take *any action* to influence conditions in the economy. Even today, many Americans stand strong against almost any kind of government involvement in the economy.

CLASSICAL ECONOMICS, AND SMITH'S "INVISIBLE HAND"

Adam Smith's book marks the beginning of "classical economics." It tells the world that *laissez-faire can work.* It explains the market process.

It says that if the government leaves the people free to make their own economic choices, people who seek to follow their own best interests will be guided "as though by an invisible hand" to do the things which are best for the whole society.

In *Wealth of Nations,* Adam Smith explains how self-interest will drive individuals—as though guided by "an invisible hand"—to do those things which others want them to do. He explains how people will be financially rewarded for the good things they do for society. He explains how the market process will generate savings and investment and bring economic growth, more output, and more good things for everybody. He explains how a nation which follows laissez-faire will automatically become more wealthy, more powerful, more productive —how the people will enjoy higher standards of living if *market forces* are in control than they would if the *government* tried to control things.

Smith Was Optimistic About the Future Outcome

Adam Smith thus explained the misery and hardship of England and the Western world in terms which seemed to make it all worthwhile in the long run. He was optimistic. He explained how businesses, making profits, would reinvest in more capital to try to make even more profits. The result: more growth, greater production, and (eventually) higher wages and better conditions for the common people.

Adam Smith's work was greatly appreciated by the capitalist industrialists during the hectic days of the Industrial Revolution. *Wealth of Nations* gave them a way to justify their self-serving activities and a respectable explanation for their great wealth and profits. The wealthy business leaders could explain that as they were being selfish in seeking profit, they were really working for the good of society. Adam Smith had told them so!

Natural Laws of Economic Behavior

Adam Smith explained a kind of "natural law of economic behavior." If the government followed any policy other than laissez-faire, it would thwart this natural law. The government would keep the economy from working properly. How stupid that would be! Talk about an effective argument against the government controls of mercantilism! With the natural laws of economic behavior controlling things, it made sense to permit individuals to be free to make their own economic choices.

Adam Smith didn't invent the natural laws of the free market. The market process was already there, busily at work. Tradition had already given way to the new order of things. There was a new kind of control over the economic choices—a new kind of influence directing economic life. Smith just showed it to people. He gave them a way to look at and recognize it—a way to understand and explain what was going on. He gave the world the first systematic explanation of how the market process works—of how all individuals, working for their own greatest benefit, will automatically bring the greatest benefit to all of society.

His thesis was that the nation will be most wealthy and the people will "fare best" if they are left free to follow their own selfish interests. He emphasized the need for free markets, for competition, and for the factors of production to move freely in response to market prices—for each person to produce whatever will bring the most income, or profit.

Division of Labor, Specialization, Trade

Smith emphasized the essential role that trade plays in bringing about the most productive, most efficient uses of the society's resources. He explained the importance of specialization, of division of labor. A jack-of-all trades can't be as productive as one who specializes. But it's obvious that a person who is going to specialize, must be able to trade the output produced—to sell it and get some other things in return. Smith emphasized the indisputable fact that specialization requires trade —that only with *trade* can people specialize.

The Functions of Government

Smith said the functions of government should be closely restricted. Since the natural laws of the market process could direct things so well, the government could only hurt things by interfering. People left alone would generate their maximum income (and wealth, well-being, and all that), so that in total, the nation's wealth and well-being would be maximized. Interference by the government could only reduce the nation's wealth and cut down on the economic well-being of the people.

Smith said the government should maintain law and order, protect the rights of private property, regulate the monetary system, and under-take the few necessary public projects—building harbors and highways and such things. But the government should *not* use the resources of the society for things the people would not want to spend their own money to pay for. The government should stay out of it and let the natural forces of the market direct and control the society's productive activities and resources.

Adam Smith's Impact on Economic Thinking

Adam Smith's book was a great book at the time it was written. It is still a great book. It explained what was going on. To the business leaders of the day, Smith gave a justification for selfish profit-seeking. To the poor he gave a promise of a better life through economic growth: Profits would be reinvested; more capital would be built; eventually there would be more income and a better life for everyone.

Smith showed how all the painful and seemingly heartless conditions could be justified by this larger picture—by long-run benefits for everybody. He showed how all this misery was really leading to something good in the future—something good in which all people would share. He explained that there was some *purpose,* and some *ultimate relief* for all the hunger and misery in the world. Looked at from Smith's point of view, perhaps the miserable conditions of the early years of the industrial revolution weren't quite as hard to take.

Smith's explanation of the natural laws of economics—of how free market forces can control the economy and direct things into desirable directions—were destined to live on to the present time, and almost certainly, far beyond. But his optimistic conclusion about the outcome —about the *ultimate relief* for all the hunger and misery—about the long-run betterment of the economic welfare of the masses—this idea was soon to be challenged. By whom? By the next two great classical economists: the Reverend Thomas Robert Malthus and the self-made millionaire David Ricardo. But before we get into the ideas of Malthus and Ricardo, there's someone else who needs to be mentioned: Jeremy Bentham.

JEREMY BENTHAM

In the very same year the *Declaration of Independence* and the *Wealth of Nations* appeared, young Jeremy Bentham also published his first book. But it wasn't until thirteen years later (in 1789) that his major work, *Principles of Morals and Legislation,* appeared. Bentham's book was not a book on political economy. It was not on the question of the wealth of the nation, but on "the welfare of the society"—how to measure it and how to achieve it.

Bentham's book was a very different kind of economics book—but it was an economics book, just the same. It talked about how the wealth (the good things of the society) *might be shared* among the people for the greatest *total welfare*—for the "greatest good" the society could achieve.

Bentham's "Pleasure Measure"

Bentham's "Felicific Calculus" (his "pleasure-measure") was based on the idea that the greatest total welfare of the society would result from the greatest *sum total* of the welfare of all the individuals. If I might *lose* some "welfare"—and thereby you might *gain more* "welfare" than I lost, then there would be a net gain for the society. Get the idea? It's the idea of "the greatest good for the greatest number."

What's so important about Bentham's contribution to classical economics? Just this: He explained the motives of the individual—the driving force which directs each individual's activities and behavior. Bentham said that each person is essentially a self-serving unit—that all individuals are powered by the desire to do things which serve their own best interest—the desire to seek pleasant experiences and to avoid or escape from painful ones.

Bentham Analyzed the "Motive Force"

Remember how Adam Smith explained how the market system worked? How all people would act to serve their own best interests, yet each would be guided "as though by an invisible hand" to serve the best interests of the society? How the only way people could get more of what they wanted would be by doing or making something somebody else wanted? Now you can see how Bentham's ideas fit in.

Smith talked about *how* individual self-interest is automatically directed toward improving the welfare of the society. Bentham *dug into* the self-interest question; he analyzed and offered new insights into the motive force—the "engine" which powered Smith's economic machine. He did that, and he did much more than that.

Bentham tried to explain human behavior and the things which influence the welfare of mankind in society. Some of his ideas can be found deeply imbedded in all of today's social sciences. Certainly his ideas influenced the next classical economists we'll be talking about— men who were greatly concerned about the record-breaking, historically unprecedented rate of population increase during the late 1700s and early 1800s. What men? Malthus, Ricardo, and John Stuart Mill. You'll be reading about them in the next chapter.

Chapter 6: Malthus, Ricardo, and Mill

Thomas Malthus was only ten years old when *Wealth of Nations* was published. David Ricardo was only four. Obviously neither of them was very impressed with Adam Smith at the time! But as they grew up and observed the chaotic, miserable world in turmoil around them, they began to study, and to think. Then each in his own time decided that he had something to say. And each said it—to each other, and to the world.

MALTHUS AND RICARDO WORKED WITH "NATURAL LAWS"

Essentially both Malthus and Ricardo agreed with the natural laws of economics as presented in Smith's *Wealth of Nations.* They agreed that there was a *natural order* in economic affairs and that the government should follow a policy of laissez-faire to let the natural laws operate freely. Both Malthus and Ricardo published books called *Principles of Political Economy,* both about the same time (around 1820), not quite half a century after *Wealth of Nations* was published.

Both Malthus and Ricardo carried forward and added to what we call *classical economics.* Both writers helped to further explain the process of the market—how the free market forces can control and direct the economy. But both disagreed with Smith about the optimistic ultimate outcome of laissez-faire economics in the real world. Both said that *population expansion* would prevent the improvement of mankind's economic welfare.

Malthus said that for the poor, hard times were here to stay. He said that population would expand so rapidly that people always would be going hungry. The gains from increasing food production would be eaten up by the expanding population.

The Malthusian Law of Population

The population of Europe had more than doubled in the 1700s. In the 1790s Malthus wrote his *Essay on Population.* He said there was a tendency for the population to expand *more rapidly* than the food supply could expand. Therefore, most people's food consumption always would be held down to bare subsistence. Malthus admitted that people might voluntarily limit their reproductive urges and dodge this unpleasant outcome, but he didn't expect that they would.

This idea expressed by Malthus—that population expansion would keep the people poor and hungry—is called the *Malthusian Law of Population.* It made a lot of sense at that time. It makes a lot of sense now.

In most of the less-developed nations of the world today, population growth is the greatest single obstacle to economic development and improved standards of living for the people. Whenever gains are made in production or in living conditions, population seems to expand and wipe out the gains.

Malthus dealt with more than just the population issue. He had more than that to say about economics. But he will always be best remembered for calling the attention of the world's thinkers to the population problem—a problem which today is much more serious than it was then—a problem which some people now consider so serious as to threaten the continued existence of mankind on earth.

RICARDO'S THEORETICAL MODEL OF THE "PURE MARKET SYSTEM"

Ricardo was a brilliant economic theorist. He developed a theoretical model to show the intricate way in which the market process directs and controls an economy of "laissez-faire and competition." He emphasized the importance of the growth of capital, through savings and investment. He could see that widespread poverty was contributing to growth. But, like Malthus, he was pessimistic about the future welfare of most of the people.

The Iron Law of Wages

Like Malthus, Ricardo agreed that the population would continue to expand and force wages to stay very low—at or near (sometimes below) the level of bare subsistence. Like Malthus, Ricardo agreed that if wages were *less* than subsistence, the population and the labor force would get smaller. People would die—more children would die of malnutrition and old or sick people would not survive as long. Young people would delay marriage and/or have fewer children. The work force would shrink. The shortage of workers would cause businesses to overbid each other—to offer higher wages to try to hold on to their workers. Wages would be pushed upward to the subsistence level.

If wages ever got *above* the subsistence level, population would expand. People would marry earlier and have larger families. More children would be healthier and would survive and become workers. There would be more workers around than the businesses wanted to hire. The surplus workers would be trying to get jobs, underbidding each other. Workers would accept lower wages in order to get jobs, or to hold on to their jobs. Wages would be pushed down to subsistence again. Economic misery would be perpetuated.

This bare subsistence theory of wages is sometimes called "the iron law of wages." No wonder economics in the early 1800s was called "the dismal science"!

High Food Costs Force Up Wages

Here are more of the results of Ricardo's model: Since wages must hover around the subsistence level, the higher the subsistence cost of living, the higher wages must be. If grain and other foods are cheap, the cost of subsistence will be low; the wages the manufacturer will have to pay will be low. The manufacturer's profits will be high. But suppose the cost of living is high. Then the subsistence level of wages will be high. The manufacturer's profits will be low.

With high living costs and therefore high wages and low profits, manufacturers will not have much money to invest in new capital. Economic growth will be stunted. Can you see why Ricardo fought against the high import tariffs on grain (the corn laws)? The corn laws increased the cost of living and therefore kept wages up. The higher wages reduced industry's profits and stunted economic growth! (Leave it to a sharp thinker like Ricardo to figure out something like that!)

The Profit Squeeze

Ricardo's analysis went much further. He went on to show that as the population expands, the cost of living will increase. As there are more and more people eating up the food supplies, more land areas will have to be cultivated. But the new land areas will be less and less fertile. Intelligent farmers will cultivate the best land first. No one will cultivate any *more* land (the poorer land) unless the price of grain goes high enough to pay the cost of growing the grain on the poorer land. Obviously! And it costs more (obviously) to grow grain on poor land. So the subsistence cost of living must go up. Then wages must go up. This squeezes profits and slows economic growth.

Ricardo's Theory of Rent

Something else happens, too. When the price of grain goes high enough to justify cultivating the *very poor* land, think of the high profits the owners will be making on the *very best* land! If you own a lot of good land and you have been making a pretty good rent from your wheat-growing tenants, think how much rent they will pay you so they can keep using your good land after the price of wheat goes up! This was Ricardo's "differential rent" theory.

Ricardo talked about the "marginal" land on which the farmer would just make enough to break even. This land could command no "rent." But any land which is more fertile than the marginal land would bring its owner a "surplus"—a *rent.* So as population expands, you see what is going to happen. Poorer and poorer lands will have to be cultivated. But higher prices will have to be paid for grain in order to get this to happen. Now, as the grain prices go up, the people who own the *fertile* land (and who were doing okay already) will find that they are beginning to make a lot more money.

The Landowners Receive Surplus Income

You can see that as the grain prices rise more and more, landowners will receive larger and larger *surplus incomes* from their fertile lands. This will put the landowners on easy street. The more the population expands, the more of the poorer lands must be farmed. So the higher must go the price of grain (and the cost of food, and the wages of labor), and the bigger will be the surplus incomes (rents) of the landlords. Can you see that rent is "price-determined" (determined by the demand for and the price of grain)? Sure. Oh to be a landlord!

What does Ricardo's model predict for the manufacturers—the ones who are making profits and investing in more and better capital and bringing about economic growth—adding more and more to the wealth of the nation? For them the prediction is not so good. As wages go up to pay for the high cost of food, profits are squeezed. As profits shrink, the boom slows down and stops. The industrial expansion gets choked off.

According to Ricardo, the economic deck was stacked in favor of the landowner and against everyone else. Ricardo concluded that by the very nature of the market system—by the natural laws which guided it —the landowners were bound to be big winners over the long run. The workers would be receiving just enough to live on, the capitalist-industrialists would be struggling to survive, and the wealthy landowners would be getting richer and richer as the rents for the land went higher and higher. (After Ricardo made his fortune in stocks, he invested in good land. He must have really believed in the real-world relevance of his theoretical model!)

THE LONG-RUN IMPACT OF MALTHUS AND RICARDO

As history would have it, many of the predictions of both Malthus and Ricardo didn't come true exactly as they had expected. Both were making assumptions about the *permanence* of the world as they saw it in their lifetimes. They didn't allow—they *couldn't have* allowed—for the explosive rate of change which at that time was already well underway. As it turned out, population in the advanced countries has not expanded exactly as expected. Wages have risen *far* above subsistence. And technology and productivity in both agriculture and manufacturing have gone forward so much more rapidly than Malthus, Ricardo, or anyone else could have expected. It shows something about the perils of predicting. It was perilous then. It's just as perilous—maybe even more perilous—now.

Both Malthus and Ricardo made important contributions to the development of our present understanding of economics. The Malthusian Law of Population focused early on a problem which today is very real and very serious. Hunger in the poor nations and pollution in the cities are only two of the many present-day manifestations of rapid population expansion.

Ricardo's theoretical model identified and explained in detail many of the economic forces which previously had been understood only in general terms. His model helped us to see some of the "economic laws" at work in the world. Ricardo is considered by many to be the greatest economist of his time. Some call him the greatest economist *of all time.* He was that good. His theoretical model of how the pure market process would work has had a profound influence on economic thought and policy, from Ricardo's day to the present. And certainly Ricardo's influence on economic thought isn't all used up yet. It will go on, far into the future.

OTHER CLASSICAL ECONOMISTS

During the time of Malthus and Ricardo many others were thinking and writing about economic matters—about "political economy." Jean Baptiste Say and James Mill were both about the same age as Malthus and Ricardo. J. B. Say was nine in 1776 when *Wealth of Nations* appeared. James Mill was three. Both these men published "Political Economy" books in the early 1800s. Both wrote in the classical tradition of Smith, Malthus, and Ricardo, explaining how the market process works—explaining the intricate workings of the market system.

And there were several others—before, at the time of, and after Smith, Malthus, and Ricardo. But we just don't have time to talk about them all.

Say is best known for his "Law of Markets"—the idea that *supply* creates its own *demand.* The more a producer takes to the market (supply), the more he can get in trade (buy) and take home with him (demand). Say's law explains an important "natural balancing tendency" in the way markets operate. (As with other economic theories, Say's law doesn't always work out exactly right in the real world. But the tendency is there, and sometimes it's helpful to know about it.)

James Mill is not best known for his contributions to economics, but for his contributions in history and political theory. But probably he is even better known as the father and teacher of a truly unique, great philosopher and economist of the nineteenth century—John Stuart Mill.

JOHN STUART MILL

John Stuart Mill was born in 1806. He was not yet fifteen years old when his father and his father's friends, Malthus and Ricardo, were coming out with their political economy books. But even at fifteen, he was ready for them. Very ready.

Ever since he had been about old enough to talk, John Stuart Mill had been studying under the demanding tutelage of his father. It is said that he was reading classical Greek at the age of three. (I don't know how well.) By the time he was thirteen he had finished his studies of Aristotle and Plato and the other philosophers who wrote in Greek and Latin. He had read profusely in English history and in other areas, had mastered calculus, had written history books and, among other things, was then studying the writings of Smith, Malthus, and Ricardo. All by the age of thirteen, would you believe!

Although he was writing on economics and various other subjects from the time of his teens, it was not until 1848 (when he was 42) that his *Principles of Political Economy* was published. This book became the leading text on economics for several decades. Much of John Stuart Mill's *Principles* was orthodox classical economics. It integrated much of what had been done by the various writers from Adam Smith on. It further clarified Ricardo's theoretical model of the pure market system. But it wasn't all orthodox. It challenged classical economics—specifically, the Ricardian model—on a very basic, fundamental point—on "the laws of distribution."

Mill Challenged Ricardo's Model

The Ricardian model described an economic system in which the pure market process was allowed virtually complete control over everything. People owning productive factors would produce. Those who produced could have something to consume. The iron law of wages kept the worker's share low. Increasing rents kept the landlord's share high and rising. All this happened as the result of natural market forces. To tamper with the results would be to interfere with the system. And that would only make matters worse. The poor people would stay poor, and that was that. John Stuart Mill challenged this conclusion.

Can the Society Redistribute Income?

Mill's point was this: It isn't necessary to let the natural market forces decide how much each person is going to get to eat. It is possible for the *society* to decide whether or not it wants some of its people to starve, while others (the landowners) are filthy rich and getting richer. He pointed out that the laws and customs of the society (that is, the political process and the social process—not just the market process) can have a lot to say about how the output is distributed.

At least to an extent, it's obvious that Mill was right on this point. In all modern societies the market forces are modified to take something away from the productive people and give a share to the nonproductive ones. But, of course, we have no way of knowing how much these "income redistributions" may have stunted growth, and contributed to low wages, high unemployment, and other undesirable effects. Economists wonder about things like that, but there's no sure way to find the answers to "what might have been."

POSITIVE ECONOMICS AND NORMATIVE ECONOMICS

Mill sort of straddled the line between what we call "positive economics" and "normative economics."

Positive Economics

Positive economics deals with the "laws" of economic behavior—that is, with general statements of fact: "If you don't *pay* a person to work for you, then that person will not work for you." "If you offer a lot more money for corn than wheat, then people will grow and sell you more corn than wheat." "If the fried chicken price doubles and the hamburger price goes down, people will buy less of the high-priced fried chicken and more of the low-priced hamburgers." These are statements of positive economics.

Positive economics doesn't say it's good or bad—it just tries to tell "what would happen if . . ." It just tries to "tell it like it is."

Normative Economics

Normative economics gets into questions of how things *ought to be*—of how things ought to be changed—how to make things better. Normative economics is what John Stuart Mill was talking about when he suggested that the society could distribute and share its products and resources among the people in the way they *wanted* to—in the way they thought *best.*

Mill addressed some of these normative issues—the "value" issues —the issues of good or bad, right or wrong, better or worse, and of how to make the economic choices *better* for society. He sort of "straddled the positive-normative fence." Perhaps that was the best thing for him to do—or perhaps not. Who knows? Certainly many (perhaps most) economists are doing it today.

Should Economists Deal with "Normative" Issues?

What do you think? Should economists get involved in the issues of "what's best"? Or only "what is"? The "scientific tools of economic analysis" are tools of positive economics—of finding out and explaining "what is," and "what would happen if."

When the economist gets into questions about how much income a family of four *should* have, and how high wages of unskilled workers *should* be, the scientific tools of economic analysis don't help at all. Still, economists can talk about such things as guaranteed annual incomes and minimum wages, and be at least one step ahead. At least the economist can work up a pretty good answer to the question: "What would happen if the government decided to set up this program or that program?" or "What kind of program might we set up to achieve the normative objective?" Unless you know some positive economics, you don't know what's going to happen when the government (or somebody) starts making normative changes in the economic system.

Economists are no better than anyone else at deciding what objectives we'd *like* to achieve. (No worse, mind you. But no better.) But economists are (or at least should be) better at working out feasible ways (and throwing out unfeasible ways) of getting to the objectives. Still, there are many economists who prefer to bypass these issues entirely and spend their energies finding out more about the interrelationships among the variables in Ricardo-type models.

Which is the proper role for the economist? That question has been at issue for quite some time. It isn't likely to be solved anytime soon.

Chapter 7: The Utopian Socialists

There were several philosophers about John Stuart Mill's time (and some before and some after) who didn't straddle the fence any more than Ricardo did. They were clearly on the *other* side of the fence—the normative side. We call these philosophers the "utopian socialists."

The Utopian Socialists Were Not Classical Economists

Most of the utopian socialists really didn't know much about the natural laws of positive economics. But they saw that the world looked like a miserable place for most people. They saw many rich and powerful people—industrialists, entrepreneurs—being very cruel to a lot of poor and hungry people. Men and women—and children too.

The utopian socialists responded in various ways. But most of their responses were not very realistic. The problem? They didn't understand some of the real-world limitations imposed by the natural laws of positive economics.

Most of the utopian socialists weren't bothered by the restricting influences of the laws of positive economics. But it's a fact of life that the economic laws which do hold true in the real world *are real.* Anyone who goes along trying to change things and ignoring these laws is inviting failure. Several of the utopian socialists did that.

There Were Several "Utopian Socialists"

There were several different, unique writers who can be grouped under the broad heading "utopian socialists." Who were they? What were their similarities? Their unifying characteristics?

All of them were people who looked at the world, didn't like what they saw, and set about the task of trying to change it. Each had a different idea, a different approach. But generally, all were interesting and dedicated, but not too realistic people who were trying to reorganize the society to get rid of some of the harshness and cruelty—to build more love, friendship, sharing, and mutual assistance into peoples' daily lives. They worked for reforms to improve the conditions of the common people. This chapter gives the highlights of the ideas of three of them.

SAINT-SIMON AND FOURIER

In France there were two utopian socialists who were contemporaries of Malthus and Ricardo: Count Saint-Simon (pronounced SOHn-see-MOHn) and Charles Fourier (Foo-ree-A). Saint-Simon, an aristocrat himself, attacked as unjust the high incomes of the unproductive aristocrats. He founded a small religious sect—a sort of industrial religion.

Fourier worked for the reorganization of people into communes, called "Phalanxes." Small groups of people would live in a big hotel—or those who preferred could live in a cluster of houses—and all would work for the good of the group.

Both of these French socialists had followers; people really did attend the Saint-Simonian churches, and Fourierist Phalanxes were actually set up in several places. Would you believe there were some forty of them in the United States in the early to mid-1800s? You may have heard of the Brook Farm community in Massachusetts (mid-1800s). Nathaniel Hawthorne joined it for awhile. Brook Farm was one of these Fourierist "utopian" communities. Two other well-known ones were the North American Phalanx at Red Bank, New Jersey, and the Wisconsin Phalanx.

The Utopian Socialists Worked for Social Change

We really don't need to go into much detail about the utopian socialists. The important thing is to be aware that while the classical economists were accepting certain things as given and trying to understand and explain what was going on, the utopian socialists were *refusing to accept* the givens. They didn't ask why, or where it was all going. They jumped right in and tried to change things. Each one approached the task in his own unique way.

One of these utopian socialists stands out, because he did accomplish some things. Not all that he wanted to accomplish—not by a long shot —but he did accomplish some things. The man was Robert Owen.

ROBERT OWEN

The Englishman Robert Owen was one of the most interesting and versatile of the utopian socialists. Owen was in the same age group as the several classical economists we have been talking about. Owen, Malthus, Ricardo, Say, James Mill, Saint-Simon, and Fourier were all approaching or in their 30s at the beginning of the 1800s. They were all observing the same real-world conditions, but they certainly were interpreting them differently! Owen set out to improve the world.

Owen Was a Successful Mill-Operator

Robert Owen started out as a poor boy and worked his way up in the textile industry. Eventually he owned and made a fortune operating a textile mill in Scotland. His mill and the local town were operated on policies which were, at that time, unbelievably humane. He was trying to prove that people would respond favorably to a benevolent environment. The profits of his mill seemed to prove his point; but no one else rushed to follow his example.

Owen's "Villages of Cooperation"

Like Fourier, Owen suggested that society be reorganized. He suggested that people set up "villages of cooperation." To prove that these villages would work, he sold his factory in Scotland, came to the United States, bought some land, and (in 1826) established a utopian community in Indiana.

Owen's new community was named New Harmony. Too bad it didn't live up to its name. Owen placed much trust in the people who came to join. As it turned out, it appears that there was too much trust and too little planning. In less than two years the community had fallen apart.

Owen Had a Lasting Impact

After the failure of New Harmony, Owen became a leader in the co-op and trade union movements in England. He never ceased to work, to write, and to press political leaders, to try to achieve reforms to help the common people. He worked hard at the task of improving the world, and he generated a sizeable following. His writings inspired several cooperative communities; he had a lasting impact on the labor and co-op movements in Britain. He is credited with coining the word "socialism."

THE EFFECTS OF THE UTOPIAN SOCIALISTS

Both the utopian socialists and the classical economists were looking at and thinking about all the hardship and misery in the world around them. Some of the classical economists (Adam Smith and others) explained that all this hardship was *necessary* to serve the long run good of the society. Other classical economists said it was *inevitable*—that any attempt to ease the hardship and misery of the poor would only bring more suffering. The natural laws of economics said so. There could be no escape from these natural economic laws!

But the utopian socialists refused to believe this. They would not accept and give in to the natural laws of economics. Really, most of them didn't even study these laws. They were too busy trying to change things —trying to improve the economic conditions of the common people.

The writings of the utopian socialists generally carried none of the precise and scientific analysis which is found in the writings of the classical economists. The utopian socialists weren't theoretical analysts. They were impatient activists. All of them had their followers, and all of them had some influence on the lives of some people.

There Were Many Utopian Communities

In the United States alone, more than 150 utopian communities were established, inspired by the philosophies and teachings of the utopian socialists. Most of the communities didn't last long—probably because they refused to recognize some basic laws of economics and some basic facts about the nature of human beings. But a few of the communities still exist (in modified form) even today.

The utopian socialists didn't help us much to understand the sweep of economic evolution, or to understand the natural economic forces at work in the world. But the lives of some people were influenced— perhaps improved. Some of the ideas and dreams of the utopians are still living, influencing the lives of some people, even today. These utopians cared a lot. And they fought hard. It's pleasant to think that some lasting good may have come from it all.

Enter: The Communist Revolutionaries!

Now it's time to move on and take a look at a very different "breed of cat"—people who were not nearly so mild and gentle, so optimistic and dreamy as the utopian socialists. These were angry, bitter, coldly logical people who were ready for the violent overthrow of the social, political, and economic systems which were permitting such hardships and misery to exist. Who? The communist revolutionaries. You'll be reading about them and about the problems of big business and growing monopoly power in the next chapter.

Part III: Rapid Changes in Theory and in Society—
The Evolution Becomes Explosive,
(1850s - 1920s)

*Marx Attacks Capitalism,
Monopoly Power Grows, Marshall
Rebuilds Economics, and the World
Keeps on Changing*

Chapter 8: Karl Marx, and the Emerging Monopoly Problem

In 1848 the kind and gentle philosopher John Stuart Mill published his *Principles of Political Economy.* He raised a question about the Ricardian model and its natural economic laws of distribution. Remember? Well, in that same year there appeared a much different, most outspoken pamphlet which mounted a major attack on the market system. The pamphlet was *The Manifesto of the Communist Party.* Its principal author was a man you have already heard of: Karl Marx. In the *Communist Manifesto,* Marx and his colleague Friedrich Engels called for revolution —for the workers to violently overthrow the governments in Europe, and take over the factories from the capitalists.

In 1848, Times Were Bad

Marx and Engels were looking at Europe in the mid-1800s. Conditions were bad. Very bad. There was hunger. Starvation. Popular revolts against the governments of several European countries seemed very likely. People were rioting in several cities—Paris, Brussels, Berlin, Prague, Vienna, and elsewhere. In France, King Louis Philippe was forced to resign. It was in this turmoil that Marx and Engels called for the workers of the world to unite, to forcibly overthrow their governments and to take over the factories from the capitalists.

At that moment in history it looked very much like this Marxian revolution might really happen! But somehow things held together and ultimately began getting better for most people. You need to know about this remarkable man who has had such a profound impact on the lives of all of us—this brilliant, angry "classical economist-revolutionary"—Karl Marx.

KARL MARX

Marx was in radical protest against "the system" throughout most of his life. He was born in Germany in 1818. That was when John Stuart Mill was twelve years old and the *Principles* books of both Malthus and Ricardo were about ready to appear. Before Marx was twenty-five years old he was already in trouble.

Marx had studied philosophy (and had become an atheist). He went into journalism, began writing radical articles and got himself expelled from the German city of Cologne. Then he went to Paris, developed an association with socialists and other radicals, wrote more radical things and wound up getting kicked out of Paris. Then he went to Belgium. But after the *Communist Manifesto* appeared in 1848 (when Marx was thirty) he was exiled and went to England where he spent the remainder (the last thirty-five years) of his life.

Marx Lived in Poverty

During most of his life Marx was very poor—frequently hungry—often angry. During his thirty-five years in England (until his death in 1883) he studied the writings of the classical economists, the socialists, and other philosophers. And he thought, and wrote. In 1867, almost twenty years after the *Communist Manifesto,* he completed and published the first part, or "book" of *Das Kapital* (in English, *Capital*). The second part was not published until almost twenty years later—in 1885, two years after Marx's death. The third part did not appear until nine years later, in 1894. Parts two and three were published by Marx's long-time friend, colleague, and supporter, Friedrich Engels.

Marx Studied Ricardo, for a Purpose

During his years of study and thought (and poverty) in England, Marx became one of the great economists of the last century—and, really, of all time. But he was a revolutionary and an angry man long before he was a great economist. Marx studied the classical economists (especially Ricardo) long and hard, for a purpose. He was building a case to support his conviction—a conviction he had already stated (most forcefully!) in the *Communist Manifesto.*

Marx learned and then used the precise concepts, the "natural economic laws," of the Ricardian "market system" model to show that the economic system described by the model contained within itself "the seeds of its own destruction." Marx used the Ricardian model to prove that his (Marx's) already-stated convictions really were supported by natural economic laws—that the outcome was predictable. *Inevitable.*

It shouldn't surprise you that different people can look at the same real-world conditions and use the same economic concepts and principles and yet arrive at very different conclusions about the ultimate outcome. Think back. Smith, Malthus, Ricardo, other classical economists all more or less agreed about the basic concepts—the "natural laws" of economics. They all agreed about laissez-faire and competition, and about the responsiveness of the factors of production to the demands of the society. Yet each came to a somewhat different conclusion about the future.

To Smith, everyone was going to share in the economic growth. To Malthus, the industrialists would do fine but the people would be poor. To Ricardo the landowners would ultimately be the really fat cats and their high surplus incomes (rents) would choke off economic growth. What Marx did (in his *purely economic* writings) really was not so different from this. Smith, Malthus, and Ricardo all observed the same "natural forces" at work. But each came to a different (and, as history would have it, wrong) conclusion about the ultimate outcome. And so did Marx.

Marx Was a Classical Economist

Marx "the economist" was really a classical economist, dealing with positive economics—even more than, for example, John Stuart Mill. Mill challenged some of the "natural economic laws." Marx worked within them, and with them. Marx understood and used the principles of classical economics to support his conclusion about the ultimate collapse of the market-directed system—the collapse of the system which he had the honor of naming "capitalism." What did he say in his big economics book?

DAS KAPITAL

Das Kapital is a most remarkable book. Just as *Wealth of Nations* at times shows us the thoughts and feelings of Smith the economist, and at other times Smith the antimercantilist; so *Das Kapital* reflects the several faces of its author. We see Marx the visionary, the revolutionist, the rejected philosopher, the hungry, angry, sometimes bitter man. But we also see Marx the meticulous, precise economist—the one who set out to build the airtight case showing the inevitable collapse and oblivion of this "most dastardly" economic system—capitalism.

Revolution Was Inevitable

In *Das Kapital,* Marx undertakes economic analysis with the precision of Ricardo. He uses the Ricardian laws to build his system and to explain the "inevitable sequence" of economic change—change that, to Marx, was predetermined within narrow limits by economic laws—by the natural economic forces at work in the society.

The Marxian theoretical system shows how the economic forces will lead to *inevitable revolution*—to the overthrow of capitalism. The careful, logical, precise explanation of how capitalism will lead itself to its own destruction is presented in detail in *Das Kapital.* The essence of the argument isn't difficult to understand. Here are some of the highlights.

Surplus Value

Marx agreed with Malthus and Ricardo about the iron law of wages —that wages will stay at about the subsistence level. But, said Marx, workers doing a long day's work can produce more than enough for their subsistence. That is, workers produce more "product value" than they receive in wages.

Workers may work a fourteen-hour day (not particularly unusual in the mid-1800s) but they may produce enough "product value" to cover their wages in only eight hours. Everything they produce after that (the six extra hours' worth of output) is *surplus value.* The "surplus value" goes to the capitalist. The capitalist *exploits labor* by keeping this surplus —when the surplus really belongs to the workers who produced it. (So said Marx.)

Capitalist Exploitation of Labor

Marx said that the capitalist gets profits from exploiting labor—from forcing workers to work longer than they should work to earn their subsistence wages. Next, the capitalist invests this profit (surplus value) in more capital—factories, machines, equipment. Then, with all the new capital equipment, the expanding businesses need more labor. So they try to hire more people. This increases the demand for labor and pushes up the wage rate. So what do the capitalists do? They buy even more capital to replace some of the high-wage workers. With more labor-saving capital, the capitalists can get by with less labor.

Ah, but the trap! To Marx, surplus value comes *only* from labor, and surplus value is the *only* source of profit for the industrialist. So, in the Marxian model, as the number of *workers* declines, *surplus value* falls. So profit falls. When profit falls, capitalists will try to cut costs by introducing *even more* labor-saving equipment. But in the Marxian model this only makes matters worse. Obviously. The more the capitalists try to fight the fall in profits, the worse things get. So what's the answer?

Only a Few Capitalists Will Survive

Eventually times will get very bad. Depression. Some businesses will go broke. When they do, other businesses will buy up their capital for almost nothing. According to Marx, there will be one crisis after another until a very few, very large and powerful businesses are in control of all the capital. They will own just about all of the means of production.

The wealthy people who own these businesses will have great monopoly power over all the others in the society. Also, they will have gained control of the government so they can make sure that the government will protect their *private property* rights—their rights to own and control their monopolistic businesses and to keep their monopoly profits for themselves.

Almost all of the people will be poor, hungry, wretched. The only way for this bad scene to be improved will be for the poor people—the "proletariat"—to overthrow the government. Then they can (and will) take back "their" capital from the "bourgeoisie" (BOOR-zhwa-ZEE)— the wealthy monopolists. The capital was built out of the surplus value "stolen" from the workers (the proletarians) in the first place. It's rightfully theirs. So they take it back. Thus endeth capitalism. So says Marx.

A Beautiful Society Will Emerge

What happens after the overthrow of capitalism? Marx doesn't have much to say about that. At first things will be a little rough. The capitalist-types must be eliminated. But after that, things are going to be much better.

Ultimately a beautiful society will emerge. It will be built on the high productivity of the "reclaimed capital." All will share in the output, and without the selfish greed of the capitalists there will be enough for all of the people to have all they want of everything. A beautiful world, right? Some communist "true believers" are still waiting for it to happen just as Marx predicted. How utterly ridiculous. If Marx himself were alive today he would laugh (or be distressed) that anyone could be so out-of-touch with reality.

Instead of continuing down the harsh and bitter road which Marx expected, capitalism has been continually tempered more and more to soften the harshness—to lessen the socially unacceptable conditions of "raw capitalism." And some progress has been made in limiting the monopoly power and controlling the market behavior of big firms. Certainly Marx never could have foreseen the extent of social justice that now exists in the world's "mixed economies of modified capitalism"!

Marx blamed the misery of the times on the capitalist system—not on the effects of a rapidly industrializing society caught in the early years of disruptive, explosive change.

Marx was looking at the same world that the other classical economists were looking at. But because Marx looked at it in a different way he saw different things. The theories, ideas, concepts, and other preconceptions a person has when he or she looks at something, often *determine* what that person will see. This was as true of Marx (and of the other classical economists and of the Utopian Socialists) as it is of you and me.

The Lasting Impact of Karl Marx

Marx really gave the economists some things to think about. He made some contributions to our understanding of how the market system functions. But, of course, his predictions did not come true.

Did Marx have an impact on economics? On the world? You know the answer to that. It would be difficult to find anyone who has had more impact. He inspired and gave a rationale, a justification, for the revolutions in the Soviet Union, China, Cuba, and elsewhere. His writings have been carried forward by several neo-Marxist philosophers and revolutionaries—Lenin and others in the Soviet Union, Mao Tse-tung and others in China, Castro and others in Cuba, and others who can be found in most nations throughout the world.

It was Marx who first gave these people a logical position—a way to justify revolting and taking over the private property of the capitalists—and of eliminating the capitalists in the process. There is no question that Marx has left an indelible imprint on the world.

MONOPOLY POWER AND THE NEW ANTITRUST LAWS

During the late 1800s and early 1900s, two kinds of problems were emerging. One was the problem of increasing monopoly power. The other was the problem of recurrent financial panics and depressions. According to the theories of the market system, neither of these was supposed to happen. But both of them *were* happening.

During the decades when Marx was studying and writing, the rate of economic change seemed to become more and more explosive and more violent—rapidly expanding production of coal, oil, and steel; rapidly expanding use of steam power, railroads, and ships; the growth of industrial centers—truly phenomenal! And trade within and between nations was growing rapidly. The rate of change surpassed anything the world had ever known.

A Few People Got Very Wealthy

While the industrializing nations were growing explosively, some businesses were doing the same thing. They were developing and using new technology, becoming more efficient, making big profits—and building more capital to make more profits.

By the end of the 1800s the names of such Americans as John D. Rockefeller, Andrew Carnegie, and J. P. Morgan were household words. These were some of the powerful industrial and financial giants who were building mammoth business organizations, with monopoly positions in oil, steel, railroads, and other industries. Some people were becoming concerned about all this bigness—all this concentration of economic power in the hands of a few individuals and families.

Throughout the 1800s in the United States, England, and Western Europe, wages remained low. Profits were often very high. The rate of industrial invention, innovation, and growth was phenomenal. Output continually expanded. Some of the increased output consisted of consumer goods for the rapidly growing population. But much of the output was made up of new industrial machinery, basic materials, steel rails, new factories, and so on—the essential inputs for economic growth.

Increasing Concern about Growing Monopolies

By the late 1800s, many people began to be concerned about the rapid growth and mammoth size of some of the industrial corporations. More than a hundred years had passed since Adam Smith's *Wealth of Nations* had appeared, and more than half a century had elapsed since Ricardo developed his theoretical model of the pure market system. The laissez-faire idea was strongly embedded in the philosophy of the Western world. Still, people were beginning to worry about the growing power of big businesses.

It was well known that for laissez-faire to work, effective competition was required. Only competition prevents big businesses from exploiting their workers, the consumers, the resource suppliers, the landowners, and everyone else. The writings of Marx helped to emphasize the need for concern about big business—about industrial monopolies. Various groups began to call for limitations on the monopoly powers of businesses.

The Antitrust Laws

In 1887 the United States Congress passed the Interstate Commerce Act, regulating the railroads. The Act established the Interstate Commerce Commission to set rail rates and to see to it that the railroads provided adequate service to their customers. This was a start. Three years later the basic antitrust law of the United States was passed—the Sherman Antitrust Act.

The Sherman Antitrust Act (1890). The Sherman Act made it illegal for businesses to put their assets into a "trust," or to otherwise pool their assets to eliminate competition among themselves. This Act made it illegal for businesses to reduce competition either (a) by getting together with their competitors, or (b) by destroying their competitors. Businesses were using both these tactics to gain monopoly power to restrict supply (that is, restrain trade) and push up and hold up prices.

The phrase "restraint of trade," which means businesses stop selling in competition with each other, was used in the Sherman Antitrust Act because there had to be some constitutional justification for the federal government to pass laws regulating businesses. The U.S. Constitution does not give this specific power to the federal government. But the Congress found the constitutional justification they needed in Article I, Section 8. This section grants to the federal government the specific power to regulate interstate commerce (interstate trade). So the Congress just made it illegal for businesses to combine or conspire to restrain interstate trade. That made the Sherman Act constitutional.

The Sherman Antitrust Act was not noted for its success. In the 1890s and on up to the beginning of World War I, big businesses in the United States (and throughout Britain and Western Europe as well) continued to combine and expand. In 1911, two big monopolies in the United States—Rockefeller's Standard Oil Company and the Duke brothers' American Tobacco Company—were broken into smaller units by order of the Supreme Court. But other big businesses continued to grow.

The Clayton and FTC Acts (1914). In 1914, the U.S. Congress passed two more antitrust laws—the Clayton Act and the Federal Trade Commission (FTC) Act—to try to further restrict the powers of businesses to get together to eliminate competition and/or to deceive their customers or engage in other "unfair" or anti-competitive activities.

HOW BAD IS THE MONOPOLY PROBLEM?

Neither the Sherman Act nor the Clayton Act nor the FTC Act was really effective in maintaining a high level of competition in American industry. In most of the other countries of the Western world, even less action was taken to curb the growing monopoly power of the industrial giants. There is no question that considerable monopoly power existed, and still exists, in the United States and throughout the industrialized world. How bad is this? How much does it interfere with the proper working of the market process? No one really knows.

Everyone knows that without some kind of effective competition, laissez-faire is a license to steal. On the other hand, everyone knows that we aren't going to have so many sellers and buyers in every market that no one has *any* monopoly power at all! Of course not.

In today's world, purely competitive markets with hundreds of small producer-sellers of everything, are completely out of the question. Arguments about whether or not a real-world economy made up entirely of such markets would result in efficiency or inefficiency, stability or instability, growth or stagnation, or whatever—are just no help at all in getting the answers to the questions: "How bad is the monopoly problem today?" and "What should be done?"

The Basic Dilemma of "Bigness"

The monopoly issue presents the policymakers with a dilemma: We want all the advantages of bigness: stability, financial security for workers and for local communities, social responsibility, outstanding management, research and development and innovation—all that and more. But at the same time we don't want to let anyone escape from "effective competition." We don't want anyone to get a license to steal. We would like to have our cake and eat it too—to have the *efficiency* advantages of bigness, and the *competitive* advantages of smallness at the same time. But of course we can't.

Many economists say that for the most part some kind of effective competition does exist in the modern world of "mixed socio-capitalism." Various explanations have been offered as to how this effective competition works. Other economists (and noneconomists, too) charge that big businesses have *too much* power and that they should be either (a) broken up into smaller, more competitive units, or (b) more closely regulated by the government, or (c) taken over by the government. It is not likely that these conflicting views are going to be resolved soon. (You'll be reading more about the present-day monopoly question in Part VII.)

Chapter 9: Neoclassical Economics, General Equilibrium Theory, and Some Dissenters

Judged by almost any measure you can choose, the "developed" world of 1900 was truly a different world from that of 1800. Never before in history had there been anything like it. In one short century (less, really) the total number of human beings in the developed countries more than doubled. In the most rapidly growing places the population expansion was as high as tenfold or more. The techniques of production were almost completely different. The total outputs of industrial and agricultural products were many times as great. The rate of change had become explosive!

THE EARLY 1900S: HEYDAY OF CAPITALISM

Some economists like to say that it was during the first decade or so of our century—during the period from 1900 to about the beginning of World War I—that old-style Western capitalism reached its peak of glory. Outputs had expanded greatly. Businesses had very few restrictions and paid very little taxes. Economic growth was rapid.

The trading nations were on "the international gold standard." This meant that international trade could move easily. Since all the countries used gold as their basic money, anyone could use gold (if necessary) to buy things from foreigners. World trade was carried on with very little restriction. The trading nations were prospering. The industrial and commercial enterprises were profiting and growing. Every nation was enjoying economic expansion, and every nation seemed to be benefiting.

World War I brought an end to all this. It marked the end of an era. Many people have tried to bring back the old era. Some are still trying. But it has never and will never work that way again. You, with your awareness of the explosive change which has been (and is now) going on in our world, could have guessed that. Measured by the extent of change, the years before World War I (in historical time) were many centuries ago! If some people want to be nostalgic about it, okay. But bring it back? No chance.

It's natural to want things to settle down and stabilize someplace.

When so many things are changing so fast all the time, we get confused
—it's hard to know what's going on. But that seems to be the nature of
our moment in history. And if that's the way it is, best we recognize it
and somehow learn to live with it.

The Problem of Depressions

Throughout the late 1800s and the early 1900s, a series of financial
panics and depressions occurred. Periods of depression have been noted
as far back as the 1700s. Malthus recognized the possibility that "general
gluts" (overproduction) might sometimes present a problem.

Ricardo and others considered depression conditions to be temporary, short-run, and automatically self-correcting. Nothing to worry
about. If there was a surplus of anything—labor, or products—the price
of whatever was in surplus soon would go down. Then, at the lower
prices, the surpluses would be bought up, and presto! No more surpluses! It was as simple as that. Depression just wasn't a matter of much
concern to the classical economists.

So during the late 1800s and early 1900s while the problems of
monopoly power and repeated depressions were bombarding the world,
what were the economists doing? Addressing themselves to these issues?
Generally, no. Economists continued to argue with each other and to
refine their models of how the pure market process works. It was not to
be until the 1930s that major breakthroughs were made by the economics profession in the analysis and understanding of these two problems
—the problem of depression and the problem of monopoly power.

ALFRED MARSHALL AND NEOCLASSICAL ECONOMICS

During the time the last parts of *Das Kapital* were appearing (the late
1800s) the neoclassical (new classical) school of economics was adding
its modifications and refinements to the Ricardian model. Also, a number
of schools of economic thought were developing. Each one was aiming
off more or less in its own direction.

Disillusionment with Economics in the Late 1800s

During the late 1800s there was a good bit of confusion and some
disillusionment about economics. Economists were busy disagreeing
among themselves, and the theories of economics didn't seem to be
much good in explaining the urgent problems of the real world.

Three major schools of thought arose: the German historical school,
the Austrian marginalist school, and the neoclassical school. It was an

Englishman of the neoclassical school—the Cambridge University economics professor Alfred Marshall—who "rebuilt" economics. By drawing on the works of the classical economists and integrating the marginal concept from his contemporaries of the Austrian school, Marshall pulled it all back together again.

The Classical "Economic Laws" Didn't Seem to Fit

Neoclassical economics pushed aside and/or modified several of the natural economic laws of the classical economists. Something had to be done about the idea of the inescapable inevitability of the laws—of the Malthusian Law of Population, of the iron law of wages, of the labor theory of value (Marx's law that value comes only from labor), and several others.

In the industrializing world of the *earlier* 1800s these "laws" had seemed to fit real life, to be perpetual, immutable. But in the industrialized and rapidly changing world of the *late* 1800s, anyone could see that these laws simply weren't holding true. No wonder the esteem of economics (and economists) was slipping!

It was becoming obvious that some of the basic ideas and concepts of economics needed changing. And the *marginal concept* needed to be brought in. The neoclassical economists took care of these problems for us. But that isn't all they did. They sharpened the theoretical model of the pure market system. And they used the model to show how free people and free markets (laissez-faire and perfect competition) would bring maximum welfare for the whole society. Alfred Marshall made a major contribution to this "reconstruction of economics."

Alfred Marshall's Principles of Economics

Marshall's *Principles of Economics*—"the new Bible," the complete integration, synthesis, and explanation of neoclassical economics—came out in 1890, the same year the U.S. Congress passed the Sherman Antitrust Act. Marshall's *Principles* was the latest word on neoclassical economics. It explains the workings of a laissez-faire, competitive market system. It shows very precisely and in detail how the total welfare of the society would be maximized in a "theoretical model economic system" of laissez-faire and perfect competition—that is, in a model economy directed entirely by the market process and the price mechanism, in the absence of any government regulations, or monopoly power.

Marshall's *Principles* explained—and used supply and demand graphs to show precisely—how the market process directs the economy in response to the wishes of the society. Marshall's *Principles* lets you actually *see* (graphically) how the price mechanism directs the resources of the society into the best places—how it gets all the resources to do the things the people of the society most want to be done.

Marshall's *Principles* went through eight editions. It was *the* economics book throughout the world for some thirty years. It was widely used up to and beyond the time of Marshall's death, in 1924. It is still a good book to study, to see how the theoretical model of the pure market system works—how it brings maximum welfare to the people of a society.

Marshall Had Many Contemporaries

There were many other neoclassical economists, and many challengers, in the late 1800s and early 1900s. In England, France, Germany, Austria, Italy, Scandinavia, and other countries, there were scholars, teachers, business executives, politicians, and others, all working to develop new economic ideas and to influence economic thinking. Some made important contributions to our understanding of economic theory —of the cause-and-effect interrelationships at work in an economic system.

LEON WALRAS AND GENERAL EQUILIBRIUM THEORY

One who made a very important contribution was Leon Walras (val-RAHs). You probably don't know it, but *neoclassical* economic theory rests on what we call *"partial* equilibrium analysis."

Partial Equilibrium Analysis

"Partial equilibrium analysis" means we assume that "everything else stays the same." Then we try to see what would happen if there was too much corn and not enough tomatoes. You know what would happen. The price of corn would go down and the price of tomatoes would go up. People would start eating less and growing more tomatoes, and eating more and growing less corn. Pretty soon the problem would be solved. This is partial equilibrium analysis.

Partial equilibrium analysis doesn't tell us anything about what happens to the price of Iowa corn land, the demand for tomato pickers, the number of pickup trucks running from Ames to Waterloo, the demand for steel to make farm tractors, or any of the other hundreds of things which, in fact, will *not* "stay the same." Suppose there was some kind of theoretical system which could take into account all these simultaneous changes and show how it all works out. That would be a *"general* equilibrium analysis." Now can you guess what Walras did? Of course. He developed a *general equilibrium analysis.*

General Equilibrium Analysis

Walras built a theoretical model which tied the whole economic system together. It shows how any change in one thing will cause changes in other things and how all these changes will work themselves out throughout the entire system. And after all the changes have worked themselves out, the economy will be in a new general equilibrium.

Walras used a system of mathematical equations as his model of the total economic system. Each equation represented one part of the economy, and all the equations were tied in with each other so that any change in one caused changes in all the others.

Walras enabled economists to see the total picture. He showed that the theoretical model of a pure market economy really does all fit together, that it really is a self-contained, "mutually determined system" —that everything really does work out right. For this, Walras deserves to be listed among the greatest economists of all time.

SOME DISSENTING VIEWS

There were many economists who made important contributions to economic theory during the 1800s and early 1900s. Also, during the classical period of the late 1700s and early 1800s and even before that there were many economic thinkers who made significant contributions to the advancement of economic thought. Only a few of the most outstanding ones have been mentioned in this book.

Many Great Economic Thinkers Are Not Mentioned Here

The purpose of the first half of this book is to give you a quick and easy "overview understanding" of the historical development of economic events and ideas so that you can see the issues and ideas of the 1980s in historical perspective. That purpose requires that many important people be left out along the way.

There are several good books on the "History of Economic Thought." All of them describe the contributions of many people who helped in the development of economic ideas and theories. I hope this book will capture your interest and you will go to your library and get one of those books and look more deeply into this interesting subject. But for now I doubt that you would gain any lasting understanding from memorizing a long list of strange-sounding names—with a list of "major contributions" to go with each.

Only two more people who were writing about economics in the late 1800s and early 1900s will be mentioned here. Both of them were dissenters: Henry George, and Thorstein Veblen.

Henry George and the Single Tax

In the late 1800s Henry George wrote his very popular book *Progress and Poverty.* The one point of his book was that the economic system should not permit lucky landowners to get wealthy just because they happened to own some land in a good place—like Manhattan Island or some other place where a city is going to grow up, or where a railroad is going to come through, or where oil is going to be discovered, or where something else lucky is going to happen. He said these landowners do nothing to deserve their wealth. Their wealth is unplanned, unnecessary, and *undeserved*—a rip-off.

Henry George suggested that the money landowners get from this kind of undeserved good luck should be taxed away. This land tax should be the "single tax"—the only tax necessary. The land tax revenues would be great enough so that no other taxes would need to be levied. Henry George had an interesting thesis and a large number of followers. He gave all of us something to think about.

Thorstein Veblen and Conspicuous Consumption

Thorstein Veblen was an unusual and interesting person and a brilliant and challenging economist. He was a professor at the University of Chicago in 1899 when he wrote his very popular book *The Theory of the Leisure Class.* Veblen criticized the whole approach of materialistic society—the "keeping up with the Joneses" hangup which he saw in American life.

One of Veblen's best known phrases is "conspicuous consumption." It's the idea that people buy and use up things unnecessarily, just to show off. Veblen thought that conspicuous consumption was inherent in the market system, and that it results in a great waste of resources.

In the early 1900s, Veblen wrote several more books. All of them carried forward his initial thesis—that the market economy as it works in the real world is aimed off in the wrong direction. It's wasteful, and too much influenced by rich people with vested interests. He predicted continuing, rapid technological and sociological changes and readjustments in the society. His impact on economics and on economists was (and is) great. Many of today's economic policies and programs—for consumer protection, income redistribution, and others—have deep roots somewhere in Veblen's theories and philosophy.

OLD-STYLE CAPITALISM'S LAST BURST OF GLORY: THE 1920s

To be sure, capitalism had its dissenters. There were many in addition to Henry George and Thorstein Veblen. The neo-Marxists continued to be active, to be sure! The Bolshevik (communist) Revolution occurred in Russia in 1917. But for the most part the Western world was little touched by the dissenters.

The Social Ethic Supports Capitalism

Capitalism was strong, productive, growing, and clearly justified by its religious and social ethics. By now, everyone had somehow learned the Protestant Ethic: "God helps those who help themselves." "The idle mind is the Devil's workshop." *"Work* for the Night is Coming." Everyone had learned to believe that people who are poor *should be* poor. They are poor because that's what they deserve. They haven't worked hard enough—haven't been productive enough—to deserve anything better.

You can tell a person's worth by what he or she owns. Poverty is a sign of worthlessness. Poor people are not much good. But rich people are honorable and respectable. A wealthy person is good and worthy and should be looked up to. Such were the generally accepted values of the capitalism of the 1920s.

I'm sure you know that such value judgments still exist today. The economic philosophies and theories of "capitalism" have contributed to the acceptance of value judgments such as these—such ideas as the relationship between the "value" of something and its price, and the idea of the "productivity principle of distribution" (those who produce a lot should earn a lot and those who don't, shouldn't).

Prosperity, Then Depression

In the United States in the 1920s, economic expansion continued. The conditions of most of the people seemed to be improving, and (with the exception of some problems in agriculture) economic harmony and a happy life for most people seemed to have arrived. Of course, nothing was said about the "invisible members" of the society. But it is only in more recent years that people seem to have taken much notice of the minority people—the very poor, the dispossessed, the underprivileged, the discriminated against, or the incapable and unsupported ones.

By the late 1920s the American economy was heralded as being on a "high plateau." People talked about how difficult it would be to think of anything better. The economies of Britain and all of Western Europe had largely overcome the destructive effects of World War I. It seemed for a moment that economic conditions in the world were going to be all right again—that the golden age of the early 1900s was about to remanifest itself. But as you know, this was not our destiny. Instead, the whole economic structure was about to fall apart. A sudden, powerful, bewildering change was coming. The American—and world—economy was about to move into the Great Depression of the 1930s.

Probably you've already heard a lot about the Great Depression. What a confusing, bewildering time of social, economic, and political turmoil that was! We'll get into that in the next chapter. But before we go on, here's one more brief glance back into history—one more look at this explosive change we're all caught up in.

THE FRUSTRATIONS OF RAPID CHANGE

It's difficult to realize how much change has occurred just in the past 20 years—just during your lifetime. Throughout almost all of the history of mankind it would have taken several centuries to accumulate the total amount of change which has occurred since you were born—or even since you were in the fourth grade! It's no wonder that our understanding of economic happenings has had some difficulty keeping up with the changing times.

For Many Centuries, Change Was Very Slow

Here's something to think about. Back in history, how long do you expect it would actually have taken to bring about as much change as you have seen in your lifetime? Just think about the degree of sameness— the very, very slow rate of change—for so many centuries.

There was very little change over the twenty-five centuries from Babylonia to ancient Rome and Greece (about 3000 B.C. to 500 B.C.); and then during the five centuries of the Greek and Roman city-states (about 500 B.C. to 1 A.D.); and then during the five centuries of the Roman Empire (about 1 A.D. to 500 A.D.); and then during the next ten centuries of the Middle Ages, up to the discovery of America (about 500 A.D. to 1500 A.D.); and then even in the three more "mercantilist" centuries which led up to the beginning of the United States (about 1500 A.D. to 1800 A.D.).

The pace of change was quickening somewhat during the mercantilist period. But throughout most of history, just think how very long it took for even the smallest change to take place! In any one *century* there might not be enough change—economic or any other kind—to notice.

Now the Rate of Exchange is Explosive

Approaching the 1800s, the Industrial Revolution somehow got started. During the 1800s it burst forth, breaking everything loose, disrupting and changing everything. We have been blasted off on a journey of increasing speed, away from the world of yesterday. And toward what? Toward an unknown—an unknowable—tomorrow.

As you read in the chapters coming up about all the changes happening in our own century, stop to think once in a while about how *unbelievably fast* it's all happening. Perhaps that will help you to understand this brand new ball game in which humanity suddenly finds itself forced to play. Perhaps it will help you to be more tolerant of your parents, your government leaders, your college administrators, your professors—and perhaps yourself—when you find that the game doesn't seem to be going as you think it should.

*Neoclassical Economics Didn't Seem
to Explain the Depression, So Some
New Ideas and Theories Were
Developed*

Chapter 10: The Great Depression and the "New Deal"

When the year 1929 began, everybody was sure that the booming American economy was in great shape. Then in October of 1929, the bubble burst. The decade of the 1920s had been one of growth, prosperity, good times, high employment, happy days for most people. The total real value of the nation's output (value of goods and services produced) had increased from about $73 billion in 1920, to more than $100 billion in 1929—a total increase of more than forty percent.

Population was expanding, of course. More people were sharing this larger output. But even so, output *per person* increased by about 25 percent over this decade. When Herbert Hoover accepted the nomination of the Republican Party in 1928 he said: "We shall soon with the help of God be in sight of the day when poverty will be banished from this nation." But as you very well know, things didn't turn out that way.

THE STOCK MARKET "BOOM AND BUST" OF THE 1920s

Throughout the decade of the '20s, while employment and output were increasing, prices of stocks on the stock markets were going up faster and faster. Throughout the first half of the decade, stock prices increased only moderately. Then the speedup began. A person holding an average group of stocks in 1925 would have seen the value of those stocks increase by about 50 percent before the end of 1926—a 50 percent increase in about one year. And the same thing happened again in 1927.

Ten thousand dollars invested in "an average group" of stocks in

1925 would be worth about $20,000 before the end of 1927. Before another year had passed, that $20,000 would just about double again—to about $40,000 before the end of 1928. And by August of 1929? Would you believe it doubled again? And more? That $10,000 investment in stocks in 1925 would very likely have reached a value of $100,000 before the crash came in October 1929.

Here's another thing: A person could have bought that $10,000 worth of stocks for as little as *10 percent down.* So for an actual cash investment of $1,000 in 1925, the "average person" would have wound up with $100,000 in 1929. Is it any wonder that everyone was "playing the stock market"?

The Stock Market Collapse

By 1929 the ever-growing demand for stocks had pushed stock prices up far beyond the *real* values of the assets which the stocks represented. Many people knew they were holding overvalued stocks. But as long as stock prices kept on going up, why sell? Then, in the fall of 1929, some investors began to sell, to get their cash. This selling pushed down stock prices and caused others to lose confidence. There was more and more selling until finally, on October 29, the market collapsed. Everyone was trying to sell but no one was buying.

Economic Conditions Got Worse and Worse

For the next three years stock prices kept falling. Suppose a person had owned $100,000 in General Electric stocks in 1929. By 1932 those stocks would be worth about $3000. As stock prices fell month after month, businesses all over the country were failing. Unemployment was increasing. More and more banks were failing. Economic collapse continued to visit one company after another, one place after another, one family after another. There seemed to be no end to the downtrend.

THE GREAT DEPRESSION OF THE 1930s

Each year it seemed that conditions were so bad they couldn't get worse. But the next year *was* worse. Some people were actually starving in the cities. Food—grain, potatoes, livestock—was going to waste on the farms. Crops were rotting in the fields. Sometimes food prices were so low in the cities that it didn't even pay to ship the goods to market. Farmers couldn't get enough for the potatoes they shipped to pay the freight bill!

People in the cities were hungry, all right. But they didn't have any money. They couldn't buy the potatoes which were already there in the city, getting old in the grocers' storerooms. The economic system just wasn't working.

During this period many people in the United States joined the Communist Party. Veterans of World War I marched on Washington demanding that the government do something to help. The people didn't understand what was going on, but they knew they were hungry. Surely *any kind* of economic system must be better than this! An economic system that lets people starve while goods go to waste is obviously not doing a very good job. A person doesn't have to study economics to figure that out!

The Market System Wasn't Working

The market system is supposed to work by getting people to produce things for other people. That's the way people get the things they want —by producing things "for the market." It's all supposed to work out neatly. But during the depression the markets weren't working. So the system wasn't working.

The people in the cities were wondering how they could get some potatoes to feed their families. The farmers were wondering how they could sell their potatoes so they could get some money to pay their debts and keep going. But the city people had no jobs and no money so they couldn't buy, so the farmers couldn't sell. When nobody's buying, then nobody's selling. The market system just isn't working.

The potatoes rotted in the fields. The city families went hungry. What had gone wrong with the world? What was causing all these bad times? What could be done to get the system working again? Nobody seemed to know.

No One Knew What Was Happening, or What to Do

The nation's leaders asked their economist-advisors what was happening, and why—and when things would start getting better. But the economists didn't know. This was a new situation. Neither the classical nor the neoclassical nor any of the other theories of economics were of much help in explaining how such serious and prolonged depressed conditions could exist—or what (if anything) might be done.

It was easy to see that the model of the pure market system didn't help much to explain what was going on. This was some kind of new problem—a brand new ball game—a game the economists hadn't learned to play.

Conditions Were Really Bad

The U.S. economy and the economies of the other free nations of the world kept getting worse and worse throughout the early 1930s. Then in 1933 things leveled off at a very low level. There was serious depression—U.S. and worldwide. There were some improvements over the next five or six years, but not much. The recovery of the U.S. economy was painfully slow.

In 1933 the total output of the U.S. economy was only about one-half the size of the 1929 output. The "normal" unemployment rate when the economy is healthy is somewhere around 3 or 4 percent of the labor force. But in 1933 more than 25 percent of the people who wanted to work couldn't find jobs. So they (and their families) had no incomes.

The families of most farmers and fishermen were living in serious poverty. Some of the lucky ones who had jobs were getting paid *less than* (would you believe?) $10 a month. Sure, $10 then would buy a lot more than $10 now—maybe as much as 7 or 8 times as much! But how would you like to try to support a family today on $70 or $80 a month? In many parts of the country a wage of $20 a month was considered very good. People were begging for jobs—for *any* way to make money, at *any* wage.

Between 1929 and 1933, some 85,000 businesses failed. One bank out of every five went out of business. Some *nine million people* lost their savings as the banks collapsed. On March 4, 1933, the U.S. government ordered all the banks in the country to close—that was to keep *all* the banks from failing under the increased assault of panic-stricken people withdrawing their deposits, demanding cash.

Things really were miserable. There were millions of hungry, desperate people. It's no wonder that some committed suicide—and that many joined the Communist Party. And it's no wonder that some committed crimes just to be sent to jail—where they could get shelter and food. I don't suppose freedom or liberty has very great appeal to one who is freezing or starving to death. Many Americans found that out in the 1930s.

The Depression Went on for Many Years

It's hard to believe how long this Great Depression lasted. It never got any worse than it was in March 1933, but as the years passed it didn't get much better. The government was trying out all kinds of programs. But the economy just didn't seem to respond very much.

Things got somewhat better in '35 and '36, but then in '37 and '38 there was another sharp drop. Unemployment all this time had been more than 15 percent of the labor force. In 1938 it was up to almost 20 percent. Also, in 1938 big surpluses began piling up on the farms again. Farm prices fell again.

Government Military Spending Overcame the Depression

It wasn't until 1939, when the government began to increase spending for military production, that total recovery began. By 1944 there was virtually no unemployment. The value of the nation's output was double that of 1929. Half the total output was being produced in response to the huge military spending program of the government. The government alone spent as much in 1944 as *total spending in the economy* had been in 1929 (about $100 billion).

See what happened when the government began its unlimited spending for World War II? How quickly the economic system began running full speed again! No more depression. No more unemployment. No more idle factories or unused surpluses of farm products or labor or anything else. A miraculous recovery! This experience taught us one thing: If the government is willing to spend enough money to employ enough people and buy enough output, it certainly can overcome a depression.

Did the government wait for World War II before it tried to do anything about the depression? Of course not. Lots of things were tried. Some seemed to help. Some didn't. What was the government doing? And what new ideas were economists coming up with during this long, miserable, bewildering decade of the 1930s?

THE "NEW DEAL": BASIC CHANGE IN THE ECONOMIC SYSTEM

With things so bad and getting worse following the stock market crash in October 1929, people were urging the government to do something. Many voices clamored for government action. The clamor came from businesses large and small, from state and local governments, from welfare agencies and private charities, from religious organizations, from groups of irate citizens, from just about everybody. The veterans of World War I marched on Washington demanding relief. But no one seemed to know what to do.

When Franklin D. Roosevelt was inaugurated on March 3, 1933, he promised to do something. He promised a "New Deal." He promised *action.* A real flurry of action is what he delivered. When he was all through, the American economic system was a *different* economic system than it had been before. A *better* system? Perhaps. Some people disagree on this. But everyone agrees that it was different.

What Was Roosevelt's "New Deal"?

What was meant by the "New Deal"? You can answer that question in many different ways. One way would be to list the fifteen or so major pieces of legislation which were pushed through Congress during the first 100 days after Roosevelt took office, and to describe the impact of these important federal acts on how the American economic system functions.

Another way to answer the question "What was the New Deal?" is to say that it was an idea, a concept, a vision of major change in the American economic system—a change away from the philosophies and policies of laissez-faire. The idea was that we were going to "reshuffle the cards and deal them out again"—to give the people with "bad hands" a chance to do better—that is, a "new deal."

This New Deal means that we will give the farmers some help, and some economic power to protect themselves from economic adversity. We will let workers join unions and bargain with (and if they wish, strike against) their employers. We will establish a social security program so that the welfare of each individual will be (to some extent) a responsibility shared by all members of the society.

The New Deal tried to do something specific, something direct to help those who were in difficulty—and that included farmers, workers, businesses, young people, old people, city people, country people: just about everyone. The government started programs to employ people, and to buy up the surplus food and give it to people.

Increasing the Economic Role of Government

Ideas about the proper role of government were changing fast. The New Deal idea was that wages and farm prices need to be kept high enough to support people adequately; that people have a right to live in decent housing—and that the government has a responsibility to *do something* to bring about these results. The New Deal also included the ideas that the banks and stock markets and other financial institutions should be watched over and regulated by the government to be sure the interests of the people are protected; and that the government should watch over and regulate employment practices—should prohibit child labor, should set limits on the length of the work week, and should require that higher wages be paid for overtime work. And there were many other changes to the economic system—all away from laissez-faire toward more influence and control by government in the economy.

A New Philosophy: Challenge to Laissez-Faire

Perhaps we could summarize the philosophy of the New Deal this way: "It is the responsibility of the government to be concerned about the operation of the economic system, and about the material welfare of the people. The government has a responsibility to keep the system running properly, to oversee all of the activities within the economic system which might adversely affect the lives and conditions of the people of the society, and to see to it that everyone has an opportunity to share in the high level of well-being which this 'modern economic system' can produce. Even those people who are unproductive—because of health or age or unemployment or some other misfortune—should still get a share of the output. The government should take some income from the productive people and give it to the unproductive ones."

What a basic change this New Deal was! The American economic system *before* the New Deal was quite a different system from the American economic system *after* the New Deal. *Quite* a different system! It's no wonder that many people—especially those who had been enjoying most of the benefits of the pre-New Deal system—were strongly opposed to President Franklin D. Roosevelt's New Deal.

But in 1933 and the years following, almost everyone was feeling the squeeze of the depression. Most of the people were disillusioned, confused, bewildered. The depression had been dragging on, getting worse and worse each year. People who in 1929 would have considered the New Deal subversive and un-American (or maybe even a Communist take-over!), in 1933 were ready to try anything. By then it was obvious to most people that sitting around waiting for the natural forces of the laissez-faire market system to solve the problem just wasn't the answer.

The real world wasn't behaving the way the neoclassical model said it should. The model just didn't fit the reality of the 1930s. So what happened? What *always* happens when the theoretical explanations don't offer workable solutions to the real world's economic problems? Pragmatism takes over. That's what happened.

THE NEW DEAL LEGISLATION AND PROGRAMS

It has been said that when Roosevelt took office he mounted his horse and galloped off in several directions at once. And really, that's sort of what he did. So many programs, each aimed at overcoming some visible problem, and some of the programs inconsistent and conflicting with each other—but there was no question that something was being done. *Action* was being taken.

The depression years of the Roosevelt administration are a truly unique period in American history. The things which happened during these few years brought major changes both in economics and in politics. The greatest changes were in the rapidly increasing functions of government in the economic system.

Many vital pieces of legislation were passed during the 1930s. It would be easy for you to spend an entire semester or an entire year studying the effects of the New Deal legislation on the economic system. Several books have been written about the changes wrought during these few hectic years. I hope that some day you will have the opportunity to study the interesting things that were going on then. But this book is not the place for that.

But you need a quick overview of the kinds of changes which were made by the New Deal legislation and programs. Many of the programs were temporary, but many initiated permanent changes in the nature of the American economic system and in the role of government in the economy.

Roosevelt had to do several things *immediately.* He had to get the banks open again, and make the people confident that they would *remain* open. He had to somehow get some emergency funds to the state and local governments throughout the nation, almost all of which were in bad financial shape. And he had to get some food (or some money) into the hands of the unemployed and hungry people. All three of these objectives were worked on immediately.

The most difficult objective was getting money into the hands of people—getting them employed. The government started creating new money and undertaking all kinds of programs, including local conservation projects of all kinds and, later, public works projects. What to build? Build anything anybody can think of that seems to need to be built! Even if it didn't really need to be built, maybe it was better to build it than to leave the people unemployed. (Maybe someday, some use for it could be figured out.)

The National Industrial Recovery Act

After the banks were reopened and the state and local governments were provided some emergency funds and the first steps were made toward overcoming starvation and unemployment, then attention was turned to the task of industrial recovery. The National Industrial Recovery Act was passed. It included "something for everybody."

The Act provided for minimum prices and production limits in agriculture; it permitted labor to unionize and bargain with employers; and it permitted the business firms in each industry to get together and work out a "code of fair competition," which, in effect, gave them monopoly power over outputs, marketing territories, prices, and other things.

Truly, the National Industrial Recovery Act (NIRA) was one of the most far-reaching pieces of legislation ever passed by the U.S. Congress. It was a radical departure from the concept of competition—in the agricultural markets, in the industrial-product markets, and in the labor markets. The NIRA was based on the idea that if everybody had enough *market power,* they could keep their prices up, thus keep their incomes up, thus keep their spending up, and thus assure prosperity in the economy.

The Act also established a public works program which provided for the construction of highways, dams, housing, post offices, other public buildings, water and sewer systems—any kind of public works project anyone could think of.

The NIRA, and the National Recovery Administration (NRA) which it created, lasted only about two years. In 1935 the Act was held unconstitutional by the Supreme Court. But soon, new acts were passed reestablishing and expanding many of the provisions of the NIRA. Agricultural markets were again placed under government control, and the monopoly powers of labor (to unionize and bargain and strike) were reaffirmed and strengthened. So it's true that although the NIRA was held unconstitutional in 1935, many of the changes initiated in that Act were reestablished by new legislation and still live on today.

Social Welfare Legislation

During the early days of the Roosevelt administration, emergency funds were provided to the state and local governments to bail out the welfare programs in the state and local areas. People needed relief, but the local governments didn't have much money for relief programs. Even with the federal grants the welfare programs couldn't meet the needs. Soon it was clear that the people wanted the government to take a stronger, more continuing role in providing for economic welfare.

The Social Security Act In 1935, the Social Security Act was passed. This Act set up the old age and survivor's insurance program which has continued and been expanded repeatedly to the present time. This is a program of income redistribution: income from the wage earners (through social security taxes) and from the public (through taxes on businesses, which are ultimately paid by the public through higher product prices) is redistributed to people who are retired or disabled or sick or dependent survivors of wage earners. This is the OASDHI (also called the "Retirement, Survivors, and Disability Insurance and Medicare Program) which now redistributes billions of dollars of income every year.

The Fair Labor Standards Act In 1938 the Fair Labor Standards Act was passed. It established minimum wages, set the forty-hour workweek, and established various other "fair labor standards." This Act has also been continued and expanded to the present time.

The Full Employment Act of 1946

One of the important pieces of New Deal legislation—legislation committing the government to an increased and continuing responsibility for the welfare of the people and for the functioning of the economy —was not passed until after the depression was over—not until the year after the sudden death of President Roosevelt in 1945.

As World War II came to an end, many people were aware that massive government spending for the war had brought an end to the great depression. So now that the war was over, what was going to happen? Many people expected another depression. It was in this atmosphere that Congress passed the *Full Employment Act of 1946.*

This 1946 Act did not spell out any program. It simply stated that it is the continuing responsibility of the federal government to see to it that the economy will keep operating fast enough so that people can get jobs and incomes—so that employment and production and output will be maintained. If the economic system doesn't appear to want to run at the right speed on its own power, the government is responsible for doing something to keep it running at the right speed. This Act set up the Council of Economic Advisers to keep the administration in touch with conditions in the economy, and to advise the President whenever action should be taken.

THE LONG-RANGE IMPACT OF THE NEW DEAL

It would hardly be correct to say that following the years of the depression and World War II, laissez-faire was dead in the American economy. But certainly in many ways laissez-faire had been significantly reduced. The influence of the political process on economic choices had been greatly expanded. Most of the changes that were made were more "pragmatic," trial-and-error changes than changes directed by either theory or philosophy.

But what were the economists doing all this time? If the economic theories couldn't help to explain what was going on and couldn't provide any guidelines as to what the government might do, then what were the economists doing?

You remember that back in the late 1800s economists weren't held in high esteem by laymen and policymakers because their "economic laws" didn't seem to be working in the real world. That's what happened again in the 1930s, when the accepted economic theories didn't seem to help to understand what was going on. But some economists were working on new explanations—trying to develop new ways of looking at and explaining what was going on in the world.

The economist who made the greatest contribution—the one who has had the greatest impact on economic thinking in this century (perhaps in any century) was John Maynard Keynes (KAYns). It's time now to talk about the evolution of economic ideas during the 1930s—especially about the new ideas introduced by this brilliant and outspoken Englishman, Lord John Maynard Keynes. You'll be reading about who he was and what he did in the next chapter.

Chapter 11: The Economics of John Maynard Keynes

The experience of the Great Depression made it obvious that economists had some rethinking to do. Economists needed some new ways of looking at and explaining the economic forces at work in the modern industrial economic system of the twentieth century.

NEOCLASSICAL ECONOMICS DOESN'T DIRECTLY ADDRESS THE PROBLEM OF DEPRESSION

Neoclassical economics didn't help much to explain what was happening during the 1930s. Economists, politicians, business and finance experts *all* were trying to figure out and explain this new real-world happening: prolonged, persistent depression. To get at it, things had to be looked at in a new and different way.

For more than 100 years there have been times of boom and slump —some times when employment was high and wages were rising, prosperity was in the air; then other times when people found it hard to get jobs, incomes were low, and businesses had trouble surviving. These recurrent periods of prosperity and depression—these ups and downs of business—had been recognized as "normal cycles" in business activity. For a long time economists had been talking about and explaining these business cycles.

Business Cycles Were Natural and Self-Correcting

Neoclassical economics explained these recurrent depression periods as a necessary part of the system. There were several different theories, but all of them explained how a depression was a short-term, self-correcting condition—how depression conditions soon would move on into a period of recovery and then prosperity. But what about the 1930s? The U.S. economy (and the economies of most of the modern world) went into a devastating economic slump that just kept going on, year after year. What about that?

Neoclassical economics had no way to explain an entire *decade* of continuous depression. And without the massive government spending required by World War II, when might it have ended? And how?

Neoclassical economics really didn't offer any good answers to these questions. Can you see that economists had some rethinking to do?

Neoclassical Economics Describes "the Market System at Work"

There must be a thousand different ways of looking at the world. And how you look at it determines what you will see. The classical and neoclassical economists looked at it as "a market system at work." They saw people buying things and they saw businesses producing the things people were buying. They saw the demand of the people controlling the uses of the society's resources. They saw everybody seeking more—workers seeking higher wages, landowners trying to get better rents, owners of money and capital trying to maximize their incomes, and businesses working for maximum profits. They saw all these "owners of the factors of production" seeking more for themselves and thereby automatically responding to the demands of the society.

The businessman was supposed to make profits, then invest the profits and bring more economic growth. Competition was supposed to keep each business, each worker, each landowner, and everyone else doing the most productive, most valuable things for the economy. Competition was to keep everyone in line. That's the way Adam Smith and the other classical economists, and Alfred Marshall and the other neoclassical economists looked at the world. And when they looked at it that way, of course that's what they saw.

Even the theories of Marx and the other radical critics of the laissez-faire market system were aimed in the wrong direction to help to explain the persistent, prolonged depression. Generally, *all* economists were concerned with the *interworkings of the parts* of the economic system. How do the pieces fit together? How are society's choices made—about what to produce, which inputs and techniques of production to use, and how much "distributive share" each person will get? These were the kinds of questions economists were prepared to answer.

The Depression Question Wasn't Considered Relevant

To the classical and neoclassical economists, these "production" and "distribution" questions seemed to be the relevant issues, since neoclassical economics explains how depression will take care of itself automatically. But the 1930s presented the world with some new kinds of questions. And on these new questions the old ways of looking at the economy didn't help very much.

With surplus farm commodities, prices were supposed to fall so that people would buy up the surpluses. With surplus workers, wages were supposed to fall so that more workers would be hired. With surplus industrial output, prices of products were supposed to fall until people would buy them all. With surplus savings, interest rates were supposed to go down until investors would borrow all the savings, and invest.

All of the surpluses of everything—food, workers, products, money —were supposed to be automatically cleared away by falling prices. But that didn't happen. The surpluses persisted. The economy slowed down more and more. Hungry people couldn't get the surplus food. People experienced "starvation in the midst of plenty."

The goods weren't moving across the market. Why not? The otherwise very useful concepts of classical and neoclassical economics simply couldn't answer this kind of question. The neoclassical explanation of "how the system works" is just great—so long as the system is working. But when the system *breaks down* that's something else! And sure enough, the system had broken down.

Neoclassical economics has excellent explanations of why the market system must work—why it will not break down. So when the system did break down, neoclassical theory was not in a position to help very much. According to neoclassical theory it couldn't happen. The automatic price adjustments would not let it happen. But it *did* happen.

Needed: A New Way of Looking at the Economy

Explanations of how the market functions when it is operating properly are not very helpful in understanding what's wrong when the market breaks down. The world needed to be conceptualized differently— to be looked at in a different way.

Think back. Every era in history which has created a new set of conditions and problems has seen philosophers and activists arise to try to explain things and/or to change them—Adam Smith and Malthus and Ricardo and Saint Simon and Fourier and Robert Owen and Karl Marx and so many others—all arose more or less as products of their times. Each of them took on and tried to explain and/or change the real conditions of their day.

In the 1930s we needed a new way of looking at the total economy. We needed to better understand what keeps it running—and what makes it speed up or slow down. We needed to understand what is now called "macroeconomics." John Maynard Keynes gave us the new approach— the new principles and theories. He gave the world a good start toward finding some of the answers it was looking for.

JOHN MAYNARD KEYNES

John Maynard Keynes gave the world a new way of explaining the depression problem. His book *The General Theory of Employment, Interest, and Money* (1936) explains how it is possible for the economy to go into a persistent depression. And it explains what governments can do to overcome depression.

Keynes offered *positive* suggestions. He didn't suggest (as neoclassical economists did) that we suffer along and wait for the "natural economic laws" to work things out. The Keynesian *General Theory* recommended increased government spending. And it explained why.

The General Theory of Employment, Interest and Money (1936)

The first chapter of *The General Theory* consisted of a single paragraph in which Keynes slapped the economics profession in the face. Even now, more than forty years later, some economists are still smarting from the blow. What did Keynes say? Only that neoclassical economics didn't happen to fit the real world of the 1930s—that neoclassical economics was "misleading and disastrous" if we tried to use it to guide public policy. Nothing timid about Keynes!

The economics profession scurried around trying to defend its position. But as time went on, more and more people came to accept "Keynesian economics" as an essential addition to our understanding of how the market system works in the real world.

It was not that Keynesian economics invalidated neoclassical economics. Of course not. The most basic, most essential principles of economics are described and explained in neoclassical economics. But Keynes said that there are times when that model—that way of looking at the world—is more *misleading* than helpful—that sometimes the real world doesn't behave the way the model *assumes* it will behave. When that happens, the neoclassical model may lead its followers off in exactly the *wrong* direction. Keynes said that's what was happening in the 1930s.

Keynes Gave Us Macroeconomics

What Keynes did was comparable, in a way, to what Adam Smith had done about 160 years earlier. Keynes looked at the real world and gave us a new way of looking at what was happening.

Most economists have exhibited much greater brilliance in dealing with models than in dealing with real-world issues and problems. But

Keynes saw and understood the real world. And more than that. He had the unique ability to understand the real-world forces which influence and control the level of economic activity—the speed at which the economy runs.

Keynes explained the forces which control the speed of the economy. He built a theory explaining the depression—a theory which was aimed *directly* at the problem, and which offered avenues of *positive action* for dealing with it. Keynes gave us much of what we now call "macroeconomics."

Keynes' Earlier Writings

Keynes was about fifty years old when *The General Theory* appeared in 1936. But much earlier, before he reached thirty-five, he had indicated his ability to see and understand the economic realities of the world. In 1919 he wrote a book called the *Economic Consequences of the Peace.* In this book he explained why the World War I peace agreement was unworkable. The book was straight from the shoulder; it named names, and it left no doubt that Keynes thought the whole agreement proceeding was an exercise in stupidity. He said that the agreement would break down, and he predicted serious economic disruptions as a result. The book cost him some friends. But as it turned out, he was right.

During the 1920s, Keynes was the editor of the *Economic Journal* (one of Britain's most honored economic publications). He continued to write articles criticizing the government. In the mid-1920s he attacked Britain's decision to return to the gold standard. He predicted that this move would be harmful to the nation and that it would fail. But no one seemed to be listening. Again, as it turned out, he was right.

In 1930, Keynes published his two-volume *Treatise on Money.* This *Treatise* explained many of the concepts which later were integrated into his *General Theory* in 1936. But in 1930, no one was ready for a "new look" in economics. Everyone expected the depression to be short. Soon everything would be rolling along again. Keynes disagreed. He saw some serious fundamental problems. Some of these are explained in his *Treatise on Money.* But at that time no one was listening very well.

As the years passed and the depression deepened, Keynes continued to give advice to government leaders. He wrote an open letter to President Roosevelt (published in the *New York Times* in 1933) and he served as occasional advisor to Roosevelt in the 1930s. In 1936 *The General Theory* was published. But it would not be until several years later that most of the economic theory expressed in that book would become integrated into the thinking of most economists.

Keynes at Bretton Woods

From the time *The General Theory* appeared in 1936 until his death ten years later, Keynes continued to play an active role as an adviser to governments on national and international policy. One of his last major involvements was in the Bretton Woods conference (at Bretton Woods, New Hampshire) in 1945. There the postwar system of international exchange was worked out.

At Bretton Woods, Keynes suggested that some alternative to gold should be used in international finance. He suggested using some kind of "paper credits" instead of gold. But at that time the idea of using paper credits was just too far out. He predicted that the time would come when the world would have no choice but to move to some such system. Almost twenty-five years later the major nations agreed that it was essential to establish paper credits as an alternative to gold in balancing international financial accounts. A system of "special drawing rights" (SDRs) was initiated in the late 1960s and is now playing an important role in international finance.

John Maynard Keynes was one of the great economists. It isn't likely that any economist who ever lived has had a more clear understanding of how economics works in the real world. Most of the economic concepts and principles we now call "macroeconomics" have their roots in Keynes' *General Theory of Employment, Interest, and Money.*

We needed a new image of the world— a different perspective. John Maynard Keynes gave us that perspective. His ideas have had a very real influence on the lives of all of us. No economic discussion, no prescription for attacking an economic problem, no economic policy has been quite the same since. Even those who have consistently opposed "the Keynesian way" of looking at the world have been unable to ignore Keynesian economics.

KEYNESIAN ECONOMICS

What is Keynesian economics? It's a different way of looking at the world. It looks *directly* at the questions: What determines the *speed* of the economy? What determines *how much* (in total) will be produced? What determines whether or not all the labor, capital, land (the factors of production) will be employed as fully as their owners (and the society) want them to be employed?

Keynesian economics focuses on *the rate of spending* in the economy. Spending is what pulls forth the *output,* and thus supports *employment* and *incomes.* Keynesian economics tells us that if we can understand what determines the level of spending, we will know what determines the level of employment and production—of output and income in the economy.

Keynesian economics tells us that public policies which *change the level of spending* in the economy will *change the level of employment and production, and output and income* in the economy. Keynesian economics offers the government a *positive* approach to overcoming depression:

Make total spending increase and the economy will speed up. Increase government spending. Cut taxes so people and businesses will have more money to spend. Permit the money supply to expand. As the government and the businesses and the people all spend more, people will all receive more income. As people's incomes increase, their spending will increase. The result: prosperity!

If the Keynesian prescription works, the economy will boom. Soon the government will need to cut down on its spending and raise taxes to keep the boom from running away into inflation.

The Market System Was "Flooded Out"

During the depression, people were unemployed. They were receiving no income, so they weren't spending to buy anything. They couldn't buy anything because they didn't have any money to spend! The market process wasn't working.

The markets were "flooded out." Surpluses existed in all the markets, but no one was buying the surpluses. Businesses weren't employing people. Why produce more output when you can't sell what you already have?

No one wanted to build new factories, homes, or anything else. Everyone was taking a defensive position—trying to hold on to what little bit of money they had for as long as they could. Not much money was being spent, so not much income was being generated.

When businesses collapsed, workers lost their jobs so they couldn't buy things. So the farmers couldn't sell their products. They couldn't buy tractors, gasoline, or fertilizer. The tractor, gasoline, and fertilizer companies had to cut back. Banks couldn't collect on their loans so many of them failed.

The moving finger of economic ruin touched each unit in the economy—each household, each industry, each firm. Things just kept getting worse. Why? And what could be done? These are the questions that Keynesian economics came forward to answer.

Keynes Focused on the "Spending Sectors"

Keynes focused *directly* on the problem: not enough total spending. It's obvious that if the people and businesses and government are spending enough to buy up all of the output of the economy, then the economy will keep producing: Full speed ahead! And it's just as obvious that when the total amount that the people and businesses and governments are buying *decreases,* then total output and employment will slow down. If businesses can't sell enough to keep all their workers busy, then they will lay off some workers. This obvious fact is what Keynes focused on.

Keynes analyzed total spending. He took it apart and looked at *who* was doing the spending, and why. Essentially, he split the "spending stream" into two sectors—spending for consumer goods, and spending for capital goods. Then he tried to get at the *motives* underlying each kind of spending—to try to see what underlies, what determines how much *each sector* of the spending stream will spend. If we can understand the *causes* of spending increases or decreases by each sector, then maybe we can induce total spending to adjust to the desired level. See what a neat approach Keynes thought of? (Like so many things, it seems quite obvious once someone else works it out and explains it to us!)

So Keynesian economics is the economics of understanding *why* each sector of the spending stream (essentially consumers and businesses) spend as much as they do, and what makes their spending change. Also, Keynesian economics tries to explain how adjustments in government spending and taxes (and other things) can influence the total spending flow and thereby influence the speed at which the economy will run.

THE KEYNESIAN "SAVINGS GAP"

There was another important principle in Keynesian economics which challenged one of the basic conclusions of neoclassical economics —the conclusion that the forces of the market system would automatically maintain full employment in the economy. According to the neoclassical economists, *price adjustments,* if permitted to occur without interference, would move the economy to full employment. The prices (or wages) of any "surplus" (unemployed) resources (labor, or other inputs) would go down until it became profitable for businesses to employ them. These price adjustments would continue until full employment was achieved.

Keynes challenged this neoclassical conclusion by introducing the idea of the *savings gap.* The idea is that as the economy grows and prospers, most people enjoy rising incomes. As this happens they tend to save more—to spend a smaller proportion of their incomes on consumer goods. As people save more, this amounts to a withdrawal—a drain from the "spending flow" (the "income stream") of the economy.

When a person earns $100 in a week, that means that person has been responsible for adding at least $100 worth of output into the economic system. But suppose that person only buys $80 worth of the output. That leaves $20 worth of output still in the market, unbought (unless someone else buys it).

Investment Can Offset Savings

Suppose businesses decide that they want to increase their investment spending. Perhaps they will buy up all of the unbought (surplus) output left in the economy by the savers. If so, the total or "aggregate" demand in the economy will be great enough to buy up all of the output and there will be no surplus (unbought) products left in the market. When that happens, it means that *investment injections* in the economy are great enough to offset the *savings withdrawals*. When investment spending equals savings, there is no problem of excess supply (or insufficient demand) in the nation's markets.

The "Savings Gap" Tends to Get Larger

As the economy keeps growing and people's incomes keep rising, the percentage of their incomes which they withdraw from the spending stream (by saving) increases. This causes a larger "savings gap" which must be made up by more investment spending. If businesses don't decide to increase their investment spending enough to offset this growing "savings gap" then all of the output will not be bought. Surpluses will develop in the economy. When businesses can't sell all of their products they cut back production and lay off workers. So there will be increasing unemployment.

Unemployed people don't spend as much money. So as unemployment increases, total spending decreases even more. This causes businesses to cut back production even more and results in even more unemployment. So the economy winds up with a recession. Maybe depression.

According to Keynesian analysis, the unemployed workers *might* be willing to try to get jobs at lower wages and thereby increase their chances of getting rehired. But in the "real modern world," (as contrasted with the "model world" of neoclassical economic theory) Keynes did not expect wage and price adjustments to solve the problem. Wage and price adjustments did not seem to be doing much to overcome the depression in the 1930s when Keynes was writing.

What Can Be Done About the "Savings Gap"?

If we accept the Keynesian theory of the "savings gap," what can be done? Keynes prescribed government fiscal policy—adjusting taxes and spending—to offset the savings gap. The government should cut taxes and leave people more money to spend. Also the government should increase its own spending (with newly created money) to offset the deficiency of investment spending. It should buy up the surplus products, employ the unemployed workers, and get the economy moving again.

In short, the Keynesian idea was this: "If private investment is not great enough to offset the savings gap, then government spending should be increased enough to make up the difference. Then full employment and full production in the economy can be maintained." You can see how different the Keynesian prescription was from the "hands-off" recommendations of the neoclassical economists. You can see that each approach looks at the world in quite a different way than the other.

THE PRAGMATIC KEYNESIAN PRESCRIPTION

See the great importance of Keynesian (and neo-Keynesian) economics? It tells us how to prevent and how to overcome depressions! How? By doing things to keep total spending high enough to keep the economy prosperous.

Once we focus on the *spending flow,* then the most *direct* government policy to overcome depression becomes obvious: Spend more money. Do things to get businesses and consumers to spend more money. In a nutshell, this was the Keynesian prescription.

Much of what was done during Roosevelt's New Deal went along (more or less) with the Keynesian prescription—not because the actions were theoretically inspired, but because they were pragmatic—they seemed to be aimed in the right direction. When people are unemployed in every little town in the country, it's quite obvious that if the government will create enough money and spend it to hire all the unemployed people to build new post offices and other things, unemployment will be overcome.

See how obvious and pragmatic the Keynesian prescription was? Maybe it wouldn't be too far off to say that Keynes gave Roosevelt and the Congress a theory to justify what Roosevelt and the Congress were already doing anyway!

Remember how that's sort of what Adam Smith did, too, for the industrialist capitalists? He gave them a theory to justify what they were already doing.

It's interesting that the two men sometimes referred to as the greatest economists of all time—Smith and Keynes—did not make their contributions by refining and making more precise the theoretical models of economics. Instead, they conceptualized and explained critical, yet previously unexplained or inadequately explained conditions in the real world. Both left the refinements to the generations of economists who would follow.

Did the Keynesian Prescription Work?

Did the Keynesian prescription work for Roosevelt? To some extent, maybe. It wasn't really tried. Not *really.* There were lots of anti-Keynesians around in the 1930s. The depression lingered on until the government began its massive military spending program for World War II.

When the wartime spending began, the depression came to a rapid end. Almost immediately the government had to start working on the opposite problems: shortages, and inflation. During World War II, tight controls were established on wages and prices. Most consumer goods and industrial products were placed under direct government allocation and carefully rationed among the competing, high-priority uses.

Economic Conditions After World War II

After the war the economy kept on booming. What about the widely expected postwar depression? It never came. During the 1950s and '60s there were a few periods of economic slowdown (recession) but never a threat of serious, prolonged depression. Technological progress was phenomenal—from propeller planes to trips to the moon in only about *two decades*— and from account books to modern electronic computers in less time than that. Truly phenomenal.

The late '40s and the '50s and '60s were generally good years in the U.S. and world economies. Not flawless, but not bad. Much progress was made. Most people were living better and better, having more things all the time.

Quietly, mostly unnoticed, some serious problems were ready to erupt and force themselves on the attention of the world. And so they did. The chapters in Book Two (which follows) give the highlights of how it all happened. Also those chapters tell about what the economists were doing and thinking as they tried to keep up with this explosively changing world of the third and beginning of the fourth quarters of the twentieth century.

Book Two

THE TROUBLED WORLD AND DISAGREEING ECONOMISTS OF MODERN TIMES

Part V: Recent Developments and Current Controversies in Economic Theory

The Emergence of Post-Keynesian Economics, The Ascendency of the Monetarists, Rational Expectations Theory, and Supply-Side Economics

Chapter 12: Post-Keynesian Economics and the Monetarist Challenge

After World War II, the economy just kept on booming. The government cut back its spending, but consumers and businesses spent enough to more than make up the difference.

People Spent Their Wartime Savings and the Economy Boomed

During the war years, consumers were making good incomes. But they couldn't buy the consumer goods they wanted because the goods weren't available. The nation's resources were being allocated to the war effort—not to the production of consumer goods.

So after the war, people's savings (mostly in government bonds) were huge. The people cashed their bonds and bought the things they wanted—new houses, new automobiles, appliances, everything. Businesses invested in new plants and equipment and hired workers and tried to meet the strong consumer demand. This created a strong business demand for new capital and for raw materials and labor. Total spending in the economy was high. Inflationary pressures were great. When the wartime price controls were removed, prices moved up fast. Inflation!

The Federal Reserve bought the bonds that the people, businesses, and banks were cashing. This poured money into the economy. The new money went into the banks, creating new reserves and permitting the money supply to expand rapidly. Then in 1949 demand slacked. This lessened the inflationary pressures. But in 1950 the Korean War caused government spending to increase, and prices again began increasing rapidly. So what happened? Price and wage controls were imposed. The controls were kept on until the end of the Korean War.

The Economy Was Sluggish During the Late 1950s

During the eight years of the Eisenhower administration (1953–1960) the economy experienced three recessions. Growth was not as rapid as many economists thought it should be. During much of that period, unemployment was higher than most economists considered necessary.

As the Eisenhower administration was coming to an end, the economy was suffering a fairly serious recession—the worst of the postwar era. It was in this setting that John F. Kennedy defeated Republican candidate Richard Nixon and was elected president. Nixon said it was the recession that cost him the presidency.

THE EVOLUTION OF POST-KEYNESIAN ECONOMICS

Kennedy entered the White House with the pledge to "get the economy moving again." During the Kennedy-Johnson era the theories of post-Keynesian economics ("post-Keynesian" meaning the ideas of Keynes, as further developed by other economists in the 1940s, '50s, and '60s) were, for the first time in the post-War period, relied on to guide public policy. But before you get into that you need to know about how the post-Keynesian ideas were evolving in the years following World War II.

The Keynesian Prescription: Unbalance the Budget

The basic idea of the Keynesian prescription for overcoming unemployment and depression was to unbalance the government budget. The government would reduce its "tax withdrawals" from the income stream at the same time that it would increase its "spending injections" into the income stream. The idea was for the government to unbalance the budget, run a deficit, create more money to finance its expenditures, and thereby push more money into the spending and income flow of the economy. How was this idea of "unbalancing the budget on purpose" received following World War II?

Many economists accepted the Keynesian prescription in the 1940s and '50s, but *public policy* did not fully reflect this attitude. Many political, Congressional, and business leaders—and ordinary citizens too—had strong "balance the budget" attitudes. During the sluggish years of the 1950s there was no *purposeful* budget unbalancing to try to speed up the economy.

The Post-Keynesian Prescription: The "New Economics"

It was not until the early 1960s—actually, not until 1963, the year of President Kennedy's death—that post-Keynesian economics was explicitly stated as public policy. It was stated by President Kennedy in his speech at the Harvard graduation in June 1963. This is the basic idea of what he said:

> Even though we are already running a government deficit, we are going to cut taxes and even further unbalance the budget. The economy will be so stimulated by the tax cut that soon people and businesses will be making so much more income that they will be paying much *more* to the government in taxes. The extra *tax revenues* will be big enough to bring the budget into balance.

A radical idea! Cut taxes in order to collect more taxes? (The idea was that *raising taxes* to try to balance the budget—which was what the Eisenhower administration had done—would only slow down the economy even more, and make the deficit *larger!*)

What had happened during the years following World War II to prepare the nation to accept such a radical idea?—the idea of *further* unbalancing the budget *on purpose?*—the idea that *cutting* taxes will produce more revenue than *raising* taxes? What had happened to ready the policymakers for such an unorthodox economic policy? Such a policy would have been considered nonsense only a few years earlier. What brought about the change in thinking?

THE SYNTHESIS OF KEYNESIAN ECONOMICS INTO NEOCLASSICAL ECONOMICS

Perhaps the most important influence was the synthesis, or integration, of Keynesian economics into the general body of accepted economic principles. As time went on, most economists (and apparently most people) came to accept Keynesian economics—not as a substitute for, but as a necessary complement to neoclassical economics.

But *note this well:* Not *all* economists accepted Keynesian Economics into their "theoretical models" of how the economy functions. Milton Friedman was the leader of the "anti-Keynesian school" of economic thought. He and his followers held out and ultimately emerged with the powerful "monetarist challenge" to Keynesian economics. You will be reading about that soon.

How did it happen that Keynesian economics became acceptable to most economists?—and integrated into their thinking, and their economic models? Probably the greatest influence was Professor Paul Samuelson's *Principles of Economics* book.

Samuelson's Economics Book

Samuelson's *Economics* (first edition, 1947) did an exceptionally good job of explaining the ideas and principles of Keynesian economics, not to the *exclusion* of, but *together with* the orthodox principles of evolving neoclassical economics.

Samuelson's book was widely used, and soon widely imitated. Even today, more than a quarter-century later, the Samuelson book (now in its eleventh edition) and other, similar books are the ones used to introduce most college students to the concepts and principles of economics.

During the 1950s and '60s most of the graduates pouring out of the colleges and going into business or public administration or law or politics or most other worldly pursuits had been exposed to Keynesian economics. Most of them had some understanding of the Keynesian (post-Keynesian) prescription for overcoming unemployment and recession and for keeping the economy running along at a proper clip.

See what happened? Many people had come to understand the ideas and principles of Keynesian economics. So it wasn't so mysterious any more! An increasing number of leading citizens were able to understand the Keynesian prescription and to call on the government to apply it to keep the economy going at a healthy pace.

Neoclassical Economics and the Post-Keynesian Synthesis

Exactly what was this post-Keynesian synthesis?—this integration of Keynesian and neoclassical ideas? Quite simple, really. The neoclassical model was still accepted as a valid statement of the *market forces* which are constantly at work in the society. But the post-Keynesians emphasized that there were many other forces, too—forces *outside* the neoclassical model—some outside of *economics* even—which sometimes would be strong enough to overpower the neoclassical market tendencies to maintain full employment—maybe even carry the world in the *opposite* direction. And when that happened, the neoclassical model would not be the best place to look for an explanation.

The Focus of Neoclassical Economics. Neoclassical economics is based on a different set of assumptions about the world and how it works, than is Keynesian economics. Neoclassical economics focuses on the forces which, if left free to operate without impediment, will always bring the economy fairly quickly and smoothly into a "long-run equilibrium" of full employment and stable prices.

In this long-run equilibrium, all resource uses will be optimized— that is, all labor, land, and capital will be directed in the most efficient ways toward the true objectives of the society. A beautiful system! But not everyone believes that it works out that way in the real world.

The Focus of Post-Keynesian Economics. The post-Keynesians also believe in the neoclassical model as an essential tool for explaining what the market forces are and how they work. But they don't believe those forces always work out in the same predictable ways. They don't believe in the "inevitable mechanistic determination" of real-world economic events, as described in the neoclassical model. They don't believe that the normal real-world economic condition always looks like the long-run equilibrium of the neoclassical model. Therefore, when they see high unemployment and other signs that the economy isn't running as it should, they look to the ideas of Keynesian economics to help them to understand what's going on.

Keynesian economics focuses on the spending flow—on what speeds it up and what slows it down—and on what the government can do to influence the spending flow. To the Keynesians, the spending flow is what supports employment, production, and prices. When it slows down, the economy slows down. Recession.

As an economy grows and prospers, people's incomes go up. People with high incomes save a lot. They may pull so much savings out of the income stream that a depression will result. Prices may not easily adjust to end the depression as the neoclassical model says. That's when the Keynesians say the government should *take action:* follow the Keynesian prescription! Spend enough to offset the savings withdrawals. Or cut taxes so people and businesses will be able to spend more. Or promote "easy money" (low interest rates) so businesses and people may borrow and spend more.

Many economists with widely differing views can be grouped together under the post-Keynesian label. Most economists these days agree with some Keynesian ideas. John F. Kennedy was the first U.S. President to publicly announce his commitment to Keynesian economics.

The Kennedy Tax Cut Proposal (1963)

In 1963 Kennedy called on Congress for a tax cut, but it was not until 1964 that the tax cut actually came. And did it work? The answer to that depends on who you ask—a monetarist or a Keynesian. The economy really did speed up, and tax revenues really did *increase.* The American economy enjoyed an unprecedented period of prosperity and growth.

Some economists were critical. They didn't think the tax cut *caused* the prosperity. It's true that there were many things going on, influencing the economy in the mid-'60s. For one thing, the growth of the money supply was fairly slow and stable—exactly what the monetarists would prescribe for prosperity and growth. Another thing was the Vietnam war. We'll talk more about that soon, but first, here's something else to think about.

The Keynesian Prescription May Give People Confidence

Throughout the '50s and early '60s almost everyone who took economics in college learned about the Keynesian prescription. Everyone learned that the government knew how to prevent a serious depression. Perhaps people's *confidence* that the economy was depression-free actually helped to make the economy depression-free. Consider this: As long as people are confident that depression won't come, depression can't come!

Did people's understanding of the Keynesian prescription help to stabilize the economy during the '50s and '60s? Nobody knows for sure, of course. But it's interesting to think about.

We know that in general, if people expect times to be good, times will be good. But if enough people *expect* bad times—either inflation or depression—then that's exactly what we are likely to have.

People *spend now,* to protect themselves from inflation. Their increased spending brings shortages, and soon we have the inflation they feared. People *save* to protect themselves from depression. When people save more (spend less), businesses don't sell as much. They cut back production and lay off workers. So what happens? Depression. See how it works? As people try to protect themselves from inflation or depression, they tend to bring on or worsen the inflation or the depression they're worrying about.

Confidence is essential. Yet without *Keynesian economics,* what prescription can the economist offer as "economic stabilization insurance"? Not much. Only that if we leave things alone and wait, eventually the natural market forces will correct the problem.

Without Keynesian economics we are right back where we were before the depression of the 1930s, with no way to prescribe effective action to revitalize the system. So who, pray tell, would throw out Keynesian economics? Milton Friedman and the other *monetarists,* that's who. Why? Because they don't think it's needed. And they don't think it works. They think the Keynesian prescription, although perhaps *seeming* to help to stabilize the economy, actually has the effect of *worsening* the problem of economic instability.

THE CHALLENGE TO POST-KEYNESIAN ECONOMICS

In the way the monetarists perceive the world, Keynesian economics is unnecessary, irrelevant, wrong, harmful. If the monetarists' perception of the world is correct, then Keynesian economics *is* wrong and harmful. But if the monetarists' perception of the world is *not* correct, then the monetarists are doing mankind serious harm by discrediting these prescriptive tools which the Keynesians offer for dealing with economic instability, economic stagnation, and depression. So in the real world of the 1980s, this issue is very serious business.

The Anti-Keynesians: Milton Friedman and the Monetarists

Throughout the period of the 1940s, '50s, and '60s, while Keynesian economics was being integrated into the mainstream of economic understanding, a few economists were speaking out loud and clear against Keynesian economics. They were arguing and building their case against the whole idea of government fiscal policy—of adjusting taxes and spending to influence the economy.

The leading challengers have been (and are) Milton Friedman and his colleagues who make up "the Chicago School" of economic thought —or, more specifically, the "monetarist" school of economic thought. Friedman and his followers weren't the first monetarists. Far from it! The philosopher David Hume, one of Adam Smith's contemporaries, fairly well explained this idea more than two hundred years ago—and even Hume was not the first to explain it.

Irving Fisher's Monetary Economics

In the early 1900s the Yale University economist Irving Fisher took up the cause and further refined monetary theory. Fisher explained in detail how the *quantity of money* influences both the *level of prices* (inflation or deflation) and the *rate of production and employment* (depression or prosperity) in the economy.

In the 1920s the Stable Money Association was formed to push forward Fisher's monetary theory. Here's the basic idea. A change in the *size* of the *money supply* is the thing that causes *prices* to change. If the money supply increases, people have more money to spend. So they start buying more things. Soon shortages appear. People have money but can't find the things they want to buy. So they start offering *more* to get what they want. Prices start going up.

The economy can't produce more goods to satisfy the increased demand, because the economy is already at full employment. The neo-classical model says so. Remember? So prices just go up. This process continues until prices are high enough to bring everything back into balance again. If the money supply doubles, prices will double. It's as simple as that.

It works the other way, too. If the money supply decreases, people will have less money to spend, so they will buy less. Surpluses will begin piling up in the markets. Business will slow down. There will be a (temporary) depression.

When the depression begins, sellers will cut prices so they can sell all their products. Workers will work for lower wages so they can get jobs. Banks will lend for lower interest so they can get investors to borrow. *All* prices come down (by varying amounts) until everything is back in balance and the economy is humming along again. .

PUBLIC POLICY IMPLICATIONS OF MONETARIST ECONOMICS

The public policy implication of the basic monetarist idea is obvious: Keep the money supply the right size and everything will be all right. An expanding money supply brings rising prices. A contracting money supply brings falling prices. It's inevitable!

The Monetarist Prescription: Hands Off!

So what do Milton Friedman and the monetarists of the Chicago School have to say about the new economics—that is, about the Keynesian prescription for influencing the economy? They disagree strongly. The monetarists insist that neoclassical economics is all we need. If the *money supply* is properly adjusted, spending and prices and employment will adjust automatically and the economy will run properly.

To the monetarists, there's just no need to get involved with the Keynesian prescription. To do so would do more harm than good. The government's *only* economic policy should be to control the size of the money supply and its rate of increase. As total output and trade increase, the money supply should be permitted to increase enough to finance the increased trade. But that's all.

The government's role should be to keep taxing and spending in proper balance, to work out flexible international exchange rates so international trade can come into natural balance, and to keep the money supply expanding at about 4 or 5 percent per year. Those are the *only* economic stabilization policies the government should have. Beyond that, the policymakers should just relax and let nature take its course.

Even the neoclassical monetarist members of the Chicago School admit that the neoclassical model doesn't work out *exactly right* in the real world. But they think it comes out close enough. And they think that if public policy follows the Keynesian prescription or tries in any other way to influence the economy, things will be made worse—not better.

Economic Conditions Are Determined by Market Forces

To the modern neoclassical monetarists, macroeconomic conditions are to a very large extent *mechanistically determined*—that is, determined by the natural forces of the market mechanism (the forces of demand and supply and price) which are so clearly illustrated in the neoclassical model. The natural laws of economics determine what result will follow from each cause. Any attempt by government to alter the results would interfere with the natural forces and therefore would be harmful, and doomed to failure.

The Monetarist Creed: Keep Your Eye on the Money Supply

According to Milton Friedman and his followers, the government should never take any kind of direct discretionary action to influence employment or spending or wages or prices. The 4 or 5 percent limit on expansion of the money supply will take care of the problem of inflation; automatic price adjustments and the automatic forces of the market system will take care of unemployment and depression. The government shouldn't do anything to try to make the economy run better than it runs naturally.

"Keep your eye on the money supply. Let everything else alone. If times are bad, there's nothing the government can do. If the government tries to do something it will only slow down the natural adjustments and delay the coming of good times. The government has no business fooling around with the economy." So say Milton Friedman and his colleagues, the monetarists.

The Effects of Monetarist Economics on Public Policy

What effect has "Friedman economics" had on U.S. public policy? Perhaps a little during the Eisenhower administration, but certainly none during the Kennedy-Johnson era. During the Kennedy-Johnson era, excessive inflationary pressures were dealt with by direct government influence. Wage-price guideposts were set up and the power of the presidency was used to coerce businesses and labor into going along with these guideposts. This general approach came to be known as "jawboning"—an unofficial but usually quite effective technique of arm-twisting to prevent labor and businesses from getting big wage or price increases.

Then, when Nixon took office in January of 1969, the scene changed. President Johnson's economic advisers were replaced. President Nixon spoke out strongly against any kind of direct controls— jawboning or otherwise.

The Congress passed a law giving the president legal powers to establish direct controls on wages and prices. But Nixon vowed that he would never use those powers. He vowed, right in the beginning and repeatedly thereafter, that as long as he was President no direct controls would be imposed. His "more-monetarist than-Keynesian" advisers assured him that holding down the size of the money supply would solve the inflation problem and that no direct controls would ever be necessary.

President Nixon was very slow to change his mind. But as it turned out, he did change his mind. You'll be reading all about that later. But for now, here's another idea in the Keynesian-monetarist argument.

HOW DOES THE ECONOMY ACHIEVE "STEADY MONEY-GROWTH?"

One question which the monetarists have not answered to the satisfaction of some of their post-Keynesian critics, is this: "Exactly how do we get the money supply to stabilize, and grow at a gradual, constant rate, year after year?"

The growth of the money supply depends mostly on the rate at which businesses and individuals are borrowing (and repaying their loans). Borrowing depends on "the desire to spend"—either for consumer goods, or for investment. Keynesian economics says that this depends a lot on people's *present* economic conditions and their *expectations* about short-run *future* economic conditions.

Suppose the economy is depressed and the money supply isn't growing at its "specified 4 or 5 percent" annual rate. Money may be very easily available for loans. Because of the available supply and slack demand for money, interest rates would be very low. So people and businesses "should" be enticed to borrow more and cause the money supply to resume its expansion at the prescribed rate. But suppose the people *don't* borrow more, even at the very low interest rates? Suppose their outlook is so gloomy that they wouldn't borrow and spend even if you offered to lend them the money interest-free! What then?

Experience has shown that in the short-run, "borrowing and spending" decisions often are not very sensitive to interest rate changes. During the very high interest rate environment of the late 1970s, businesses continued to borrow and spend at a high rate. But during the depression of the 1930s, even though interest rates were very low there was no rush by businesses or consumers to borrow and spend.

If people don't borrow and spend, then the money supply will not expand by the "steady annual rate" which the monetarists prescribe. That is, the money supply will not expand *unless* the government takes some "Keynesian-type" fiscal policy actions—such as reducing taxes and creating new money and increasing its own spending.

Most Keynesians would agree that the monetarist objective of keeping the money supply growing at a slow and steady rate is (under "usual" or "normal" conditions) a desirable objective. But the post-Keynesians don't think it can be achieved under all circumstances without some "Keynesian-type" fiscal policy actions on the part of government. The Keynesians don't believe that the money supply will always maintain its slow and steady growth as an "automatic result" of the operation of the natural forces of the market.

SHOULD WE FOCUS ON THE LONG-RUN?—OR THE SHORT-RUN?

One basic question which explains a lot of the disagreement between the post-Keynesians and the monetarists, is this: Does the economy in the real world approximate the long-run results which are described in the neoclassical model? Or does the economy operate in each period, in each year, *partly* as a result of the influences described in the neoclassical model, but *also* partly as the result of various short-run influences?—shocks, and short-run fluctuations—which government stabilization policies *can* and *should* be used to compensate for and help to overcome?

The monetarists agree that shocks and short-run influences do have an impact on the functioning of the economy. But they say that the natural market forces will work out these shocks and short-run fluctuations by themselves in the best possible way. They say that any attempt by government policy to "help the process along" will not succeed, but instead will result in *further destabilizing* the economy.

Why do the monetarists believe "Keynesian-type" action will be destabilizing? And what do the post-Keynesians have to say about that?

And how have recent public policies been influenced by these conflicting theories? These are things you will be reading about in the following chapters. But from what you know already you can see quite clearly why the monetarists are arguing as strongly as they can *for* a "hands-off" policy by government—and *against* the use of any Keynesian-type actions to try to overcome recession or inflation.

Chapter 13: The Post–Keynesian—Monetarist Debate, Rational Expectations Theory, and Supply-Side Economics

During the past fifteen years or so—ever since the late 1960s—it seems that the world has been in some kind of turmoil. The American economy was experiencing high unemployment and rapidly rising prices —that is, stagnation, and inflation ("stagflation"). By looking at what's been happening in the world, you would think that perhaps some of the "basic ground rules" by which economies function—both individual economies and the world economy—have changed. And you might wonder: "If so, how can we figure out what's going on?—and what's going to happen next?"

This chapter and the ones that follow deal with these issues. In this chapter you will be reading more about the conflicting ideas of economists, and about some new theories which try to give better explanations of how modern economic systems operate. Then in the two following chapters you'll be reading about what has actually been happening in the U.S. and world economies. There you will gain some insight into the ways that modern economic theories may help to understand what happens in real-world economic systems.

This chapter begins with more explanation of the "Great Debate" between the post-Keynesians and the monetarists. Then it introduces and explains some new ideas and new emphasis in economic thought— it explains "rational expectations" theory, and "supply-side" economics.

KEY ISSUES IN THE KEYNESIAN-MONETARIST DEBATE

The very basis, or "root cause" of the disagreement between the monetarists and the post-Keynesians stems from a basic difference of opinion about how to view the economy, and how the macroeconomic forces in the economy actually operate.

The Monetarist "Long-Run" View

The monetarists take a long-run view, and assume that the short-run ups and downs of the economy—inflation, unemployment, etc.—are just that—short-run conditions which the natural market forces will work out in due time.

The monetarists assume that the economic forces of price and competition described in the neoclassical model will work more effectively than would any government attempt to stabilize or offset undesirable changes in prices or production and employment.

Because of the great power and effectiveness of the "natural market forces," these forces should be allowed to control the economy. We should not try to offset or overthrow them in order to achieve short-run price-level or production and employment objectives.

The Post-Keynesian "Short-Run" View

The post-Keynesian view of the economy is different. The post-Keynesians accept the proposition that the natural market forces are powerful, even as they work in the "impure" real world. But they believe that much of the time these forces *will not* be sufficiently powerful to force the economy to "approximate the long-run equilibrium conditions" described in the neoclassical model.

The post-Keynesians agree that if we waited long enough, and if there were no additional short-run "shocks" or developments which would push the economy away from the long-run equilibrium situation described in the model, then ultimately a long-run condition described by the model *might arrive.* But the post-Keynesians focus on the fact that the world operates all the time in the short-run.

Keynes said it this way: "In the long-run, we are all dead!" So according to Keynesian economics, whether or not *in the long-run* the equilibrium conditions (of full employment and stable prices) described in the neoclassical model *might arrive* is irrelevant—and certainly should not be used as the *only guide* to government policy in macroeconomics.

Post-Keynesians Emphasize "Unresponsive Prices"

The post-Keynesian position is that actual conditions in the modern economy are quite different from the *assumed conditions* in the neoclassical model—that the model therefore cannot be relied on as the "complete guide" to appropriate public policy. Post-Keynesians emphasize the condition of *inflexible prices,* and the constant upward pressure on prices from business and labor organizations, many of which have enough power to succeed in pushing their prices up.

The post-Keynesians would agree with the monetarists that if spending in the economy slows down *enough*—so that surpluses in markets are widespread and unemployment is very high—then it isn't likely that very many prices will be going up—not under such depressed circumstances —not unless perhaps some prices are "shocked upward" by uncontrollable cost increases such as the oil price increases.

Post-Keynesians also would agree that when the economy is in a depression, some workers would be willing to take jobs for less than their previous wages, and some businesses would be willing to sell their products for lower prices. But the post-Keynesians hold that in order for these conditions to arrive, the economy must be in a *serious* depression. The Keynesians don't believe that such suffering and misery are necessary. And they don't believe that such misery should be forced on the people—not when appropriate Keynesian-type government policies and programs are available to overcome such depressed conditions.

The Post-Keynesians Emphasize Fiscal Policy

Those who accept the post-Keynesian view of the economy and of the macroeconomic forces at work, see an important role for government in economic stabilization. They focus on the flow of spending, and they prescribe government action to try to adjust this flow of spending as near as possible to the "full employment and stable prices" level.

The government is supposed to maintain a stable, growing economy primarily through fiscal policy—taxing more and spending less to hold down excess demand; taxing less and spending more to speed up spending when the consumer and business sectors are not spending enough to maintain full employment. The government is supposed to support its fiscal policies with appropriate monetary policies—tightening money and raising interest rates to help to hold down excess demand; easing money and lowering interest rates to speed up spending when the economy is depressed.

The Monetarist Fear of "Overkill"

The monetarists hold that if the government tries to follow the Keynesian prescription, not only will it be unsuccessful, it will *worsen* the short-run fluctuations in employment and prices. The monetarists say that whenever the economy has problems of either unemployment or inflation, the government should do what is necessary to maintain a slow and stable rate of increase in the nation's money supply. Then the problems soon will be corrected through natural market forces.

The monetarists say that if the government tries to come in and offset a "too fast" or "too slow" rate of total spending, it will be adding its "corrective" influence into the economy *at the same time* that the natural market forces are exerting *their* corrective influence. The total effect will be to *over-correct* the situation and force the economy to respond too fast. So the economy will overshoot the "desired equilibrium" rate of spending and wind up with *the opposite* problem.

If the government tries to correct for *too little spending* (recession and unemployment), soon the economy will find itself with *too much spending.* Serious inflation is likely to result. If the government tries to correct for *too much* spending (inflation), soon it is likely to wind up with too little spending (recession and unemployment).

The Monetarist Problem of "Response-Lags"

The monetarist position is that there is a natural pattern of almost "mechanical relationships of causes and effects" in the economy. ("When you pull this lever, then this result is certain to occur.") But the important problem is this: No one can tell you *how soon* these results will occur.

The monetarists say that when we have inflation, if you bring down the rate of growth of the money supply, you will bring down the rate of inflation. They agree that the reduced money supply will result in reduced spending and some increased unemployment—a recession—but they are absolutely certain that the inflation rate will come down. But there are "lags"—some time delay—between the slowing of the money supply growth rate and the slowing of the inflation rate. The monetarists believe that in general these lags are not very long—no more than a few months—so we should hold tight on the money supply and wait.

The Experience of 1979–80

In the late 1970s and early 1980s, money supply growth was held down to a very slow rate. There were periods of several months when the rate of money growth was approximately zero. During that time several post-Keynesian economists (and some business leaders—and Senator Edward Kennedy) were saying that the reduced growth of the money supply *alone* was *not sufficient* to handle the serious inflation problem. They were suggesting that other government policies (such as direct controls on wages and prices) were also required. But the monetarists were saying that maintaining the slow growth rate of the money supply *was* a sufficient policy—was in fact the *only* effective policy available—and that other government action to try to stop inflation (such as any kind of direct controls on wages and prices) ultimately would do much harm, and no good.

The monetarists blamed the apparent lack of responsiveness of the inflation to the tight money policies and slow money growth on "lags."

They said that the lags between the slowing of the money supply growth and the slowing of the inflation rate turned out to be longer than they had expected—probably because of the "built-in inflationary psychology" which was causing people and businesses to behave as though they *expected* inflation to continue.

It is true that in this period, buyers were finding all kinds of ways to get around the money supply restrictions and to continue their high rates of spending. Everyone seemed to be trying to "buy now before prices go up even more." This high level of spending certainly contributed to the inflationary pressures.

In the first half of 1980, money was tight and there was very little growth in the money supply. The economy was slowing down. Unemployment increased from about 6 percent to 8 percent, and the inflation rate seemed to be responding to the deepening recession. The inflation rate (the annual rate of increase in prices as measured by the consumer price index) dropped from almost 20 percent in early 1980 to about 10 percent by midyear.

THE FUTURE OF THE "GREAT DEBATE"

The macroeconomic developments in the economy by mid-1980 were exactly the kinds of developments the monetarists had been predicting for the previous two years. They had been explaining that the *lags* were much longer than they had expected.

Perhaps the events of the next year or so will provide experiences which will shed more light on these macroeconomic questions and help to resolve the Great Debate between the post-Keynesians and the Monetarists. But it isn't likely that events in the near future will resolve the issues.

There will be many government actions taken to try to "help the economy"—tight money, taxing and spending adjustments, regulatory changes, direct efforts to prohibit large wage and price increases, and others. So if the economy performs well, *both sides* of the "Great Debate" can find a way to take the credit. But if the economy performs poorly, each side can find a way to blame the *other side's policies* for negating the effectiveness of their own recommended policies. So the "Great Debate" will continue . . .

A NEW THEORY: "RATIONAL EXPECTATIONS"

During the 1970s a new attack by the monetarists was mounting against the Keynesians. The monetarists put forth the theory of "rational expectations." This new theory leads to the conclusion that any government stabilization policy which the government might decide to undertake (and which the spending units in the economy—businesses, consumers, financial institutions, etc.—might have "rationally expected" the government to take) would be doomed to failure.

The basic idea of the "rational expectations" theory is this: When economic decision-makers (consumers, businesses, etc.) expect the government to initiate a certain economic stabilization policy, then these decision-makers will take action to protect themselves—to "maximize their own positions" in the light of the "rationally expected" effects of the government policy. As they do this, they will make it impossible for the government's stabilization policy to work.

The Logical Steps of the Theory

The theory of "rational expectations" is quite complex. But the basic outline of the theory can be summarized in the following steps:

1. First, we must assume that the old saying, "Everybody makes mistakes but only a fool makes the same mistakes over and over," is true. Not very many people would disagree with that.

2. After the first basic premise, the theory goes on with a series of steps with which not everyone would agree. The second step is that when government takes Keynesian-type actions to try to stabilize the economy, that tricks people into doing things which *ultimately* will hurt them—that is, ultimately will worsen their economic condition.

3. After the government has done its "Keynesian-type stabilizing tricks" once or twice, people catch on. They realize that if they do what the government policymakers expect them to do, they will wind up being hurt again, just as before.

4. Since people (and businesses, financial institutions, etc.) "rationally expect" to be harmed if they respond to the government policies in the way that the government policymakers *expect* them to, they look at the situation differently now. They *do not* do what the government stabilization policymakers *wanted* and *expected* them to do.

5. Because people's "rational expectations" tell them not to respond to government stabilization policies in the "expected way," the government stabilization policies are doomed to failure. The only significant effect of stabilization policies under these circumstances would be to interfere with the efficient operation of the economy.

In the case of anti-recession policies the only effect would be to cause inflation—not to increase production and employment which was the objective of the policies in the first place. So any attempt to use Keynesian-type stabilization policies to overcome recession would not help at all—would only make matters worse.

6. Following these logical steps the conclusion is obvious: Government should *never* introduce any Keynesian-type stabilization policies. Instead, government should make it quite clear that it is *never going to use* any Keynesian-type stabilization policies.

The government should emphasize that its only "stabilization policy" will be to permit the money supply to expand by a slow and constant rate (four or five percent per year). Then the economic decision-makers (consumers, businesses, etc.) will make their decisions based on this assurance that the government will not "meddle" in the economy to try to overcome or lessen the effects of any recession which might appear.

The "rational expectations" theorists (now led by Robert Lucas of the University of Chicago) put forth the hypothesis that when everyone in the economy knows that the government will maintain slow and constant money growth, then they will know that they have no cause to "rationally expect" continued inflation. In this stable environment they will be able to make proper decisions. They will follow the "natural laws" of the neoclassical model and thereby ensure that the economy will be as stable as it ever could be—that recessions which may occur will be short-term and self-correcting.

Recessions are thought to be a natural part of the functioning of the market system. People should learn to accept them as that. They should not call on government policy to try to do anything about them because active government stabilization policies can't help and will make matters worse.

Rational Expectations, and the Traditional Monetarist Position

You can see that the rational expectations theory as currently developed leads to exactly the same government policy recommendations as Friedman and the monetarists have been advocating all along. But rational expectations theory arrives at the same conclusion in a different way.

The logic of the more traditional monetarist position is this: The natural market forces for overcoming recession and inflation are *powerful,* and *effective,* but they operate with *time lags.* The economy *ultimately* will correct itself—but not *immediately.* If the government undertakes any stabilization policies to try to achieve a *more immediate* correction of either recession or inflation the *ultimate* result will be overkill. The government's corrective actions will be added to the already powerful corrective forces of the market. So the economy will overshoot the objective of long-term stability and growth. Government anti-inflation efforts will cause recession; anti-recession efforts will cause inflation.

The rational expectations theory doesn't focus on the effect of these "time lags." It focuses on the way in which people's *expectations* of the effects of government stabilization policies cause them to behave differently—and how this "change of behavior" renders the government's stabilization policies not only ineffective but also destabilizing. The following section gives some examples so you can see how the rational expectations theory explains this.

Examples of "Rational Expectations" at Work.

Exactly how do the "rational expectations" of people and businesses prevent government stabilization policies from working? This section gives two examples of ways in which Keynesian-type stabilization policies are *supposed* to work. Then for each it explains the way in which the new theory says that people's "rational expectations" will prevent these policies from working.

Example 1. One way government trys to overcome unemployment and recession is to create new money and increase its own spending. It spends on such things as public works projects and it buys products from businesses. This stimulates businesses to hire more labor and buy more material inputs and increase their outputs.

The Keynesian theory says that as the government does this, the spending flow in the economy will increase. The newly-employed workers will spend more money, and demand throughout the economy will increase. Soon the recession will be overcome as business activity (production and employment) speed up. The "rational expectations" theory says this won't happen. Here's how the theory explains why not:

1. Suppose government increases its spending to try to induce production and employment to increase. Businesses will respond by producing and selling more to government. They will do this because their "rational expectations" tell them that government spending will cause their output prices to go up *faster than* their costs will go up. Workers will be working for wages which don't go up as fast as prices go up. So businesses will make more profits. This is what stimulates businesses to expand their operations, employ more workers, and speed up the economy.

Note: Post-Keynesian and other non-monetarist economists would argue that this is not a picture of the real world—that in the real world, businesses will sell more as government stimulates demand even if prices do not rise—or even if wages rise as rapidly as do prices.

2. The "rational expectations" theory says that after the government has used its "increased government spending" approach two or three times, labor catches on. They see what happens to their *real wages* when government spending increases.

   Workers soon come to realize that when the government starts creating new money and spending more, that will cause prices to rise. So they realize that unless they get wage increases right away (at least as much wage increase as the "rationally expected" price increase) soon they will wind up as losers.

   So workers demand (and get) higher wages. This chokes off the possibility for increased profits by businesses and prevents businesses from expanding their outputs and employing more workers as the Keynesian theory predicts. In this case it's the "rational expectations" of labor which doom the government's anti-recession policy to failure.

   Note: Post-Keynesian and other non-monetarist economists would argue that this also is a distorted view of the real world because:

   a. Wage rates are not under such complete control of labor—that it isn't realistic to assume that labor would get higher wages just because they decided that's what they wanted and what they deserved; and

   b. Depressed businesses would be happy to produce and sell more output even if their labor cost increased as rapidly as their output prices might be increasing.

3. The conclusion of the "rational expectations" theory, again, is that the government's attempt to overcome recession won't work. It will only succeed in forcing prices up—causing inflation.

The theory says that only if the government could count on "catching people by surprise" (so they wouldn't have any "rational expectations" about the policy) would it be possible for the policy to work. But "catching people by surprise" usually isn't possible. People are too sharp and have too much information about what's going on. So the obvious conclusion, again, is that the government should not try to overcome recession or depression by creating money and increasing government spending—so say the rational expectations theorists.

Example 2. Another "Keynesian stabilization policy" designed to speed up the economy and overcome recession or depression is the "easy money" approach. It's supposed to work like this: The Federal Reserve buys bonds from banks, businesses, and individuals, and pays for the bonds with newly created money. This increases the money supply, pushes down interest rates in the money markets, and provides banks with more money to lend.

Banks with more money to lend offer loans at lower interest rates. At the lower rates, businesses are more willing to borrow and invest. With lower interest cost, more investment opportunities become profitable. Also consumers are more willing to buy durable goods (such as automobiles, and appliances) because the interest cost is lower. As businesses spend more, the economy begins to speed up. Businesses hire more people and generate more income, so people spend even more. This is the way the "easy money" policy is supposed to overcome the depression. This process continues until the economy reaches full employment.

The "rational expectations" theory demolishes this Keynesian scenario in one sentence: "Banks will not make loans at low interest rates because their 'rational expectations' tell them that the 'easy money' policy will cause *inflation*, which will push interest rates up and make low-interest loans unprofitable." Certainly banks don't want to make loans on which they expect to wind up losing money! So the "rational expectations" theory concludes that the government should not try to use "easy money" policy to try to stimulate a depressed economy. The policy would fail and would only cause inflation.

Note: It is generally recognized by economists and other informed people that widespread *inflationary expectations* do in fact influence people's economic decisions and therefore also influence the functioning of the economy. For example, in the high inflation period of the 1970s and early 1980s, banks were making loans with "floating interest rates" so that if interest rates went up after a loan was made, the interest rate on the loan would also go up. Some savings institutions were lending to home-buyers on "variable-rate" mortgages. But this does not lead all economists to conclude that "rational expectations" prevent businesses and consumers from borrowing more when there is "easy money" and lower interest rates, or less when there is "tight money" and higher rates.

During mid-1980 interest rates dropped sharply and there was a great surge in bond sales by businesses and by state and local governments, all borrowing more and taking advantage of the lower rates. And the financial investment community was prepared to buy the bonds. But who can say if it was the lower interest rates, or reduced inflationary expectations (or some of both, and perhaps some other things too) that caused all this to happen?

Is the Rational Expectations Theory Valid?

Now you know the "bare bones" of the "rational expectations" theory. And you know what some of the post-Keynesian and other non-monetarist economists have to say about it. So what do you think? Is it valid? Is it a significant contribution to our understanding of how the economy works? Or is it no more than a "spoiler attempt" by the monetarist school of thought to destroy Keynesian economics? The answer to that question depends on who you ask. It depends on the view one takes about how a real-world market-directed economic system works—how close it comes to approximating the long-run conditions of the neoclassical model.

As one recent article says: ". . . the prevailing models of rational expectations share with neoclassical models the undesirable feature of suppressing all dynamical and short-run disequilibrium phenomena. What happens during this period of adjustment to equilibrium is of considerable interest."*

Economists on both sides of the "rational expectations" controversy have analyzed data going back several years. But their findings so far have been conflicting. So the data haven't yet revealed the "clear and indisputable truth" about the rational expectations theory.

One positive thing that economists can agree on about the "rational expectations" theory is this: It reemphasizes the importance of *expectations* in economic decision-making, and it offers us a new idea about the way in which some expectations are formed. Expectations have always played an important role in Keynesian economics. Most economists would agree that expectations will always play an important role in influencing the functioning of the economy.

Summary Analysis

The post-Keynesians focus on the *short-run changeability* of expectations as an important factor influencing economic decisions, contributing to the *short-run* instability of the economy (recession and inflation). The

---

*Anthony M. Santomero and John J. Seater, "The Inflation-Unemployment Trade-Off: A Critique of the Literature," *Journal of Economic Literature,* Vol. XVI, No. 2 (June, 1978), p. 533.

rational expectations theorists focus on the *long-run rationality* of expectations—based on the expected long-run effects of government policies—as an important factor influencing economic decisions and (assuming government policies are appropriately stable) contributing to the *long-run stability* of the economy.

So again, the basic difference in the "mental set" between the post-Keynesians and the neoclassical economists carries on into the basic difference between Keynesian economics and the rational expectations theory. That is, Keynesian economics is concerned with understanding and explaining the *dynamic short-run changes* which occur in the economy —the process by which it gets itself into recession or inflation and the process by which it gets itself out. The rational expectations theory concentrates on *long-run equilibrium* conditions and doesn't focus on the dynamic process of causes and effects which move the economy to (or away from) this long-run equilibrium position.

Perhaps (let's hope that) by the end of the 1980s we all will have a better understanding of all this. It appears that the "rational expectations" theory will help us to move toward a better synthesis of macroeconomic theory. This could be true even if the *specific* propositions and conclusions of the "rational expectations" theory (as it has been developed to date) do not turn out to be precisely accurate.

A NEW EMPHASIS: SUPPLY-SIDE ECONOMICS

Another important development in economic thinking which occurred during the 1970s and early 1980s was the shift in emphasis toward "supply-side" economics. This also was to some extent an attack on Keynesian economics. But it was a different kind of attack than the monetarist attack.

The monetarist attack says that Keynesian economics has always been basically wrong about the economy and about what the government can (and should) do to stabilize the economy. Keynesian economics prescribes stabilization policies, and monetarist economics prescribes "hands-off" policies. "Supply-side" economics doesn't focus primarily on this controversy.

What is "Supply-Side" Economics?

The basic idea of "supply-side" economics is this: If we want to slow inflation, we need to generate *more output*—more supply of products in the market. If we can succeed in doing that (assuming nothing else changes to upset the results), then the increased *supply* will help to hold down prices.

How do we increase the total (aggregate) supply of output in the economy? Primarily by increasing the *productivity* of the average worker in the economy. So "supply-side" economics focuses its attention on *increasing worker productivity,* and on ways to achieve that.

Recent "Supply-Side" Conditions in the U.S. Economy

The idea of supply-side economics is very relevant to the situation in the American economy in the late 1970s and early 1980s, because the economy was not increasing its productivity very rapidly during this period. During 1979 there was an *absolute decline* in productivity (in average output per worker).

When productivity growth is slow, that means that output per person is not increasing much. So the "amount per person" being supplied into the nation's markets is not expanding much. That's what was happening in the American economy. Productivity just wasn't increasing as it had been in previous decades. Yet employees were receiving increasing incomes for their work—even though their outputs were not increasing commensurately with their incomes. The result: People were *receiving more money* at a faster rate than they were *producing more goods.* So people had more money to spend, but there weren't that many more goods in the market to buy! You know what happens in a situation like that— prices go up.

In the late 1970s and early 1980s, economists and business, labor, and government leaders were seriously concerned about this productivity problem. Various explanations were offered as to *why* average productivity was so low, and various prescriptions were suggested as to *how* the problem might be solved.

"Supply-Side" Economics and the Keynesian-Monetarist Debate

Where does "supply-side economics" fit in the Keynesian-monetarist controversy? It doesn't, really. But it makes the Keynesian prescription somewhat irrelevant.

Keynesian economics focuses on "demand-side" economics. Keynesian economics is concerned with the forces which determine total spending (total, or "aggregate" demand) in the economy. It's concerned with the ways in which government actions can adjust this total spending or aggregate demand flow to achieve full employment and stable prices. "Supply-side" economics looks at the *other side* of the question.

Supply-side economics recognizes that the economic circumstances which exist in the American economy in the early 1980s are greatly different than were the circumstances during the depression of the 1930s

—back when Keynes was offering his stabilization policy recommendations. During the depression years, the economy was glutted with supply. The demand to buy the output just wasn't there. It made sense, both pragmatically and in Keynesian theory, to concentrate on the demand-side problem. The question then was: "How do we increase the spending flow enough to get all these surplus products bought up and get the economy back into production again?"

Does the World Need a "New Keynes"?

In the American economy of the early 1980s the situation was very different. A slow rate of productivity growth throughout most of the 1970s, together with constantly increasing incomes of the people, had clearly led to a "supply-side" problem. In the early 1980s some people were suggesting that what we need now is a "new Keynes"—someone who will focus on the new, different situation and provide a new theory —and a new policy prescription for the government.

But the monetarists are not calling for a new Keynes. The monetarists are sure that we already have the theoretical understanding we need. We already know what to do: Cut back the influence of government in the economy. Maintain a slow, steady rate of increase in the money supply. Then let everything be controlled by the natural market forces —the forces of supply and demand, and prices and competition.

Conflicting Ideas on How to Increase Productivity

In the late 1970s there was developing a general awareness of the seriousness of the "low productivity" problem. Then in early 1980 when the 1979 productivity figures showed an *absolute decline* in output-per-worker it became clear that this problem was becoming critical. In early 1980 the decline worsened. By mid-1980, not only the economists and business and political leaders, but also most of the informed members of the general public were aware of the problem and of the need to do something about it.

- In January of 1980 the *Economic Report of the President* emphasized the need for policies which would stimulate increasing productivity in the economy.
- In February of 1980 the Joint Economic Committee of the U.S. Congress issued a report entitled, *A New Economic Era.* In this report they emphasize the need for new efforts to increase productivity.
- In April of 1980 an important conference was held at Harvard University concerned entirely with the issue of increasing the

productivity and improving the competitive position of the American economy in world markets. This conference included academic economists, business and labor leaders, and members of Congress.

- By May of 1980 the news media were reporting on the need for, and on various proposals which were being offered for increasing the productivity of the American economy.
- The June 30, 1980 issue of *Business Week* is a "special issue" on "The Reindustrialization of America." This issue analyzes the low-productivity problem and provides recommendations on what should be done.
- During the summer of 1980 the political candidates began to identify themselves with the need for increasing productivity in the American economy, and to offer proposals for achieving increased productivity.
- By mid-1980, various suggestions on how to approach the low-productivity problem had been offered by business, labor, administration, and Congressional leaders, by political candidates, and others—including a goodly number of business, financial, and academic economists—post-Keynesians, monetarists, and others, including dissenters and "radicals."

SUGGESTED WAYS TO IMPROVE PRODUCTIVITY

By mid-1980 everyone seemed to agree on the *need* for a new focus on supply-side economics—on doing something aimed at increasing the productivity of the American economy. But everyone *did not* agree on how this might best be achieved. Almost everyone can agree that increasing productivity requires *increased efficiency* in the production process—that more efficient technology, machinery and equipment, resource management, and use of the labor force, are required. But how do we achieve that? Here are some suggested approaches which were being put forward by various individuals and groups in the late '70s and early '80s:

- A reduction of cost-increasing government regulations;
- Reduced taxes on businesses to provide more incentive and more cash flow for investment in more and better capital;
- More emphasis by corporations on long-run productivity improvement and less emphasis on "maximizing profits in the present quarter";
- Improved education and training programs and personnel policies for employees;

- Changing the "reward structure" to reward *productivity* more than seniority;
- Stimulating and rewarding truly innovative activities of any kind by anybody, either labor or management;
- Eliminating government prohibitions to competition and letting the inefficient businesses fall by the wayside to make room for more efficient ones;
- Reduced concern about "equal opportunity" and "consumer protection" and more concern with increasing productivity and competition and "let the devil take the hindmost";
- Eliminating productivity-reducing "job rules" required by some labor-management contracts which slow the introduction of high-technology production techniques;
- Reducing welfare, unemployment, and other kinds of payments which "reward people for not working";
- Developing lower-cost energy sources and reducing the dependence on high-cost imported oil;
- Eliminating government restrictions on (potentially environmentally harmful) energy developments and uses, such as nuclear power, high sulphur coal, strip mining, etc.;
- Increasing the rewards for invention and innovation;
- Convincing the labor force and the general public of the "basic truth" of the "work ethnic" and that "the good life" for an individual and for the society comes from increasing productivity;
- Working out "social contract" arrangements between management and labor in each industry and firm (with government's assistance and support) so that management and labor will become partners (not adversaries) in working for increased productivity;
- Establishing government "targets" for productivity increases in each industry and providing rewards and imposing penalties on those businesses which fail to meet their established targets;
- Establishing government "labor force plans" and inducing people to take training and to move into high productivity occupations;
- Nationalizing the big corporations and establishing government management teams to plan and manage the activities of these businesses for maximum increases in productivity;
- And the list could go on and on.

The Choices Will Not Be Easy

As you look at this list of possible approaches you can see why there would be much disagreement about what should be done. Nobody would suggest that *all* of the possible approaches should be tried. Obviously not. Several of the approaches conflict with each other. And as you can see, some of them would involve basic changes in the nature of the American economic system. You'll be reading more on this issue, and on the issues of big business, energy, and the pollution problem in Part VI.

One thing is clear. If we are going to have very much success in solving the problems of inflation, reduced productivity, and the declining competitive position of the United States and the world economy, we're going to have to do some things differently in the future than we have in the past.

During the decade of the 1980s you are likely to see an increasing number of these "possible approaches"—and some other ones too—actually being put into practice. But it will be a slow and difficult process. At this point there is no way to know how much—or how fast—success in dealing with "supply-side economics" will be achieved.

IN WHICH DIRECTION SHOULD THE ECONOMIC SYSTEM CHANGE?

As you were reading through the list of possible approaches to increasing the productivity of the American economy you probably were aware that many of the suggested approaches reflect the same basic ideas as classical economics—ideas that go as far back as Adam Smith's *Wealth of Nations* in 1776. Even in the American economy of the 1980s there is much sentiment for moving toward *lassez-faire,* increased competition, and increased reliance on the "productivity principle of distribution."

Most modern-day economists who have any faith in the neoclassical model (and that means *most* economists—including post-Keynesians) would agree with that. But not *all* economists agree with that.

There are some economists—some dissenters and some so-called "radical" economists—who think that our approach to increasing productivity should be to move in the *opposite direction*—that the government should get *more involved* in planning and directing the economy. These economists don't believe that the industrial structure which actually exists in the American economy of the 1980s is directed and controlled "as though by an invisible hand" to respond to and fulfill the wishes and needs of the society. They believe that the kinds of productivity improvements which will best meet the social needs can only be brought about by some kind of government planning arrangement.

These dissenting economists think there should be some basic changes in the nature of the American economic system. Specific suggestions have been offered as to what ought to be changed, and why. You will be reading about some of their recommendations in Part VI of this book.

The events of the 1970s and early 1980s certainly didn't clear up the controversies and disagreements among economists! But some new ideas were developed, and perhaps some significant progress in economic understanding was made. During the decade of the 1980s we will know better about that.

Before you go on with any more discussion of the recent development of economic ideas, you need to know more about how our critical macroeconomic problems evolved during the turbulent years of the late 1960s, the 1970s, and the early 1980s. That's what you'll be reading about now in Part VI.

*The "New Economics," Stagflation,
Wage-Price Controls, the "Dollar
Crisis," and the Continuing
Controversy among Economists*

Chapter 14: The Current Inflation Problem: Evolution and Outlook for the 1980s

Back in the 1950s after the Korean War ended (1953), the wartime wage-price controls were abolished. There was a minor recession; inflation didn't seem to be a problem. But then as the years went by, prices began to creep upward. When prices were increasing at about 2 percent a year, money was "tightened up" to hold down the rate of inflation. But when money was tightened, the economy slowed down.

When the economy slowed down, the government budget automatically went into a deficit. (Tax payments drop when total income falls, of course.) In 1957–58 the economy went into a recession. The Eisenhower administration tried to balance the budget—to hold down public spending and keep tax collections high. But the budget deficits continued and the economy stayed in recession. There was some improvement in 1958–59, but in 1960–61 things got worse again. In January 1961 when President Kennedy took office, unemployment was approaching 7 percent.

WALTER HELLER AND THE "NEW ECONOMICS"

Not until the early years of the Kennedy administration (1961–62) did the economy begin to pick up. But still, unemployment was high. In 1963, Walter Heller, Chairman of President Kennedy's Council of Economic Advisers, persuaded Kennedy to apply the Keynesian prescription to try to speed up the economy. Thus, for the first time since the depression of the 1930s, Keynesian economics began to play an important role in influencing economic policy for the nation. Walter Heller was the chief spokesman for this Keynesian approach, which came to be called the *new economics.*

One idea of the "new economics" is that if the government tries to balance its budget when the economy is running too slowly, then the economy will be prevented from reaching full speed. When the economy is underemployed, the government *should* run a deficit. It should set tax rates at that level at which the budget will come into balance *automatically* whenever the economy gets up to "full employment." If the economy gets "overheated"—too much spending and inflation—tax revenues will increase automatically, the budget will run a surplus, and that will hold down the excess spending.

A Tax Cut to Increase Tax Revenues!

In 1958 when the economy slowed down, the U.S. government ran the biggest peacetime budget deficit in history. When the Eisenhower administration tried to balance the budget, the economy just stagnated and the budget still didn't balance. But in 1964 when the deficit was more than $8 billion, the Kennedy administration *lowered* taxes. (President Kennedy asked Congress for the tax cut back in the summer of 1963. It was slow in coming. Congress doesn't always jump and run just when the President asks, of course!)

What happened after the Kennedy tax cut of 1964? The economy sped up. Unemployment dropped. Incomes rose. Tax revenues increased enough to reduce the deficit from $8 billion in 1964 to $5 billion in 1965. Why? Individuals and businesses were making higher incomes, so they were paying more taxes.

The booming economy helped almost everybody. State and local governments received more tax revenues, so they could do a better job of providing education and other public services. Monetary policy was "easy"—interest rates were kept low and the money supply was allowed to expand to finance the boom. Everything seemed to be going just fine. Then suddenly there was a new problem: the Vietnam war.

Spending for the Vietnam War Broke the Balance

U. S. involvement in the war expanded slowly, then more rapidly, until soon the war was making heavy demands on the economy. Government spending poured into the nation's income stream. As the government demanded more war goods, shortages developed in some markets. When the economy is "fully employed" and the government uses more of the nation's labor, resources, and products, the people must do with less. Taxes should be raised to get the people to buy less. Otherwise: Shortages. Inflation.

President Johnson and his Council of Economic Advisers urged Congress to increase taxes to pull some of the money back out of the economy to hold down total spending. But Congress did not act. Voting to raise taxes is not ever a very popular thing to do. When the tax increases were wanted to finance the unpopular Vietnam War, Congress said, "No!" But the government kept spending. So what happened? Prices began to rise. Inflation.

How much extra spending was the government pumping into the economy? In 1967 the deficit approached $9 billion. In 1968 it was $25 billion! What to do? Antiwar sentiment was growing. Congress continued to refuse to pass legislation to increase taxes to finance the war. Finally, in 1968, there was a tax increase. But it was too little and too late. The inflation fires were already ablaze.

PRESIDENT NIXON'S ECONOMIC POLICIES

Prices had been increasing for several years at a rate of around 3 percent a year. The inflation rate picked up a little in 1968, but it wasn't until 1969, the first year of the Nixon administration, that prices began to break loose and run. In 1969 prices were increasing at an annual rate of about 6 percent. Nixon vowed that he would bring inflation under control. What did his "Friedmanesque" economic advisers prescribe? Tight money, of course.

Remember the slogans? "Keep your eye on the money supply." "When inflation threatens, hold tight on the money supply." "If the money supply is not permitted to expand too much, then it follows as the night the day, prices cannot rise too much." That's what the economic advisers prescribed; and that's exactly what the Nixon administration did—at least that's what it started out to do, and tried to do.

Nixon's "Tight Money" Policy Didn't Work as Expected

The Federal Reserve (Fed) held back on credit. The Fed refused to let the money supply continue to expand. Soon there was such a shortage of money that interest rates rose to levels higher than they had been in the United States for more than one-hundred years. The stock market collapsed—the worst tumble in stock prices since the depression years of the 1930s. And what about prices? Did tight money stop inflation? No.

Prices kept on increasing faster and faster. Also unemployment increased—from 4 percent to 5 percent, then, in 1971, to more than 6 percent. Tight money, plus some slowdown in government buying, forced the economy into a recession. But prices kept on rising. Inflation kept getting worse.

More and more, people were criticizing the Nixon administration's economic policy. Many urged Nixon to stop relying entirely on his indirect, "theoretical" approach. They urged him to go beyond the monetarist approach and beyond the post-Keynesian approach—to take some *direct* action to break the wage-price spiral. Many suggested direct controls on wages and prices to break the inflation, after which perhaps more normal policy tools could be used to keep things stabilized.

Congress Authorized Wage-Price Controls

In 1970 Congress passed an Act giving the President the power "to impose such orders and regulations as he may deem appropriate to stabilize prices, rent, wages, and salaries. . . ." But the President repeatedly asserted that he would never use this authority—that he would never use the power of his office to force direct controls over wages and prices. But as everyone knows, history was to prove him wrong.

Early in 1971 it appeared that things were beginning to get better. The economy seemed to be picking up a little and Nixon's economic advisers kept assuring everyone that the tight money anti-inflation policies were just about ready to take hold. But then in the summer of 1971 things took a dramatic turn for the worse.

Conditions Kept Getting Worse

Unemployment had continued to hover around 6 percent. Consumer spending was slow and was not picking up. Prices just kept on increasing faster and faster. During the early part of 1971 wholesale prices were rising at a record rate. The stock market (which had recovered somewhat) went back into a tailspin. It was clear that economic conditions were getting worse, not better.

The deficit in the U.S. international balance of payments kept getting worse. More and more dollars were pouring into the bank accounts of foreigners. And more and more of those dollar holders began to try to get rid of their surplus of dollars. But no one wanted to hold *more* dollars. The international value of the dollar seemed almost certain to go down.

For more than two years President Nixon and his advisors had been promising repeatedly that the economy was going to correct itself very soon. But as the weeks, months, and years passed and none of the promises came true, people began to suspect that the Nixon economists really didn't understand as much as they said they did. The medicine they kept applying seemed to be doing much harm and no good.

It was in the spring and summer of 1971 that the business and financial community and many of the political leaders, both in the United States and throughout the world, lost confidence in Nixon's economic policy. The problems were getting rapidly worse, threatening serious domestic and international consequences. Something had to be done.

Nixon's Abrupt Shift in Policy

In his historic television address on Sunday night, August 15, 1971, President Nixon announced one of the most sudden shifts of economic policy that has ever occurred in this country. He placed an immediate freeze on wages and prices, announced his recommendations to Congress for tax cuts and other actions to stimulate spending, and announced that the dollar would be devalued—that is, sold cheaper to people in other countries.

Why this absolute reversal in policy? It was obvious that something had to be done. Quickly. Regardless of Nixon's philosophical leanings and the continued urging of most of his advisers (some of whom had deserted the Nixon "game plan" before he did), he knew that something immediate, direct, *dramatic,* had to be done—Nixon the pragmatist, the opportunist, realized this. When he moved, he moved decisively.

Most of the world applauded his decisive intervention. Most of his critics criticized him not for what he did, but because he had waited so long, had "let so many horses out of the stable" before taking any direct action.

The Phases of Nixon's Wage-Price Controls

The wage-price freeze of August 15, 1971, was an absolute freeze for ninety days on all wages and prices. When the freeze (Phase I) ended, Phase II began. Under Phase II, wage and price adjustments were permitted, but only within the limits of established guidelines. As the months went by, it became clear that the inflationary spiral indeed had been broken. Wages and prices were rising moderately. Confidence in the economy was being regained.

Milton Friedman, leader and most steadfast of all monetarists, criticized the control program, saying that the inflationary spiral *really* had been brought under control by the delayed action of the administration's tight money policies. Friedman said that if the controls hadn't been put on, conditions would be *even better!* Of course not everyone believed him.

What about President Nixon? Did he believe Friedman? Maybe so. In January of 1973, fourteen months after the beginning of Phase II, Nixon lifted the Phase II controls. So what happened? In the months that followed, the American economy experienced the worst inflation since 1946. There was a massive rush of foreigners to get rid of their dollars. Soon the dollar was devalued two more times.

Exactly what did Nixon do in January 1973? He announced the beginning of Phase III—the ending of mandatory controls. He wanted to move to voluntary guidelines. People didn't believe it would work, and it didn't. So what did Nixon do next?

In June of 1973 the President announced another freeze. We were almost back again to Phase I—back to August 1971—except now in a much worse position. Monetary and fiscal policies had been expansive most of the time since the freeze in 1971, and inflationary pressures were strong. Prices were much higher, and confidence in the government's ability to cope with the situation was much lower than before.

In addition, the Watergate scandal was eroding domestic and international confidence in the Nixon administration, and the energy crisis and shortages of other basic resources were beginning to push upward on prices. So this time the freeze didn't work. It was "phased out" over several months

In 1974 the wage price controls were removed and money was made very tight. The economy suffered its worst recession since the 1930s. This was the first year of quadrupled oil prices. There were worldwide grain shortages and soaring agricultural prices. The inflation rate reached 12%.

PRESIDENT FORD'S WIN PROGRAM

The year 1975 started off bad but then got better. Unemployment peaked at about 9%, but after that employment and production picked up some. President Ford called for a voluntary effort by business and labor to hold down prices and wages. He urged everyone to wear a "WIN" (whip inflation now) button to show their pledge to help fight inflation—but it wasn't quite clear what these concerned citizens were supposed to do. The "movement" never caught on. The inflation rate slowed some in 1975, but not much. It averaged about 9% for the year.

The Carter-Ford election year (1976) was not much better. The inflation rate dropped to less than 6%, but the unemployment rate was almost 8%. More than 7 million people were unemployed. The Federal government deficit for the fiscal year ending June 30, 1976 was more than $66 billion—up from $45 billion in 1975. In January of 1977 President Carter took office with a committment to reduce inflation and unemployment.

PRESIDENT CARTER'S INCREASING USE OF DIRECT CONTROLS

At first the Carter administration didn't make any basic changes in the Ford administration "game plan." Money was kept tight, the budget deficit was held down to $45 billion, and there were some programs to generate employment. But there were no direct controls, either "voluntary" (jawboning) or compulsory.

In the first half of 1977 the inflation rate was high—about 10%. Unemployment was still high—more than 7% of the labor force. But in the last half of 1977 the inflation rate slowed to less than 5% and unemployment was down a little—to about 6.7%.

In January of 1978, President Carter announced that the first domestic priority of his administration would be to reduce unemployment. There was talk of tax cuts to stimulate more spending to generate more employment. But then in the first quarter of 1978 the inflation rate picked up again—up to 9%.

Carter's Voluntary Restraints

In April, President Carter announced a major policy shift. He said that *inflation* (not unemployment) had become the nation's number one problem, and that, effective immediately, his administration was imposing "voluntary" wage-price guidelines. Labor and businesses were asked to limit their wage and price increases to *less than* their average increases over the past two years.

Did the voluntary restraints do any good? Apparently not much. The government did succeed in "talking down" the size of announced price increases in the steel industry. But the inflation rate for the second quarter (April, May, June) was back up in the "double digit" range— that is, over 10%. By midsummer of 1978, President Carter and his economic advisors were planning stronger moves to try to slow down the inflation.

Carter's "Phase II" Anti-Inflation Program

In October, President Carter announced Phase II of his anti-inflation program: tighter money, reduced government spending, and firmer direct controls on wages and prices. New "voluntary" guidelines were announced. Businesses which ignored the guidelines would not be eligible for government contracts, and several other "jawboning penalties" were threatened against those who did not comply with the guidelines. Workers who accepted the guidelines would be eligible for tax rebates if the inflation rate exceeded the wage increase guideline rate of 7%.

Money was made very tight, interest rates rose very high, and Carter announced a major cut-back in planned government spending. The planned government deficit was cut to $29 billion for the fiscal year ending in 1980, down from a planned deficit of over $60 billion for fiscal 1979. (*Note:* Planned deficits and realized deficits don't usually come out in the same place.)

For the year 1978 the inflation rate averaged about 9% and the unemployment rate, about 6%. Entering 1979 the Carter administration appeared determined to slow inflation and to do it without too much recession—that is, without too much increase in unemployment. How did they plan to do that? By using monetary policy (tight money), fiscal policy (spending cuts), and direct wage-price restraints (guidelines, backed up with penalties for non-compliance).

The Results of Carter's "Phase II" Program

How well did Carter's Phase II Program succeed? That's impossible to say, for sure, because no one knows how bad things might have been without that program. But in terms of achieving the objectives of slowing the rate of inflation, it was a failure by any measure. The average inflation rate for 1979 was about 4 percentage points above the average rate for 1978—up to 13%. Then in the beginning of 1980 prices were spurting upward at the unbelievable annual rate of almost 20%! Why?

The rapid inflation of early 1980 certainly couldn't be blamed on "easy money." Money was tighter and interest rates higher (much higher) during early 1980 than ever before.

THE FED'S NEW POLICY OF OCTOBER, 1979

In October of 1979 the Federal Reserve Board had announced a new decision about how it was going to control the money supply. Until that time, the Fed had looked more at *interest rates* as an indicator of "the tightness of money." But since October, 1979 the Fed has looked at and tried to control the "monetary base"—that is, the reserves available to banks. If the monetary base is not permitted to expand, this cuts off the ability of the banking system to make new loans.

The significance of this shift in Fed policy is this: By controlling the monetary base, the Fed can *absolutely prevent* the money supply from expanding. When it does this, if the demand for money goes very high, then interest rates are pushed up very high. That's what happened between October, 1979 and April, 1980. But even with the tight money and very high interest rates, inflation continued to speed up just the same.

SOME CAUSES OF THE INCREASED INFLATION RATE

With tight money, and very high interest rates, why did the inflation rate speed up? There are various reasons, some of which you already know. This section talks about some of them.

The Effect of Expected Inflation

One very important inflationary influence was the *existence* of inflation, and *expectations* of continued inflation. No one wants to buy a bond or to lend money when they think the value (purchasing power) of money is going to decrease by about 15% per year, *unless* they can earn interest of *more than* 15%—more than enough to make up for the loss from inflation. So in this environment of high inflationary expectations, interest rates had to be high.

Also, businesses and consumers will continue to borrow money and buy things even when interest rates are high if they expect the prices of the things they are buying to be going up at a higher rate than the interest rate. And that was happening with many products during 1979–80. You wouldn't mind paying 15% interest to borrow the money to fill your fuel oil tank if you thought the price of fuel oil was likely to go up by maybe 50%! That's the kind of thing that was happening in the oil markets in 1979.

The Effect of Increased Costs

In 1979 there was another big jump in the price of imported oil. The higher price of oil quickly worked its way into the prices of gasoline and other petroleum products—and into the costs of production (and ultimately the prices) of most other products also. The very high interest rates (higher than 20% for many borrowers) made borrowed money very expensive. This added significantly to production costs in business and agriculture. Ultimately, output prices must reflect these cost increases.

Workers pushed hard for wage increases. They realized that their *real wages* were decreasing as the value (purchasing power) of their dollars was going down faster than their incomes were going up. But the (no doubt *deserved*) wage increases even further contributed to increased costs and helped to push prices up even more.

The Slowdown in Productivity

Another contributing factor was the slowdown (the actual *decline*) of the *productivity* of the average worker in the American economy. This problem is discussed in more detail elsewhere in this book. The basic problem is that when workers are receiving *income increases* and their *outputs are decreasing,* there's more income to be spent, but less output to be bought. That's inflationary. The *supply* of output is inadequate to meet the *demand.* This problem has led to the recent emphasis on "supply-side" economics.

The Declining Savings Rate

In 1979–80, most consumers and businesses seemed to be trying to spend as much as they could—either with money, or credit. The "average savings rate" of consumers dropped to its lowest point ever.

The Creation of New "Money Substitutes"

With money so expensive to borrow, businesses and banks and other financial institutions were working out all kinds of ingenious techniques for financing transactions without actually using "money." During early 1980 the Fed considered this problem to be so serious that it redefined the money supply so that some of the ingenious new "money substitutes" would be included in the new definitions of the "money supply."

When you consider all of the factors at work in the situation, it isn't too surprising that the inflation rate in early 1980 was very high.

Did Carter's Wage-Price Guidelines Help?

What was the effect of the Carter administration's wage-price guidelines? Did they help? The answer to that depends on who you ask. The President's Council of Economic Advisors (CEA) says "Yes." The CEA estimated that during 1979 the guidelines reduced the wage inflation rate by between 1% and 1½%. And they said that the guidelines succeeded in holding down some price increases by big businesses.

But not everyone agrees with this. It's obvious that both big business and labor organizations can announce larger price or wage increases than they really expect to get, and then reduce these under government pressure to "appear to be" responding to the government's stabilization efforts. So it's not easy to say, for sure.

The Effect of the Recession of 1980

By mid-1980 the economy was moving rapidly into recession. Unemployment increased rapidly from the less than 6% rate in 1979 to about 8% by mid-1980. Unemployment in the steel and automobile industries was much higher than the national average.

As the economy slowed down, the rate of inflation dropped sharply. The rate was approaching 20% during the first quarter of 1980, but by mid-year it was down in the 10% range. Interest rates tumbled, and the growth of the money supply dropped to about zero. But at mid-year it was expected that the growth of the money supply soon would resume to help support the recovery of the economy from the sharp recession.

WHAT ABOUT IMPOSING WAGE-PRICE CONTROLS?

During the last half of the 1970s and on into the 1980s as inflation roared on, there was continuing controversy on the question of whether or not legally-imposed *direct controls* should be placed on wages and prices—perhaps a wage-price freeze—to try to stop the inflation. The argument about whether or not to impose legal restraints on wages and prices is not strictly a "monetarists vs. Keynesians" argument. It's clear that monetarists, because of their view of how the economy operates and responds to the "natural economic laws" would oppose any such government intervention, even as a short-run "emergency action."

The Post-Keynesian View

People who hold the post-Keynesian view of how the economy operates would be more inclined to accept the possibility that direct wage-price controls could help as a short-run "emergency action." The Keynesian view holds that sellers—of both *products* and *labor*—have enough economic power to push their prices up. And they believe that a properly designed and administered system of wage-price controls sometimes might be effective in preventing them from doing that. But even so, not all post-Keynesians are in favor of wage-price controls—even as a short-run emergency action.

Economists in general agree that wage-price controls distort the operation of the price mechanism, reduce the efficiency of the allocation of resources in the society, and impose unjust disadvantages on some buyers and sellers while granting unjust advantages to other buyers and sellers. But this is not the only problem.

It is very difficult (many say, impossible) to design and administer a workable wage-price control system. This would be a most difficult task even if it were done by the nation's most brilliant economists and administrators—and even if there were no political pressures to contend with. But in the real world of limited perception by economists, and strong political pressures, it takes a lot of courage and faith to embark on a wage-price control program, even as a short-run emergency measure. Nevertheless, some kind of government controls designed to limit wage-price increases have been imposed most of the time, both in this country and in other countries.

A Brief History of Wage-Price Controls

Over the past four decades, in most countries most of the time there has been some attempt to use *direct restraints* to hold down wages and prices. The United States has been no exception.

In the United States, as you know, wage-price controls were imposed in August, 1971. That was the first time wage-price controls had been imposed since the early 1950s during the Korean War. It had happened during World War II also, and during other wars. But what about the period from the mid 50s to August of 1971? Were wages and prices completely free to seek their own levels? Sometimes, yes. But most of the time, no.

President Kennedy's "Guideposts" and "Jawboning." In the early 1960s, President Kennedy set up wage-price guideposts spelling out the "appropriate conditions" for wages or prices to be increased, and by how much. The guideposts were not "legal requirements." They were only "urged upon" the industries and the labor organizations. But both President Kennedy and President Johnson used the power of the presidency to "twist some arms," to convince some businesses and labor leaders to go along with the guideposts. This "arm-twisting"—this unofficial but sometimes quite powerful technique—is known as *jawboning.*

The "jawboning" policies of the Kennedy-Johnson era were continued until the beginning of the Nixon administration in 1969. Then Nixon abolished all "voluntary controls" and relied on the limited growth in the money supply to bring down the inflation rate. So there was no attempt to apply direct pressure to hold down wages and prices during the period from 1969 until August of 1971, when Nixon announced the wage-price freeze.

"Voluntary" Restraints Have Been Used Most of the Time. From the end of the Nixon administration's price controls in the early 1970s, on into the early 1980s, there have not been any nationwide, legally-imposed controls on wages and prices. But "voluntary restraints," and "jawboning" have been used much of the time. To some extent during the Ford administration in the mid-70s, but even more in the Carter administration, the government has been applying direct pressure to try to limit wage and price increases by big business and big labor.

The government's "Council on Wage and Price Stability" tries to identify "unjustified and inflationary" price or wage increases. Then the government tries to induce the offenders to retract and "roll back" the increases.

The "Wage-Price Controls" Issue is Still Alive

In the late 1970s President Carter asked Congress to pass legislation giving him "standby authority" to impose a nationwide system of wage-price controls. But the Congress chose not to do that.

In the Presidential election year of 1980, Senator Edward Kennedy came out strongly in favor of wage-price controls. Public opinion polls showed that there was much support for Senator Kennedy's position. So in the early 1980s the issue is still very much alive.

TIP—A New "Direct Controls" Approach

In recent years a new approach has been suggested by three well known economists: Henry Wallich, Sidney Weintraub, and Arthur Okun. The idea is to use tax credits and penalties to induce businesses and workers to limit wage (and indirectly, price) increases. This suggested approach is called TIP (Tax-based Incomes Policy).

As you might guess, economists disagree about whether "TIP" should be tried. In two interviews reported in *Newsweek* (May 29, 1978) Professor Paul Samuelson comments that "some experimentation (with TIP) might be in order to improve our inflation-unemployment trade-off." But professor Milton Friedman says such plans as TIP are "another form of price and wage control (which) would prove no less monstrosities than earlier price and wage controls."

It's clear that we have a dilemma and that it isn't going to go away anytime soon. Let's hope that from our mistakes we will learn to understand it better.

THE OUTLOOK FOR THE 1980s

As this book is being prepared for press in mid-1980, conditions for the remainder of 1980 and for the years that follow are impossible to predict. Many observers fear that the recession will not succeed in bringing the inflation rate down very much below the 10% rate. Many are concerned that in the 1980 election year, both the administration and Congress may be too responsive to political pressures. They may decide to take some monetary and/or fiscal actions to stimulate the economy— and thereby rekindle the fires of inflation.

As the economy begins to recover, there will certainly be strong pressure from labor for wage increases. Most workers have already experienced declining real incomes. And it's likely that most workers expect that unless they can get wage increases in the 10%-per-year range (or higher), their real purchasing power will continue to go down because of future inflation.

Supply-Side Problems

The problem of reduced labor productivity (the "supply-side" problem) certainly cannot be overcome quickly. But labor productivity is not the only "supply-side" problem. In agriculture the very high interest rates have pushed up production costs and caused cutbacks in agricultural inputs. So we are almost certain to see reduced outputs of some farm products—which will mean higher agricultural prices.

In the housing construction industry, the high interest rates have forced nationwide cutbacks approaching 50%. That means that only a little more than *one-half* of the usual number of new houses are being constructed. This reduced supply of housing will show up in coming years and housing prices are likely to go up to reflect that.

Energy prices will be going up, too. We can be sure of that. The only thing we don't know is "how much?" An important part of this question is: "How much will we reduce our dependence on imported oil?" Nobody knows the answer to that, either.

How much impact will all these influences have on the inflation rate in the coming months and years? No one knows, of course. But it is clear that the pressures for continued inflation will be very strong—and very difficult to overcome or control.

An Adjustment of the Humphrey-Hawkins Timetable

In 1978 the Congress passed the *Full Employment and Balanced Growth Act* (known as the Humphrey-Hawkins Act). This Act provided specific target rates for *unemployment* and *inflation.* The Administration is legally bound to take the necessary steps to try to achieve these targeted rates.

The targeted unemployment rate was set at 4%; the targeted inflation rate was set at 3%. The Act says that these rates are supposed to be achieved by the end of 1983—but it says that the President can amend this timetable if necessary.

In his January, 1980 *Economic Report,* President Carter amended the timetable. He set 1985 as the target year for achieving 4% unemployment, and three years later (1988) as the target year for lowering the inflation rate to 3%. It is clear that the administration does not expect to succeed quickly in bringing down either the unemployment rate or the inflation rate.

From 1952 to 1967 the annual inflation rate *never* exceeded 4%. Usually it was in the 2%–3% range. So you can see the seriousness of the inflation problem which faces the American economy as we enter the decade of the 1980s. No one is happy with the situation. But no one is suggesting any "easy way" out.

Expected Policies and Conditions for the 1980s

It appears to be a safe bet that for the next few years you will be seeing the following policies and conditions in the American Economy:

1. Fairly strict control on the rate of growth of the money supply;
2. Fairly strict control on the government budget to reduce the inflationary pressures of government deficit spending;
3. Continuing efforts by government to exercise direct controls over wages and prices;
4. Continuing efforts to stimulate productivity and reduce production costs throughout the economy; and
5. Continuing inflation rates and unemployment rates which are significantly higher than the targeted rates in the Humphrey-Hawkins Act.

The "New World" of the 1980s

It is clear that the rapid changes of the decade of the 1970s have brought to the United States and to the world a new set of challenges —challenges which we are not well equipped to handle. We still use as our "reference point," the economic conditions which existed in the 1950s and 60s. But in terms of the *extent* and the *gravity* of the changes which have occurred during one short decade, the decades of the 50s and 60s are "ancient history."

The world of the 1980s is a *new world.* The problem is that none of us have yet caught up with it. Perhaps the future of the 1980s lies in the minds of the bright young people whose thoughts are more free to explore and less encumbered by the "ancient history" of the recent past. Let's hope that the rising generation will bring some bright, new, workable solutions to this inflation problem. Perhaps the older generation is doing everything that could be done. But it's always comforting to think that someone may discover breakthroughs which will speed the solutions to our problems.

At the same time that the inflation problem was worsening (during the period since the late 1960s) the American dollar kept getting into trouble in the international finance markets. The U.S. Balance of Payments encountered some serious difficulties. At times, "near crises" conditions existed for the dollar in the international money markets. In the next chapter you will be reading about all this—about what has been happening, and why.

Chapter 15: International Finance, "Dollar Exchange" Problems, and Outlook for the 1980s

The American economy of the 1980s (whether we like it or not) is closely tied into the world economy. What happens to the money supply, interest rates, and other economic conditions in this country will reflect —*must* reflect—the relationships between the U.S. economy and the rest of the world. What happened in the 1970s (and will continue to happen in the 1980s) with oil prices, emphasizes this fact dramatically. Recent problems of unemployment in the automobile and steel industries in this country also have brought home the fact of "international interdependence" to many people.

AMERICAN POLICIES MUST REFLECT INTERNATIONAL CONSIDERATIONS

American policies in the 1970s were significantly influenced by the position of the U.S. dollar in the international money markets. When interest rates in this country go down, foreigners who hold dollars (Eurodollars) exchange their dollars for other kinds of money—marks, or franks, or yen, or something else—so they can invest the money in other countries where they can earn more interest. But when interest rates in the United States go up, foreigners are more likely to hold dollars because they can invest the dollars here and earn more interest than in other countries.

Foreign Holders of Dollars Can Affect the U.S. Economy

Suppose the American economy slows down. There is not so much demand for money in this country, so interest rates tend to fall. The lower interest rates should stimulate more borrowing and spending and continued growth of the money supply. That should help to achieve a healthy and growing economy.

As our interest rates go down, however, foreigners shift their "liquid assets" (money) out of dollars and into other kinds of money. That causes the international value of the dollar to go down. Also, it causes foreigners who own dollars to pull their dollars out of the U.S. money supply. The foreigners' withdrawals may cause the U.S. money supply to *decline* when it should be expanding. Also, the low interest rates may trigger an "international dollar crisis." (You will be reading more about this, soon).

What about the opposite situation? When businesses and consumers in this country try to increase their borrowing and spending, that pushes up interest rates. The higher interest cost is supposed to prevent the money supply (and borrowing and spending) from expanding too much.

But when interest rates rise in this country, this causes foreigners to shift their "liquid assets" to the U.S. money markets. They want to earn some of the high interest income. When this happens, it increases the supply of available money in the American economy. So that supports borrowing and spending at a higher level than desired. In this case the money supply is growing faster than the desired rate because of the injection of foreign-owned dollars attracted to this country by the high interest rates.

Recent U.S. Policies Have "Supported the Dollar"

During the 1970s, monetary policy in this country was adjusted specifically for the purpose of stabilizing (supporting) the international value of the dollar. During the 1980s, our monetary policy (and all other stabilization policies) must continue to take into account the objective of international stability of the dollar.

It is impossible to predict the extent to which this will influence our domestic policies in the decade of the 1980s. But we can be sure that never again will it be possible for policies in this country to be carried out without some serious consideration of the international effects of these policies.

Now you have a little introduction to the importance of taking an *international view* when considering *domestic* monetary, fiscal, and/or other stabilization policies. So now you're ready to review and analyze some important recent events involving the United States and the U.S. dollar in the international trade and finance markets. That's what most of this chapter is about.

THE EVOLUTION OF THE "DOLLAR PROBLEM"

As the trend of inflation in the U.S. economy increased in the late 1960s and throughout the 1970s, what was happening to the "exchange value" of the U.S. dollar in the international money markets? It was going downward—sometimes *sharply* downward.

As prices in this country were spiraling upward, the purchasing power of the dollar was spiraling downward. If prices double, then the dollar will only buy half as much. That means, in real terms, the dollar is only worth half as much as before.

Foreigners Became Less Willing to Hold Dollars

Foreigners hold billions of American dollars. Foreign banks, businesses, and individuals have bank accounts in American banks and hold American bonds and other "dollar assets." From War II until the late 60s the dollar was a very good asset to hold—in fact, "as good as gold." Foreigners could actually use their dollars to buy gold from the U. S. government, so their dollars really were as good as gold.

As long as prices in the United States were going up only slightly (prices in most other countries were going up more rapidly), the dollar was just great as an asset to hold. But when prices in the United States began spiraling upward, it became obvious that the dollar wasn't such a desirable asset anymore. So people holding dollars began to want to get rid of them, to trade them for gold, or for some other kind of money —money less likely to depreciate in value so fast.

Another thing was happening, too. As prices of American products spiraled upward, American buyers saw opportunities to buy foreign products *cheaper.* So they did. American consumers began buying more German cars and Japanese cars and tape recorders. Businesses began buying more Japanese steel. As time went on the flood of products from foreign countries increased. Each time an American bought a foreign product, more dollars flowed into the bank accounts of the foreigners.

In the spring and summer of 1971 the desire of foreigners to get rid of their dollars began to assume panic proportions. Foreigners who held dollars were getting more and more nervous, more and more ready to sell their dollars to anyone who would buy them, with marks, or yen, or some other currency—some kind of money they could believe in. (The U.S. government had long since stopped selling gold to just anyone who wanted it, but they had been selling to the central banks of other countries. During the early 1970s gold was flowing to other countries by the billions.)

In 1971 the rapidly expanding international payments deficit and the rapid gold drain made it absolutely imperative that President Nixon take some action immediately. Perhaps the inflationary spiral could have been suffered for a bit longer. Perhaps—except for the international plight of the dollar—the "tight-money game plan" might have been continued. But as the American dollar was becoming unacceptable to foreigners, some actions were imperative. Nixon had no choice.

The Dollar Was Devalued and Allowed to "Float"

On August 15, 1971, when President Nixon announced the wage-price freeze he also announced that no longer would gold be sold to *anyone,* and he announced the devaluation of the dollar—that is, that it would be sold cheaper (for less foreign money) in the future. At first the dollar was going to be allowed to "float." That means anyone who wanted to sell dollars would have to sell them for whatever they could get from whoever wanted to buy them. Official exchange rates for the dollar were temporarily abandoned.

With official exchange rates, American tourists abroad who had traveler's checks and American dollars knew just how many francs, or marks, pounds, lire, kroner, drachmas, yen, or any other currency they could get for a given number of dollars. But after August 15, the tourist who went into the foreign bank for currency never knew what the exchange value of the dollar would be—except that it would be lower than before!

What were the effects of the devaluation and other moves to strengthen the dollar? Did they work? To some extent, yes. But as time went on it became clear that the balance of payments problem had not been solved.

In 1972 and 1973 the international problem of the dollar continued, more acute sometimes than at other times. Attempts were made to put together a new system of "fixed" exchange rates, but without success.

UNSTABLE WORLD ECONOMIC CONDITIONS OF THE 1970s

In the early 1970s there were several shocks which disrupted international trade and exchange relationships among the nations of the world. Between 1973 and 1974, prices of imported oil *quadrupled.* That forced up prices of just about everything—fuels, lubricants, chemicals, fertilizers, etc. So worldwide costs of production in both industry and agriculture shot upward.

There were a series of poor harvests which caused worldwide shortages of grain and other food products. So prices for agricultural products went higher—much higher—than they had ever been before. And so did prices of just about everything else. Prices of some raw materials went up sharply. And the prices of some things jumped up and down from year to year.

The price of sugar shot up from about $200 a ton to more than $1300 a ton, then dropped back to about $600 a ton. The price of copra (for making coconut oil) jumped from less than $200 a ton to about $600 a ton. Then a year later it was down to about $100 a ton. You can imagine the problems of the countries which were depending on sugar and copra for their livelihood! And it wasn't just sugar and copra. Many other products were experiencing similar price fluctuations.

Fixed Exchange Rates Were Abandoned

The governments of the various nations worked together to try to do something to meet the various emergency conditions brought about by the "new times" of the 1970s. They tried to work out a new system of "fixed" exchange rates between the monies of the major trading nations. But the international trade and finance markets were too unstable. Finally all attempts to put together a new system of "fixed" exchange rates (between different kinds of money in the international finance markets) were abandoned.

By the mid-1970s, not just the U.S. dollar, but also the money units of all of the major trading nations were "floating." The value of each kind of money (in exchange for any other kind of money) was "set free" to be determined by supply and demand. The exchange rate for each nation's money went up or down from day to day, depending on the supply and demand conditions for that nation's money in the international money markets.

The Increasing U.S. Balance of Payments Deficit

In the years following World War II and on into the 1960s, the United States had been exporting more goods to other nations than we were buying back from them. The foreign producers were not selling enough to us to earn the dollars they needed to pay for their imports from us. So it was necessary through loans and grants of dollars to provide money to foreigners. Otherwise they would not have been able to continue to buy these American exports. But in the 1960s this situation turned around.

As the European and Japanese economies were rebuilt, they began expanding their own outputs. So they bought fewer American products. At the same time, they began to sell more of their products in this country. Americans began buying more VWs and Datsuns and Sonys and other foreign goods—providing more dollars to foreigners. So dollars began piling up in the foreigners' bank accounts.

Then, as the inflation picked up in the late 1960s and on into the 1970s, American goods became more and more expensive. This discouraged foreigners from buying American goods and encouraged American buyers to buy more of the relatively cheaper foreign products. More "surplus dollars" poured into the bank accounts of foreigners. All of this was going on at the same time that the U.S. foreign aid programs, overseas military spending, and various other programs of government grants and loans were pouring more dollars into the hands of foreigners.

Beginning Trouble for the Dollar in the Late 1960s

In the late 1960s it became clear that the dollar was in trouble in the international money markets. The U.S. Balance of Payments was running a deficit—meaning that foreigners were receiving more dollars from us than they were using up. The "surplus supply" of American dollars in the world's money markets kept on increasing.

You know what happens when excess supplies of anything are pushed into any market—the price goes down. That's what was happening to the American dollar. The larger the deficit on the U.S. International Balance of Payments, the greater the surplus supply of dollars which is pushed into the hands of foreigners. So the greater the "downward pressure" on the international value of the dollar.

From just after World War II until the early 1970s, the international value (exchange rate) of the dollar was "fixed." During this period you always knew exactly how many marks or franks or yen (or whatever) you could get for one dollar. But as the Balance of Payments deficits continued and surplus dollars kept piling up in the bank accounts of foreigners, there became increasing pressure for the dollar to be "devalued"—that is, for its "exchange value" in buying other kinds of money, to be decreased.

As it turned out, the dollar was devalued in August of 1971. The dollar was devalued, and then allowed to "float." It has been floating ever since. In most of the years of the early and mid-1970s, the U.S. Balance of Payments continued to show a deficit. The international value of the dollar continued to float downward.

Increasing Problems for the Dollar

During the early part of 1971 (before the August devaluation) the U.S. Balance of Payments was running a deficit of some $12 billion—*much higher* than ever before. It was obvious that the international value of the dollar could not be held at its "fixed exchange rate" with this flood of surplus dollars pouring into foreign hands.

Everybody who held dollars knew that devaluation *had to come*—and no one wants to hold dollars when they know dollars are going to be devalued. No one wants to hold any asset when they know its value is going to go down! So foreigners who held dollars were trying to sell them in the international money markets—to exchange them for other kinds of money. But who wanted to buy dollars? Nobody. There was no way that this selling pressure could be withstood. A devaluation was unavoidable.

After the August 1971 devaluation, the international exchange value of the dollar floated downward. In fact, throughout the 1970s the dollar kept floating downward. In 1971 the U.S. dollar would buy 3.6 West German marks. By 1976, it would only buy 2.76. In 1971 the U.S. dollar would buy 4.3 Swiss francs. In 1976 it would only buy 2.6.

The deficits of the early and mid-1970s look small as compared to the deficits of the late 1970s. In 1977 the U.S. "Merchandise Trade" Deficit jumped to $31 billion—by far the largest deficit in U.S. history. The dollar's value in the international money markets dropped sharply. Again, there was serious danger of a "1971-type" dollar crisis.

If people holding dollars rushed to get rid of them, that could bring a total collapse in the international finance markets. If such a crisis occurred, it would cause the international value of the dollar to collapse. That would be disastrous for the world economy. International trade would be disrupted. But not only that—many nations hold their international exchange reserves (their "money to be used to buy foreign goods") in the form of U.S. dollars. Their "international money" reserves would be wiped out.

THE DOLLAR CRISIS OF 1978

It was during 1978 that the international position of the dollar became really critical. In the 12-month period ending in October, 1978 the dollar lost 36% of its value against the Swiss franc, 21% against the West German mark, and 31% against the Japanese yen. The week of October 30 opened with near-panic selling of dollars in the money markets in Europe and Japan. It was obvious that something had to be done immediately to rescue the dollar.

President Carter's "Rescue the Dollar" Package

President Carter called his top monetary advisors to the White House for a secret meeting and worked out a plan. On November 1 he announced the plan—the most dramatic package of actions (and the biggest gamble) the United States had ever taken in international finance. The package included:

- Billions of dollars worth of foreign money to be borrowed by the United States from the foreign central banks to be used to buy dollars in the foreign exchange markets—to increase the demand for dollars, and hold up the price of dollars.

- Sharply higher interest rates in this country (a) to make holding dollars more profitable for foreigners and (b) to let foreigners see that the U.S. was serious about stopping the inflationary decline in the value of the dollar. The Fed immediately raised the discount rate by a full percentage point to 9½%—the biggest single jump and the highest rate ever.
- The sale of $2 billion dollars worth of SDRs (international exchange credits) to Germany, Switzerland, and Japan to get more of their money to be used to buy up dollars.
- The sale of 1.5 million ounces of gold per month by the U.S. Treasury to hold down the world price of gold and to pull in more dollars out of the foreign money markets.
- Withdrawal of $3 billion worth of marks, francs, and yen from the U.S. reserve account at the International Monetary Fund (IMF)— more money to be used to buy up dollars from foreigners.
- Sale of up to $10 billion worth of high-interest U.S. Treasury securities (denominated in *foreign* money) in the foreign money markets to get more foreign money to be used to buy up dollars.

Was the "Rescue" Successful?

So what happened? The immediate response was overwhelmingly positive. The dollar rose sharply in the money markets all over the world. The price of gold dropped $15 an ounce in London and the New York Stock Exchange recorded its biggest single-day advance in history.

It worked in the short run, sure. But a lot of people were worried about the longer run. What if the U.S. trade deficit stays up around $30 or $40 billion dollars a year? And Americans keep investing billions overseas? It won't take long for another dollar glut to develop. And next time the U.S. government will still be deep in debt for all of that foreign money they borrowed in 1978. What then?

That would have been really bad. But luckily, it didn't turn out that way. The dollar continued to increase in value in the foreign exchange markets. By mid-November it was up to its highest level in four months. And it continued its upward trend. By mid-April, 1979, the dollar had risen (since November, 1978) more than 10% against the mark, 18% against the Swiss franc, and (would you believe?) 22% against the Japanese yen.

All this was happening at the same time that the Fed and the foreign central banks were *selling dollars* to get back the foreign money they had used to buy dollars back in November! By April, 1979 the United States had already been able to buy up enough foreign money to pay off a lot of those November loans. And foreign bankers were charging that the U.S. dollar was being allowed to increase in value too much, and too fast.

Why Did the "Rescue" Work?

How did the dollar recover so fast? Many things were involved. For one thing, foreigners found out that the United States was serious and determined about (a) protecting the international value of the dollar, and (b) fighting domestic inflation. Interest rates in the United States were high enough to make dollars a good kind of money to have. And inflation rates increased in several other countries, making the American inflation rate look not so bad. Also the U.S. balance of payments figures showed that the trade deficit was going down.

By the end of 1979 it was clear that Carter's "rescue the dollar" package of November, 1978 had been successful. But it was also clear that it had not permanently solved the international exchange problem of the dollar.

THE CONTINUING TRADE DEFICIT

The most important component of the U.S. "merchandise trade" deficit (by far) is oil imports. As long as we continue to be heavily dependent on foreign oil, we will have great difficulty exporting enough goods to eliminate the trade deficit.

During 1979 the U.S. trade deficit was more than $37 billion. But even so, the value of the dollar in the international money markets only dropped about 2.5 percent during that year. During 1979 the American dollar actually *increased* 23% against the Japanese yen. As you would imagine, the Japanese economy has been hurt by the great increases in the prices of oil and other industrial materials. That's an important reason why the yen was floating downward faster than was the dollar.

The Deficit in Early 1980

In the early months of 1980, the merchandise trade deficit continued to be very high. In the single month of February, the deficit amounted to a record—$5.6 billion. If you multiply that by 12 months, you come out with a deficit for 1980 of $66 billion! But that was not expected to happen.

In the months following February, the deficit was smaller—down to about $3.3 billion in March and $1.9 billion in April. But then it was up again to almost $4 billion in May. Economists in the Carter administration were expecting the 1980 recession to reduce imports. That would reduce the deficit during the remainder of the year. Also, the oil price increase in 1980 was not nearly as large as in 1979. That didn't *help,* because the price did go up. But at least it didn't hurt as much as did the big increase in 1979.

The Continuing Decline of the Dollar

Even with the large merchandise deficits in early 1980, the value of the dollar in the international exchange markets did not drop drastically. The very high interest rates in the United States provided foreign dollar holders with a good return on their dollar investments. But the trend of the dollar continued downward. Interest rates dropped sharply as the 1980 recession became more severe, and the downward pressure on the dollar increased.

By mid-1980, the U.S. dollar would buy only 1.8 West German marks—down from 2.76 marks in 1976 and 3.6 marks in 1971. By mid-1980, the dollar would buy only 1.6 Swiss francs—down from 2.6 francs in 1976 and 4.3 francs in 1971.

Here's an example of what the "downward-floating devaluation of the dollar" has done to the prices we now pay for imported goods. If you wanted to buy something from Switzerland that costs 10,000 Swiss francs, in 1971 it would have cost you about $2,300. In mid-1980 (assuming the price in Swiss francs had not gone up), it would have cost you about $6,300. But if the price in Switzerland had doubled (as it probably has), then in mid-1980 that item would cost you about $12,600.

THE NEW POSITION OF THE UNITED STATES IN THE WORLD ECONOMY

You can see that during the 1970s not only the American economy but also the *world economy* has gone through a period of great change. The international trade and finance situation of the 1980s is a *different scene* than that which existed in the "ancient history" of the 1950s and early 1960s. The changed position of the United States (and of the U.S. dollar) in the world economy has been one of the most significant changes.

No Longer the "Benelovent Protector"

The 1970s brought to an end the period during which the United States would play the role of "benevolent protector" for the economies of the other nations of the world. The United States has had to become a tough competitor in international markets. For many years the U.S. economy had been so strong that we had been able to get away with "breaking all the rules of prudent international finance." But not now.

Today there are several strong economies in the world. So the United States must be more careful to protect its own position in the world economy.

The United States has learned that it can no longer ignore the international consequences of its domestic economic policies. We know that if the government creates "easy money" and cuts taxes and increases government spending to try to overcome a recession, this discourages foreigners from holding dollars. This could cause a "dollar crisis" in the international money markets. But when the United States follows "tight money" and "tight budget" policies, this supports the dollar. Foreigners holding dollars feel confident about the future value of the dollar when they see strong anti-inflation policies in this country.

The International Situation Cannot be Ignored

All of this doesn't mean that the United States must let its domestic economic policies be dictated entirely by international considerations. But it does mean that the international considerations are important enough that they no longer can be ignored. If you look back at President Carter's "rescue the dollar" package of November, 1978, you will see that one important part of that package was a sharp tightening of money and a sharp increase in interest rates in this country. This was a "domestic stabilization policy" to be sure. But it was one which was undertaken for the specific purpose of preventing an international dollar crisis. Never again will the United States be able to undertake domestic economic policies without an eye to the impact on the international position of the dollar.

THE OUTLOOK FOR THE 1980S

One important factor which will influence this country's international trade and finance position in the 1980s is what happens with *energy production and consumption.* Until our dependence on imported oil is reduced we will continue to face some of the problems of the 1970s and early 1980s.

Another important factor will be what happens to *productivity.* If output per worker in this country can be increased significantly, this can make American products more competitive in world markets—and foreign products will be less competitive in American markets. Until the rate of productivity increase in the American economy can be speeded up, we will continue to face problems in international trade and finance.

Another vital factor is the *inflation rate.* If prices in the United States are increasing more rapidly than prices in other foreign countries, then American sellers will be losing their foreign markets to foreign producers. Also they will continue to lose a larger and larger share of their American markets to foreign producers.

The International Problems Will Not Be Quickly Solved

None of these conditions which contribute to this nation's "international trade and finance problem" will be easily or quickly solved. The extent to which these conditions—high oil prices, low productivity, and inflation—will hurt the position of the United States in the world economy will depend very much on what happens in the other countries. To what extent will the other countries be able to cope with and solve their own problems of energy, productivity, and inflation? In recent years the other nations generally have done better on these problems than we have. Until we turn that around and do better than they, our international trade and finance problems will continue.

SUMMARY COMMENTS ON PART VI

As we enter the 1980s we see many serious economic problems, and much turmoil and conflict. We see economists in serious disagreement with each other about what is causing these undesirable economic conditions and about what to do about them. It isn't a scene which inspires great confidence among the informed members of the society.

A 100-Year Flashback

In some ways this is a situation not too different from that which existed in the economics profession about 100 years ago—in the late 1800s when Alfred Marshall and Leon Walras and others worked within the disarray into which classical economics seemed to have fallen. They succeeded in synthesizing and refining the basic principles, and the very clear and precisely defined neoclassical model emerged. That model lives on today. It provides the basis for much of modern economics—including even post-Keynesian economics.

The apparent disarray into which economics has fallen today is not based on disagreement about the accuracy of the neoclassical model. It is based on disagreement about the extent to which the assumptions on which that model is based are accurate representations of the "real modern world"—the question of whether or not that model takes into account all of the important "causal factors" which need to be considered in understanding the functioning of a modern economic system.

Does the Model Picture the Real World?

Most economists would agree that under "model-market-system conditions" the neoclassical model would be an accurate description of the way things would work, in the long-run. But the argument is concerned with the question of *real-world conditions.* Are real-world conditions sufficiently close to the "model conditions" to verify the model?—to permit the model to be used as an accurate explanation of the way a modern economic system functions? That's the big question. And that's the major cause of disagreement among economists in the early 1980s. It doesn't appear likely that this disagreement will soon be resolved. So it doesn't appear that government policymakers are going to be able to look to the economics profession for "clear and unconflicting recommendations" on matters of economic stabilization policy. The policies recommended will depend on which economists are asked. That's unfortunate, but that's the way it is.

WHO'S WINNING THE POST-KEYNESIAN–MONETARIST DEBATE?

Who has been winning in this theoretical struggle to explain what determines macroeconomic conditions in the economy?—and what role *government stabilization policy* can and should play?

A Shift toward Monetarist Economics

During the early 1960s, post-Keynesian economists were chosen by the Kennedy-Johnson Administration for the Council of Economic Advisors. So during that time, post-Keynesian economics had a major influence on government policy. But ever since the beginning of the Nixon administration, economists with more "monetarists leanings" have been introduced into the Council of Economic Advisors and into the Federal Reserve. So "monetarist" economics and philosophy have been playing a more important role in influencing public policy.

Even with the "recent ascendency" of the monetarists, post-Keynesian economics has continued to have an important influence on public policy. Perhaps one reason for that is that when the people call on the government to "do something" (about unemployment, for example) post-Keynesian economics offers *positive recommendations* about what to do. So post-Keynesian economics has been looked at as more *relevant* and *practical* in approaching the economy's problems. But recently this situation has been changing.

New Problems Fall Outside Post-Keynesian Economics

In the late 1970s and early 80s the economy suddenly found itself facing a new and different set of problems—many of which fall "outside the range" of Keynesian economics. The declining productivity of the economy has generated a new emphasis on supply-side economics. This issue isn't dealt with by the "Keynesian prescription." But it falls very much within the range of concern of neoclassical economics. Neoclassical economics focuses attention on the basic economic choices, opportunity costs, and the kinds of trade-offs which will be required to shift resources from current consumption (and other non-capital-building pursuits) into capital investments for economic growth. So on this issue, post-Keynesian economics is less relevant and neoclassical economics is more relevant.

The Effect of Uncontrolled Inflation

Another important development contributing to the ascendency of monetarist economics has been the uncontrolled inflation. Post-Keynesian economics recommends higher taxes and less government spending to combat inflation. But political realities seem to have rendered this approach infeasible. The Federal budget continued to run huge deficits during the late 1970s. Efforts to bring it toward "balance" were having some success. But many groups were fighting to prevent budget cuts involving their favorite programs. The deficits continued.

When the government can't succeed in cutting its spending, this leaves "tight money policy"—holding down the growth of the money supply—as the key element in the anti-inflation program. This emphasis on limiting the growth of the money supply is a "more monetarist than post-Keynesian" approach. The important shift in policy by the Federal Reserve Board in October of 1979 placed increased emphasis on controlling the rate of expansion of the money supply and less on controlling interest rates. This was a move inspired by monetarist economics—which emphasizes money supply growth. It was a move away from post-Keynesian economics, which places more emphasis on the effects of interest rate changes.

Ascendency of Monetarist Economics among Economists

It is clear that in recent years monetarist economics has been having an increasing influence on public policy. But the recent ascendency of monetarist economics has not been limited to the public policy arena. Monetarist economics has been playing an increasing role among university economists, and more monetarist theory and less Keynesian theory is now being taught at many universities and discussed by economists at their professional meetings.

This ascendency of monetarist economics has resulted partly from the turbulent changes in world economic conditions—changes which have brought increased relevance of the neoclassical model in analyzing current problems. But also there is no question that with his keen analytical abilities and brilliant persuasiveness, Milton Friedman—the long-time advocate of the monetarist approach and leader of the attack on post-Keynesian economics—has played a significant role.

So what's the answer to the question: "Who is winning the Great Debate?" The correct answer is that the post-Keynesians were winning in the 1960s. But by the second half of the 1970s and on into the early 1980s the monetarists were winning. It isn't that post-Keynesian economics is dead! Post-Keynesian economics is still very much alive and will continue to have important influences on public policy. But no longer are the post-Keynesians in the driver's seat as we struggle to meet the new and urgent economic problems of the 1980s.

The Future of the "Great Debate"

What will happen on this "Great Debate" in future years? That will depend very much on how economic conditions change and on how *applicable* and *politically feasible* the recommendations of each "school of thought" may be. And it will also depend on the new developments of theory and the intellectual leadership which each "school of thought" may have to offer.

The question of which "school of thought" will have the most influence on various public policies seems likely to depend very much on how the political leaders perceive the "mood of the nation"—what the people are thinking and saying about the role of government in influencing and directing macroeconomic conditions in the economy. About the only thing we can be fairly sure of is that the Great Debate will go on and on.

THE SERIOUSNESS OF THE INFLATION PROBLEM

As you think back over the chapters you have been reading in Part V, you can see how critical the inflation problem really is. It plays a role in most of the domestic economic problems, and in the international economic problems too. The importance of bringing down the inflation rate in the United States would be difficult to overstate. Truly, it is *vital*. But the task will not be easy.

Controlling inflation may require reduced standards of living for the average person—and no one enjoys that. But many economists assure us that the reduced standards of living required to control inflation will be far less serious than the reduced standards of living which ultimately will result if inflation *is not* brought under control.

Will the political process permit inflation to be controlled? As various groups push for their programs and "desirable social objectives," the pressure to scrap the anti-inflationary programs and try to "provide more good things for the people" will be strong.

Even if all economists agreed and spoke with one voice, the political realities still would make it difficult for the government to maintain the tight budget and monetary policies necessary to bring inflation under control. But when so many differing views exist among economists, this leaves the politicians more "free to go their own course" and to respond to political pressures.

So what will happen? Will we succeed in the battle against inflation? Only time will tell about that. But it seems likely that our society is destined to suffer more than necessary as our government policymakers waver between the conflicting views of their economic advisors and as they respond to the realities of practical politics.

Chronic inflation isn't the only serious economic problem of the modern world. It's time now to look at some others—at the issues of giant corporations, environmental destruction, and the way the modern economies of mixed capitalism are evolving as they try to cope with these and other problems of modern society. That's the subject of Part VII, coming up now.

Part VII: Problems and Theories of Monopoly, Ecology, Energy, and the Continuing Evolution of Capitalism

Monopoly Power and Social Control, the Energy and Environmental Crises, Continuing Controversy among Economists, and the Rapid Evolution of Economic Society

Chapter 16: Big Business, Monopoly Power, and Social Control

The preceding chapters were concerned with the issues of depression and inflation, employment and prices, and the international situation during the years since World War II. These issues were, and still are, very serious. But there were some other serious issues also emerging during this period. This chapter talks about some of them.

The economic power of giant businesses has been increasing—some say increasing *too much* for the good of society. The explosive growth in industrialization and population threatens the environment. Resource use and waste disposal, already excessive, are increasing rapidly—at rates which are intolerable for the long run. And we have a serious energy problem, primarily because of the high price and undependable supply of imported oil.

This chapter and the next give you a quick look at each of these urgent problems: giant businesses, the ecological balance between modern industrial society and its worldly environment, and the energy problem. You will find that all three of these problems are interrelated and will require trade-offs against each other.

THE BASIC PROBLEM OF "BIG BUSINESS"

Remember how the market system is supposed to work? Adam Smith and the other classical economists explained it. Alfred Marshall and the other neoclassical economists explained it. It works through consumer demand, and competition among sellers. All the sellers try to make more profit by trying to outdo each other in serving the consumer. That way the society's wishes are served, and the producers are controlled by the demands and preferences of the buyers. This is the way the society controls its economy through the *market process.*

But what happens when big business comes into the picture? Suppose there's only one seller of a product. And suppose the product is one that most people feel is essential. Since there aren't any competing sellers, the seller may not bother to improve the product. The producer may not bother to produce as much as the people would like—may let shortages develop and raise the price and make more profits. See how the seller with monopoly power can get *rewarded* for doing a *disservice* to society?

This is the point: Competition is essential if the market system is to work right. As businesses get larger and larger and hold larger and larger shares of various markets, they have more and more power to control those markets in their own interest. They don't have to be so careful about responding to the interest of the buyers. Essentially, that is the problem of big business—of monopoly.

The Continuing Growth of Big Business

Back in the last century, big businesses were growing by leaps and bounds. The Sherman Antitrust Act was passed in 1890 to try to hold down the growth of monopoly in the markets of the American economy. But the Sherman Act didn't seem to help much. More antimonopoly laws were passed in the early 1900s. Additional laws have been passed from then until now.

The laws and the courts have had a considerable effect in limiting the growth and exercise of monopoly power. But still there's a lot of big business around. How bad are the effects? And what's going to be done about it? These are tough questions.

Back in the 1930s many people were concerned about big business. A study showed that about one-half of all the corporate wealth in the United States was concentrated in the hands of some two-hundred companies. And what has happened since that time? This concentration of corporate wealth has increased even more.

If we look only at *industrial* corporations (eliminating the transportation, utility and other service companies), the pattern of increasing concentration of corporate wealth in the hands of a few is easy to see. In 1929, about one-fourth of all industrial corporate wealth was in the hands of the top one-hundred corporations. By the early 1960s that figure had grown to about one-third. By 1970, it had increased to about *one-half.* By 1980 it was *more than* one-half.

Mergers, and the Growth of Multinational Corporations

There is no question that most of the big corporations—the ones that have been doing well—have been doing *very* well. They have been gathering more and more assets by merging other companies into their "parent corporations." Great amounts of corporate wealth are being concentrated in the hands of a relatively small number of corporations, not just in the United States but worldwide, both with big corporations in other countries and with the rapid growth of multinational corporations.

If the big multinational corporations were to grow over the next several years as they have been in the last several years (which does not seem likely), in about fifteen or twenty years almost all of the production in the world would come from three-hundred big worldwide firms, two-hundred of which would be U.S.-based corporations.

Can you see that this concentration of wealth in the hands of a few corporations might be something for economists to worry about? Can a national or world economy made up of a few massive corporations be expected to follow the laws of economics as defined in the neoclassical economist's model economy, made up of great numbers of small, competitive businesses? Of course not.

WE HAVE NO ACCEPTED THEORY OF THE "BIG BUSINESS" ECONOMY

Certainly there are advantages to bigness in business: planning and stability, long-range goals and willingness to make long-range commitments for research and development; and perhaps the development of a "social consciousness," which in modern economic systems in the real world may be an essential function. But one thing is certain: These big firms will not operate the way the small, very competitive firms of the neoclassical model are—in theory—*supposed* to operate.

So how do the big firms operate? Does some kind of effective competition keep these corporations moving toward the best interests of society? Is there effective social control over these corporations and their economic behavior, or not? And what does the future hold in store on these questions? These are not easy questions to answer.

We really don't have an accepted theory of how a modern economic system works in the real world. We know that most prices are "administered" (that is, *set by somebody*). And we know that there is a lot of planning and long-range goal seeking, both by governments and by big businesses—much more than would exist in the neoclassical model of the market system. But how does it really work? We just don't have a generally accepted theory to answer that question.

Those economists who hold strongest to the neoclassical tradition (the Chicago School) say that the real world still does approximate the neoclassical model. They say we shouldn't be looking for other ways of explaining the world.

Many economists don't think that the big modern corporations behave very much like the little "typical firms" described in the neoclassical model. So what explanation do most economists give? And what answer do they offer? That's the problem. Most of them don't have an explanation or an answer to offer. But one economist has: John Kenneth Galbraith. Let's take a look at what Galbraith has to say.

GALBRAITH'S CHALLENGE

It was in 1958 that Galbraith published *The Affluent Society,* attacking much of the "conventional wisdom" of modern-day economists. Nine years later (1967) he continued that attack in his book *The New Industrial State.* Then in 1973 he completed the attack and offered his solutions in *Economics and the Public Purpose.*

Galbraith raises serious questions about the applicability, the realism, and the helpfulness of the conventional wisdom in economics. He doesn't think the assumptions of the neoclassical model are close enough to reality. He thinks the results of the model are more misleading than helpful in understanding what really happens in the economies of the modern world.

Galbraith thinks the neoclassical model and the things conventional economists do and say are more harmful than good, because the effect is to hide the truth about the things which are really *wrong* with the system. In the foreword of his book, *Economics and the Public Purpose,* he says: ". . . on no conclusion is this book more clear: Left to themselves, economic forces do not work out for the best—except perhaps for the powerful."

Consumer Sovereignty and the Dependence Effect

Galbraith first attacks the idea of "consumer sovereignty"—the idea that the economic system is directed by and responds to the wishes of the people. He says that people's wants are not *independent* of the system, but are a *reflection* of the system. There is a kind of "keeping up with the Joneses" effect: as the economic system produces more things, new desires for those things are generated. So, says Galbraith, the system is responding to wants which it (the system) is *creating.* Galbraith calls this the "dependence effect." (Do you see how this is very close to some of Veblen's ideas?)

If the dependence effect is granted, the idea of "consumer sovereignty" as the driving force in the economic system (as in the neoclassical model) doesn't make much sense anymore. No longer are consumers rational in pursuing their objectives. As they spend they are responding to the influences of the system; they are not the ultimate source of power, the independent force, choosing the objectives to be sought and directing the economic system toward those objectives.

The Giant Corporation and the Technostructure

Galbraith's second major challenge to the neoclassical model is on the idea that businesses will adjust their behavior to try to get maximum profit. He focuses on the behavior of the giant corporations and points out that the big modern corporation is not run by a risk-taking entrepreneur. The guiding intelligence—the brain of the enterprise—is made up of many people with technical knowledge and talents who influence the group decisions which ultimately control the corporation. Galbraith calls this collective intelligence or "brain" of the organization the "technostructure"—certainly not much like the risk-taking entrepreneur of the neoclassical model!

According to Galbraith, the technostructure wants to be a part of a *successful* organization. This means the corporation must *survive.* There must be adequate earnings. Also, it is important that the corporation grow. The first order of business of the technostructure is to avoid risks that might threaten the survival or growth of the company.

The technostructure would be in favor of government policies for stability of prices and employment; would not object to labor unions which would provide them a stable supply of labor and assure that labor costs would be more or less the same throughout the industrial system, eliminating the threat of competition from other producers with low-cost labor; would be in favor of high expenditures for education and skill development by the government, thus being assured an adequate supply of labor; and would be in favor of high government spending in technology-developing activities, such as in defense or the space program.

A Government-Industrial-Labor Complex?

Galbraith's view of the "new industrial state" is quite different from the dog-eat-dog world of maximum-profit-seeking competitive activity. He sees close parallels between the objectives of the industrial technostructure and those of many political leaders and labor leaders as well. All seek reasonable success in pursuing their objectives of stability and growth. He sees businesses and governments alike planning for long-range order and stability and movement toward predetermined objectives—a far cry from the automatic operation of the laissez-faire market system described by Adam Smith and the neoclassical economists!

Galbraith doesn't see a total elimination of competition, but he sees competition more between *industries* than between firms in the same industry. The steel industry must be careful lest it lose its markets to aluminum, plastics, and other metals and metal substitutes. This is the only kind of competition that effectively operates between the massive corporations in Galbraith's "new industrial state."

Galbraith sees a tendency to overemphasize *economic* goals. The technostructure wants to increase production, incomes, employment, consumption, and all that. There is no place in the corporate planning process for placing emphasis on the *noneconomic* objectives and goals which the society might wish to pursue—goals which Galbraith says may be more important in an affluent society than the "economic" or "material" objectives and goals. So what does Galbraith prescribe?

The Galbraithian Prescription: The "New Socialisms"

In his former books, Galbraith diagnoses the problems. In *Economics and the Public Purpose,* he prescribes. What does he prescribe? A vastly different kind of economic system than the one which exists (or which most economists seem to *think* exists) in the United States today. He suggests:

- Government takeover and operation of the sectors of the economy which have not been adequately serving the needs of the society, such as housing, urban transportation, and medical care;
- Government actions to strengthen the small businesses which still operate as a market sector in the economy, but which are at a disadvantage against the giant corporations;
- Government guaranteed annual income;
- Government planning, coordination, and controls over the big corporations (including controls over wages and prices in the big corporations); and
- Government nationalization of the businesses which are big defense contractors.

Essentially, Galbraith wants (a) the industries which can't perform adequately to be run by the government; (b) the big corporations and technostructure planning to be brought under government planning; (c) the remainder of the economy to be strengthened so that it can operate effectively as a *free market* sector, and (d) more income redistribution by government to reduce "unearned" (rent, dividend, interest, etc.) incomes and to more nearly eliminate poverty.

What about these Galbraithian ideas? Are they feasible? Or too radical to contemplate? Galbraith says, "practical necessity has already forced a measure of practical action" along the lines suggested. He says that what he is really doing is providing "the theoretical justification for what circumstances and good sense have already initiated."

Here again, as with John Maynard Keynes, Adam Smith, and others, we find an economist looking at the undeniable problems in the world —watching what's wrong, seeing what's being done—and then offering an explanation. Galbraith offers mankind a new way of looking at and approaching the economic issues and problems of the last quarter of the twentieth century. But, fortunately or unfortunately, the image of the world which Galbraith describes is not the image which most economists or most people in the United States are ready to accept. Therefore the Galbraithian prescription is not likely to be taken very soon—certainly not in very large doses.

Galbraith, Keynes, Veblen—Challengers to Conventional Wisdom

Galbraith, like Keynes and like Veblen before him, has walked (and today continues to walk) a path quite distinctly different from that of the conventional economist of the day. All three of these men have broken step with the profession in order to turn their attention more directly to the problems and issues of the day. In so doing, all three have lost many friends and gained some (perhaps bitter) enemies.

I suppose that anyone who breaks ranks with his colleagues and then mounts an attack on their hallowed beliefs is bound to be criticized. Galbraith (like Keynes and Veblen) has many critics. But judging from what one can find out, neither Galbraith nor Keynes nor Veblen was bothered in the least by the flurries of criticism which their pioneering ideas generated. Likely, only people strong enough to withstand a withering fire of criticism could ever perform the pioneering function of a Veblen, a Keynes, or a Galbraith.

THE EFFECTS OF THE GIANT CORPORATIONS? ECONOMISTS DISAGREE

So what can we say about the present and future effects of giant corporations in the U.S. and world economies? And about Galbraith's new way of looking at and explaining the way a modern industrial economy functions? And about his recommended "New Socialisms" for changing the economic system to better serve the society? I'm sorry, but we really don't know. Things are changing *so fast,* it's just too early to tell.

Anyone in touch with the modern industrial society knows there's truth in what Galbraith says. But how much? And what does this tell us about the "social efficiency" of the modern industrial market-oriented economic society? And should we embark on a program aimed toward the Galbraithian prescription?

What do the economists say on these issues? Again, as you might have guessed, what they say will depend on *which economists* you choose to ask.

RECENT DEVELOPMENTS, AND THE OUTLOOK FOR THE 1980s

During the 1970s and early 1980s there were several economists, politicians, business leaders and others calling for changes in the relationship between government and big business. On one side, the objective was to get government to reduce its regulations and controls and permit big businesses the freedom to operate more efficiently—to increase the *productivity* and the *competitive position* of the American economy in the world economy. On the other side, economists were recommending that we extend *greater government control* over big businesses to ensure that they perform with maximum efficiency from a "social objectives" point of view.

Nader Calls for Federal Chartering of Corporations

Ralph Nader and his associates were calling for *federal chartering* of corporations instead of continuing to allow the individual states to approve corporate charters. In Nader's view, Federal chartering would establish more stringent requirements and would permit the Federal Government to exercise more effective control over corporate activities "for the good of the nation." But business leaders and some economists were arguing that this move would only result in further bureaucratic interference and result in further slowing the productivity of the American economy.

You already know what Galbraith was suggesting—that the major corporations be brought under the direction of government planners. Several economists (but by no means a majority) were arguing that Galbraith's recommendation (or something similar) would improve social control over big business and would improve the performance of the economy. But most business and labor leaders and most economists (and also the Carter administration) held the opposite view—i.e., that the economy will function best if entangling and cost-increasing government regulations on business can be reduced and more competition introduced into the nation's markets.

The Move Toward Deregulation

During the late 1970s and early 80s Congress passed several important "deregulation" acts aimed toward reducing costs and increasing productivity and competition in various industries. The first industry to be deregulated and "set free to compete" was the airlines. Then in March, 1980 the *Depository Institutions Deregulation Act* called for a phased deregulation of interest rate ceilings on checking and savings deposits and opened the door for greatly increased competition among banks, savings and loan institutions, savings banks, credit unions, and other financial institutions.

In June, 1980 the *Trucking Industry Deregulation Act* was passed. This sets the trucking companies free to compete with each other. By mid-1980, legislation to deregulate the railroads and to reduce government regulation of the communications industry was being considered by Congress.

In 1980 the Carter administration was trying to develop some new regulatory techniques which would reduce the "compliance costs" which businesses encounter when government regulations are imposed. Some regulations will always be required. But if the costs of complying with these necessary regulations can be reduced, businesses can then operate more efficiently.

It is clear that in the early 1980s public policy toward business was aimed more toward reducing than increasing government regulations on business. The political mood in Washington has been significantly influenced by increasing concern about the "supply-side" problem—declining productivity in the American economy and our unfavorable competitive position in the world economy. The majority view in Washington seems to be that less regulation and more competition will stimulate increased productivity.

The Outlook for the 1980s

Public policy toward big business during the next few years seems likely to be dominated by the new emphasis on "supply-side" economics. In 1980 it was becoming clear to an increasing number of people—not just business and political leaders and economists, but to the general public as well—that a healthy economy and rising standards of living depend on the success and growth of businesses. It may not be true that "What's good for General Motors is good for the country." But by the early 1980s a lot more people seemed to be thinking that there might be some truth in it. The cooperative effort between labor, business, and government to try to "save Chrysler" was one indication of the changing mood.

How long will this mood last? Probably for at least as long as people see their friends losing their jobs—and fear for their own jobs—because of competition from foreign products. Perhaps the relationship between productivity and inflation, and between our inflation rate and our ability to compete in world markets, will soon be better understood by most people. If so, then most people may become "permanently aware" of the need for productivity growth and for the healthy growth of businesses to support this productivity growth. If this happens, then public policy toward big business is likely to reflect this attitude.

There is no question that much government regulation of business will continue. But unless something in American industry takes a serious (and now unforseen) "turn for the worst," it seems *very unlikely* that any major steps toward increased government planning and control over business (such as suggested by Galbraith) will be taken. It seems much more likely that the trend will be toward deregulation over the next few years. For how long? Probably for as long as "supply-side" economics continues to occupy its present spotlight position on center-stage.

What About the Big Oil Companies?

As public policy moves toward deregulation, does that apply to the giant corporations that produce oil and gas? And if so, what will that do to the prices we will have to pay? And what about anti-pollution regulations? If those are relaxed, won't that harm our environment? Should we let that happen?

These are difficult questions. They involve unpleasant opportunity costs—trade-offs. But that's what economics is all about. Remember? In the next chapter you will be reading about these issues—energy, and pollution—and about the kinds of trade-offs which will be required and the kinds of decisions that must be made.

Chapter 17: Economic Issues and Conflicting Ideas on Energy and Pollution

This book explains many issues and ideas about which most people know very little. But everybody knows that we have an energy problem and a pollution problem. We all feel some of the effects of high energy costs and of pollution. But most people don't know much about the *economics* of either of these issues.

This one chapter can't make you an economic expert on energy or pollution. But it can highlight some of the important economic principles involved. And it can emphasize the trade-offs (the "economic problem" again!) which must be (and are being) made. This is another one of those areas in which, like it or not, "We can't have our cake and eat it too."

THE ENERGY PROBLEM

In the 1980 *Economic Report of the President,* President Carter said that during the 1980s the American economy is "dangerously exposed" to the changing supply and price conditions of oil in the world market. Nobody would argue with that statement. Everyone is already aware of the impact on the American economy of the changing supply and price of oil. The effects have touched every one of us.

Everyone is paying higher prices for gasoline and heating oil. But not everyone sees what the greatly increased cost of energy has done—and will continue to do—to production costs of everything produced in this country. Everything which is produced or constructed or transported requires energy. Oil is not the only source of energy, of course. But the productivity of the modern American economy depends more on oil than on any other energy source. So we have been (and still are) experiencing a great "shock to the system" as a result of the *tenfold increase* in the price of oil—an increase which has occurred over a period of less than ten years.

Our Increasing "Foreign Oil Bill"

In the early 1970s our "import bill" for imported oil amounted to about $5 billion. In 1974, following the first big jump in oil prices by the Organization of Petroleum Exporting Countries (OPEC), our "imported oil bill" amounted to about $25 billion. For the year 1980 it is estimated that the total cost of imported oil will amount to more than $80 billion.

What about the future? If the OPEC nations increase their prices only moderately each year, we can expect to be paying somewhere between $150 billion and $200 billion by the mid-1980s. How can the American economy withstand this constant upward pressure on prices? —and this massive cash drain from its businesses and consumers? And how can American businesses, faced with these constantly increasing energy costs, produce and sell enough (at competitive world prices) to bring our international trade into balance?

Another question is this: What will prevent the OPEC nations from restricting or cutting off their supplies of oil? Or from doubling or tripling or quadrupling the price again? In the early 1970s the average oil price was less than $4 per barrel. In 1980 it ranged from about $30 to $40 a barrel, depending on the grade of oil and where you bought it. If this rate of increase continues, the price will be more than $300 a barrel before the end of the 1980s! Nobody seems to think that actually will happen. But nobody is sure that it will not. Nobody thought the past increases were going to occur, either.

We Must Reduce Our Dependence on Foreign Oil

How do we cope with this situation?—a situation which already is having a very detrimental impact on the American economy?—and in which we are dangerously exposed and vulnerable to the decisions (perhaps whims) of the few individuals who make the oil pricing decisions in the OPEC nations? The answer is clear: We must reduce our dependence on foreign sources of oil.

The American economy must:

1. Reduce its consumption of energy as much as possible, and
2. Develop alternative sources of energy as rapidly as feasible.

How do we achieve these two objectives? No one disagrees with the objectives. But there is much disagreement about how best to do it.

The Effects of the Price Mechanism

Can the natural forces of the market and the operation of the price mechanism help? Of course. They already have. Higher prices are causing people and businesses to reduce their use of high-priced oil and of high-priced oil-dependent products. Businesses are shifting from oil to other energy sources. But conversion to alternative energy sources is expensive and sometimes it takes a long time. And there are some processes in which *only oil* can be used.

The high prices are also stimulating much more rapid development of new energy sources, including a massive exploration boom in drilling for new sources of domestic oil. So the forces of the market are at work trying to solve the problem. But market forces cannot work fast enough to solve the problem over the next few years.

The fact that oil has been so widely used by American industry and consumers reflects the fact that oil was the least-cost, most efficient energy source available. As the economy shifts to alternative energy sources, we will be moving from what was the least-cost and most efficient source, to higher-cost, less efficient sources. So as the economy converts to alternative energy sources (unless there are some important technological breakthroughs), we can never hope to get back to where we were before oil prices began to skyrocket.

What Role Should the Government Play?

Is this an issue in which the government should get involved? Should the government try to redirect resources into different channels—either by financial inducements or regulations or both—to try to help to solve the energy problem? Most people seem to think so. But people disagree widely on exactly what the government should do, and how much, and how.

THE CARTER ADMINISTRATION'S ENERGY POLICY

The Carter Administration's energy policy has a twofold objective:

1. For the *long run,* to promote an adjustment of the economy to the "new world" of more costly energy supplies, and
2. For the *short run,* to reduce as quickly as possible the nation's vulnerability to further oil price increases, or to reduced supplies.

The Short-Run Program

The government has established a "Strategic Petroleum Reserve" which it is now in the process of trying to fill with oil. This "reserve" could be used to "tide us over" if the foreign producers decided to reduce or cut off their supplies. The government is trying to promote energy conservation by requiring more fuel-efficient automobiles and buildings, lower thermostats in winter and higher in summer, and by other means. Also the administration is pushing for a "standby motor fuel rationing plan" which could be used to limit gasoline consumption in case of an oil-supply emergency.

The administration is also working with other oil-importing nations to try to get all of them to reduce their oil imports. If all oil-importing nations could succeed in cutting back their oil imports, that would reduce the world market demand for oil and reduce the likelihood of big price increases by OPEC.

The Long-Run Program

For the long run the administration's policy is aimed toward permanently reducing our dependence on imported oil. The program involves government support for energy conservation measures, support for the development of alternative energy sources, and policies which will stimulate domestic oil production. To stimulate domestic production, the administration is in favor of gradual decontrol of domestic oil and natural gas prices.

THE ENERGY SECURITY ACT OF 1980

In June of 1980—three years after President Carter had declared "the moral equivalent of war" on the energy problem—the Congress finally passed and the President signed the *Energy Security Act.* This Act —some 400 pages long—spells out the nation's energy policies and programs for the coming years.

The Synthetic Fuels Corporation

One of the major sections of the Act establishes the "Synthetic Fuels Corporation." This government corporation will be run by seven Presidential appointees. It is authorized to spend up to $20 billion (that's a million dollars, 20,000 times!) in the fiscal year beginning October 1, 1980—and up to *$68 billion more* in future years—to support the development of synthetic fuels. When he signed the Act, President Carter predicted that the effort to develop synthetic fuels ("synfuels") ". . . will dwarf the combined programs that led us to the moon and built our entire interstate highway system."

Other Provisions of the Act

The *Energy Security Act* also provides support for solar energy development, alcohol-fuel production, geothermal power plants, energy conservation measures (including weatherizing homes), and for the Strategic Petroleum Reserve.

The passage of this act was a very important event. Nothing approaching its scope had ever been done before in the energy field. It will not be the last energy act to be passed in the early 1980s, but it is likely to be by far the most important. As Congressman John Dingle of Michigan said: "This is a major step toward a National energy policy."

Carter's Oil Import Tax Proposal

In early 1980 the Carter Administration also tried to impose an import tax on oil which would be passed along (at about 10¢ per gallon) to buyers of gasoline. But the Congress defeated that proposal by an overwhelming majority. The obvious purpose of the proposal was to try to reduce consumption of gasoline and thereby reduce our dependence on imported oil. But it appears that the members of Congress did not want to be associated with approving a 10¢ price increase on their constituents' gasoline.

WHAT SHOULD BE OUR POLICY TOWARD THE BIG OIL COMPANIES?

In the 1970s and early 80s there was much controversy about the question of what should be our policy toward the giant oil corporations. This question is closely related to some of the issues which were discussed in the last chapter—questions about "big business, monopoly power, and social control." But in the case of the big oil corporations this question takes on special importance because of the energy crisis.

As world oil prices increased, the big oil companies began earning increased revenues and profits. As the news media reported the fact that oil company profits were increasing, there was strong public sentiment against the oil companies for "taking advantage of the consumers." In fact, if oil company profits were reduced all the way to zero, this would not reduce the price of gasoline at the pump by more than two or three cents per gallon—but the news media didn't mention that. Of course if oil company profits went to zero and remained there for very long, eventually there wouldn't be any gasoline available at the pump!

The Carter Administration, the Congress, and the general public were in favor of a "windfall profits tax" on the oil corporations. So that tax was passed. The Congress tried to design the tax to minimize the negative effect on investments in exploration and development of new sources of domestic oil.

Will the windfall profits tax affect future domestic oil production? The tax will reduce oil company profits and therefore will reduce both incentives and cash flow for new investments. But perhaps these negative effects will not be serious. Let's hope not.

THE ECONOMICS OF OIL PRICE DEREGULATION

As you know, the government regulates prices of domestically produced oil and gas. The Carter Administration supports decontrol of these prices. But there are strong pressures from consumer groups to maintain the controls. The "windfall profits tax" was tied in with legislation calling for phased decontrol of domestic oil and gas prices.

The economic argument for oil price decontrol is that prices for domestically produced oil and gas should be permitted to increase to equal world prices. The higher prices would discourage domestic consumption and stimulate domestic production. Both of these price-generated effects would reduce our dependence on foreign oil.

Higher prices would provide revenues and profits to the oil and gas producers, and oil and gas consumers would have to pay more. The higher prices would provide oil and gas producers with more "cash flow" for investment and more incentive to increase production.

Your "Policy Choice" Reflects Your "Theory Choice"

The question of what public policy *should be* toward the oil and gas companies depends a lot on the "theory," or "conceptual view" you choose about how these big corporations operate. Suppose you assume that these businesses operate more or less in response to the price mechanism. Then you are more inclined to recommend deregulation of prices so that the market process will be free to help solve our energy problem. But suppose you think there is too much "monopoly power" in the oil industry to permit the price mechanism to work very effectively. Then you are likely to be in favor of more government regulations and controls to direct the oil companies to do what our social objectives require.

There is much disagreement among economists on these issues. So here again (as in almost every public policy issue) the economic advice the government gets will depend on *which economists* the government chooses as advisors. Those economists who believe that the neoclassical model is a fairly accurate representation of how our "big business" economy operates (e.g., Milton Friedman) will be for more *laissez faire* (less controls). But those who think that big businesses have enough monopoly power to operate differently than the neoclassical market forces would force them to operate (e.g., Galbraith) will be for more government planning and controls.

ENERGY AND PRODUCTIVITY? OR ENVIRONMENTAL PROTECTION?

In recent years, environmental protection programs have become an important influence in the American economy. But these programs have increased costs of production and output prices throughout the economy. Increased *cost* means decreased productivity; increased *price* means inflation. In the energy field, increased cost means a reduced rate of increase in output. All of these results contribute to the major problems now facing the American economy.

Environmental Regulations Increase Production Costs

Producers are saying that they could increase productivity and outputs and sell at lower prices if they were not required to follow the environmental regulations. Some of the business leaders in the oil, gas, and coal industries are saying that the government should permit them more freedom to produce by least-cost methods, and should permit them to explore and produce on now prohibited areas of government land. They say that these changes in government policy would enable them to significantly increase their energy outputs. They say that with these policy changes, by the end of the decade of the 1980s it would be possible to greatly reduce our dependence on imported oil.

But many people take the opposite view. They don't think we should relax our environmental protection requirements—either for the purpose of increasing the productivity of the economy or for the purpose of increasing our energy output.

The Trade-Offs Are Serious and Basic

It is clear that there are some very important, very *basic* trade-offs here—that the "economic problem" is staring us in the face. The "opportunity cost" of a cleaner environment may be: (a) lower productivity of the economy, (b) continued inflation, (c) our inability to compete effectively in world markets, and (d) continued high dependence on imported oil. But the "opportunity cost" of moving as rapidly as possible to solve these other problems may be serious environmental destruction.

Which way will we go? Which way *should* we go? You can see that this is a very tough question—one which will continue to generate serious controversy among economists, politicians, business leaders, and the general public.

What about Nuclear Power?

The controversy about nuclear power—especially following the Three Mile Island accident—has brought this issue into sharp focus for many people. So has the Love Canal "chemical waste" incident.

During the 1980s the American economy could increase its efficiency and reduce its dependence on imported oil significantly by the rapid introduction of nuclear power. Nobody disagrees with that. But whether or not you are in favor of moving in this direction depends on your own personal judgment about the *safety* of nuclear power, and about the *seriousness* of the radioactive waste disposal problem.

People who believe that nuclear power presents a serious danger to present and future society would much prefer to accept the (admittedly unpleasant) alternatives. But those who believe that nuclear power is not a real danger to the society—that the necessary safety and radioactive waste disposal procedures will be worked out—will argue strongly for more use of nuclear power. Many of the people on both sides of this fence are sure that they are right. But the truth seems to be that no one knows—that no matter which road we choose to take, we will not know (until the future tells us) if it was the right one or the wrong one.

THE ENVIRONMENTAL CRISIS—A CLOSER LOOK

You have just been reading about the environmental crisis in the context of trade-offs—the very high *opportunity cost to society* of stringent environmental protection in the 1980s. Now it's time to step back and look at the environmental crisis itself. How did it arise? How serious is it? What can or should be done?

The Evolution of the Problem

Back during the Industrial Revolution, while the very efficient and highly motivating market system was supporting industrial growth by leaps and bounds, society was coming closer and closer to solving its traditional economic problem—how to provide food and other material necessities to the people. But at the same time the market system was setting the stage for the creation of this new and serious problem—the problem of the ecological balance between an industrial society and its environment.

As the Industrial Revolution broke loose, outputs expanded. Then population began expanding more and more. As the decades passed, both of these influences—increasing outputs and increasing numbers of people—began to build up the environmental problem. In recent decades that problem has become acute.

How Serious Is the Problem?

Almost everyone these days is aware of some kinds of undesirable pollution or environmental destruction going on around them. But how serious is the problem, nationwide? Consider this:

- The United States has about a quarter of a million miles of rivers and streams in its major watersheds. More than one fourth of that mileage is polluted.
- More than 100 million tons of carbon monoxide are being released into the air every year. Other air pollutants: hydrocarbon, sulphur oxides, nitrogen oxides, and others amount to millions of tons each, per year.
- There's more than 150 million tons of garbage and trash being thrown away every year. And billions of tin cans, billions of bottles, and even *several million junk cars* every year.

It would take a lot of polluting to pollute all the land and water and air of the earth and kill off all the wild life and marine life—and human life. But some scientists say we are moving in that direction at a rapid clip! Everyone knows that the trend can't be allowed to continue. Something must be done. But what? And how? These are tough questions. And the trade-offs—the opportunity costs—are going to be very difficult to accept.

Market Forces Don't Automatically Protect the Environment

How did it happen that the market system, which is supposed to direct the society's resources into *desirable* channels, allowed the environmental problem to arise? Why didn't the market system protect society against it? The answer is simple: The environmental problem is outside the market. There is no way that the automatic market process can handle this problem.

These *many* decades since the Industrial Revolution, we have been living high without paying the full costs of what we have been getting from the earth. We have been pulling natural resources from the earth without having to incur the costs of reproducing or recycling those natural resources. We have been dumping wastes into the environment without having to pay the costs of cleaning up the wastes. But now we are in a situation where we can't do as much of that anymore.

Too many resources are being pulled out of the environment and too many wastes are being put back. It is already going too fast to be sustained. To dramatize the problem some people refer to our planet as "spaceship earth." We're flying through space on a finite world; when we use up all of our supplies, then we will all die. Like it or not, that's the way it is.

Economist Kenneth Boulding is one who emphasizes this problem. Boulding says that we must begin to think of recycling *everything,* and replacing *everything* which we take from nature. We must dump *nothing* into the environment which natural forces cannot handle—that is, which nature cannot recycle.

The "Human Herd" Is Getting Too Big for the Range

What about the *population* aspect of the problem of ecological imbalance? At the beginning of this century there were only about 1.5 billion people on earth. Today there are about four billion. At current rates of growth, by the middle of the next century there will be about sixteen billion. But there's just no way that so many people can be supported on the earth! Not unless we find a lot of unbelievable ways to recycle things, and to generate something out of nothing.

What's going to happen? Two things will happen, because they *must* happen. (1) Somehow the population expansion will be slowed, and (ultimately) stopped. (2) *All* productive activities will begin shifting more and more energy toward recycling materials and toward protecting and rebuilding the natural environment. The normal processes of life in all the advanced nations must go through some changes. There's no doubt about it.

THE HIGH "REAL COST" OF PROTECTING THE ENVIRONMENT

The recycling and environmental protection efforts are going to cost a lot. Many resources, much energy, much valuable effort will be required. *All* products are likely to cost a lot more in *real* terms—not just in "inflated values" from inflation.

Higher *real cost* of products (probably meaning lower *real incomes* of people) would have been caused by the high real cost of environmental protection *even if* the current crises of energy and low productivity and inflation had never occurred. But these current crises *have* occurred. So now the real cost of environmental protection will be much higher—and decisions to stand firm on environmental protection will be much more difficult.

If a lot of resources, energy, capital, and labor are diverted toward environmental rebuilding, recycling, and pollution control, that will mean a lot more energy and resources used up as *costs of production.* So we will get a lot less output for our used-up inputs. That will mean fewer goods for the people.

Will our standards of living actually go *down?* No one knows, of course. But it's quite possible. The inputs used for environmental protection must come from somewhere. Those inputs (including human effort) can't be used to do or make what they were doing or making before.

Somehow the environmental problem must be solved. No question about it. But how fast? and how? What role will the government play? And what will be the role of the forces of the market process? What kind of "economic system" do we need—and what kind will we choose—to cope with this problem?

When Will We Begin to Pay the Costs?

As our society faces its environmental problem, some very difficult, but very critical decisions must be made. We could just decide to ignore the environmental problem and concentrate on the other problems. Maybe the government will back off and leave the market process and the price mechanism free to work for increased production.

Maybe we will say to the power companies and oil companies and all the other companies: "You are free now to use whatever production techniques you wish, to produce whatever products you wish in whatever quantities you wish and sell them at whatever prices you can get in any markets in which you can successfully compete."

If we do that, we can be fairly sure that competition (both domestic and international) will be sufficiently strong to force producers to use least-cost methods, to increase productivity in whatever ways they can, and to sell their products at prices which will enable them to compete in domestic and world markets. But we can also be sure that this approach will result in significantly increased use of nuclear power, more strip mining, use of more high-sulphur coal, more air and water and landscape pollution, and perhaps oil and gas exploration and production in Yosemite National Park.

The Nature of Our Economic System Will Be Changing

No one is actually suggesting that we should go as far as to let the big companies operate with absolutely no government restrictions! But if we did, that would be a big step toward the rejuvenation of the old-style "laissez-faire capitalist economic system."

We might move in the opposite direction. We might establish "national planning" over the big corporations. We might develop government plans to specify what inputs and production methods would be used, what outputs would be produced and in what quantities, and at what prices the products would be sold. And we might build stringent environmental protection requirements into the plans. This approach would be a move away from the "capitalist system"—toward an economic system with more "central planning."

See how easy it is for an economic system to change? But that shouldn't be surprising. Economic systems are changing all the time. That's what you will be reading about in the next chapter.

Chapter 18: The Continuing Evolution of the World's Economic Systems

Throughout history economic systems have been changing. But it wasn't until recent centuries that the changes began to become big, and cumulative—like a chain reaction, like a row of tumbling dominos.

Feudal society eroded, people were shaken loose from their land and from their traditional roles in life; trade expanded and the *market system* evolved. Remember? Then the Industrial Revolution added much more speed to the progressive changes, and the modern economic systems evolved out of all that.

THE MARKET PROCESS IS A VERY POWERFUL FORCE

The powerful forces of the market process and the price mechanism have been responsible for these revolutionary changes in economics—and in society. These forces are still very powerful in the modern world.

Decisions about which resources to use for what purposes (and which to conserve), about which products to produce in what quantities (and which not to produce); and decisions by consumers about which products to consume (and in what quantities) all still are greatly influenced by prices.

- Prices which are high always tend to discourage consumption and to stimulate production. Ultimately, prices which are "too high" result in *surpluses.*
- Prices which are low always tend to encourage consumption and to discourage production. Ultimately, prices which are "too low" result in *shortages.*

These powerful forces of price are still very much alive in the modern world and are exerting their influence on our economic choices every day. But not *all* of the output and input and consumption choices of the society are left free to be determined by market forces.

What About the Distribution Question?

The powerful forces of the price mechanism still play the most important role in answering the distribution question in the "free societies" of the modern world. People who are highly productive—or who own highly productive assets—are the ones who receive the largest incomes. But in modern society, *all* income distribution is not left free to be determined by "impersonal market forces."

Income redistribution—by government anti-poverty, welfare, and other such programs—is having a significant effect on the way in which the distribution question is now being answered. But it is still true that *productivity* is the most important factor in determining who will be rich and who will be poor. This is even true to a considerable extent in the planned economies of the Communist countries.

So the forces of the market process and the price mechanism are still extremely important in the modern world. Anyone who forgets this is likely to make foolish mistakes and wind up *worsening* their economic circumstances. And government policies which fail to consider the great power of the price mechanism are likely to have the ultimate effect of worsening the economic circumstances of the people of the society. But even so—even with all this great power—the market process still cannot solve *all* of the modern world's economic problems.

The Market Process Can't Solve All the Problems

The tough problems of this century have battered society from several sides. We have encountered wars, inflation, depression, expanding economic power of giant businesses, a world population explosion, poverty, environmental pollution, crises in the cities, international financial crises, and other difficult problems.

What about all these problems? They all require that some of society's resources be directed toward solutions. Yet how can that happen? The *market system* doesn't automatically direct resources toward wars and environmental protection and urban crises and population explosions and such. So how can the problems be handled? The government must get involved.

The government must play a more important role in the resource-directing process. That is to say: The economic system must change to include more government-directed choices. Is that what's going on in the world? Yes, that's exactly what's happening.

The Impact of the Depression, and Keynesian Economics

During the 1930s many people were out of work. Businesses and banks were failing. The economic system was not functioning as the economists said it was supposed to. During this period the self-reliant economic philosophy of many people shifted. Attitudes changed from the position: "I can always find a job—or do whatever may be necessary to take care of myself!"—to the position: "There are times when economic conditions beyond my control make it impossible for me to take care of myself. So the government must do something *to ensure* that the people have adequate employment opportunities and adequate economic security!"

This shift of the public mood away from laissez-faire and toward more reliance on the government has been reflected in the basic nature of the economic system. The result has been greater involvement by government in making the economic choices for the society.

Also you remember that it was during the depression that *Keynesian economics* emerged. This provided a theoretical explanation which specifically calls for government policies aimed toward the objective of maintaining a healthy and growing economy. Both the psychological impact of the depression, and the introduction of Keynesian economics (and the ultimately wide acceptance of the Keynesian theories) have had the effect of increasing *the role of the political process* in making basic economic choices in the American economic system.

Many people think it is *good* that the government has become more involved in directing and influencing the economic choices. But many other people think it is *definitely not good.* Perhaps the future will tell us who was right. But for now, while we're waiting to find out, of one thing we can be quite sure: The American economic system has undergone some significant changes—changes which now are affecting, and which in the future will continue to affect all of us.

The Increasing Role of the State

In all free economies of the modern world, the role of the government (the state) has been increasing. Urgent problems of modern society have required it. This trend is still going on, and it seems likely to continue. Why? Because the market process operating by itself can't deal with some of the problems that must be dealt with.

The governments will get increasingly involved in planning—in setting goals and in directing various activities in the economy. As this happens, the free market economic systems evolve into something else —something different from either the model or the reality of traditional capitalism.

How far will the market systems change in response to the "emergency needs" of modern society? No one knows. I suppose it's safe to say that it will go as far and as fast as practical necessity and political expediency take it. It's an interesting and suspenseful drama to watch.

It makes some people sad, some bewildered. But that's always the way with rapid change. As the modern economic systems change, what about capitalism? Will capitalism survive?

WHAT ABOUT THE SURVIVAL OF CAPITALISM?

Questions about the survival of capitalism really don't make much sense. What is capitalism? Capitalism *was* the economic system of the mid-nineteenth century, observed and attacked (and incidentally, named) by Karl Marx. That kind of economic system doesn't exist anywhere in the world. It hasn't for more than forty years! To talk about the survival of the system Marx called capitalism would be an irrelevant, purely academic exercise.

The names we use for economic systems these days really don't offer very accurate descriptions of anything. Capitalism, socialism, and communism have become words to argue about. The words don't describe any real-world economic systems. These words—creations of nineteenth-century social protest philosopher-prophets—have become the "banners" in a kind of worldly religious struggle.

The whole argument is far more emotional than rational, and far more political than economic. We would all understand economic systems a lot better, and likely the twentieth-century world would be a much more pleasant place to live, if everyone would forget about these worldly religions. Better we should confine our discussions to the *substance* of different economic systems and forget about the emotion-packed names by which they are known.

We've Solved the Old Problems and Created New Ones

The problems of modern civilization are pressing more and more on all people, everywhere. These problems have been visited upon us by our own progress. We have gone so far toward solving the old problems —hunger, disease, others—that we have uncovered (or permitted to arise) new problems.

The new problems have been allowed to arise only because they have not been held in check by the powerful automatic social control mechanism which brought the great progress. What mechanism? The *market process,* of course!

So now, how does society take charge and take action on these new kinds of problems? By building new kinds of control mechanisms— mechanisms which will be effective over things which the *market process* cannot effectively control.

HAS THE MARKET SYSTEM HAD ITS DAY IN THE SUN?

What powered the great thrust of economic growth which tore the world loose from its traditional past and brought us to this seething modern world of violent change? The market system—the powerful force of the price mechanism.

The Market Process Generated the Modern World

The high-living, bewildering modern world was generated by the powerful motivating and controlling forces of the market process:

- the harsh law-of-the-jungle system of rewards and punishments, where the productive people are rewarded and the others go hungry;
- the powerful incentive of *profits,* stimulating more production and greater efficiency; and
- the powerful force of prices, conserving and rationing the society's resources, and motivating the production of more of the wanted things.

These powerful forces of the market process were responsible for the economic breakthroughs which generated the modern world.

People, businesses, nations, all were striving, conserving, pushing to get ahead. They wanted the pleasure of having more things. Everyone wanted to try to get ahead of everyone else. People were highly motivated, working, producing.

As the market system stimulated the production of the things people and businesses were buying, more and better goods became available. New kinds of goods became available—consumer goods and capital goods. There were more and better machines, equipment, factories—things needed to increase productivity even more.

The market process provided a way to channel *self interest*—to use this powerful force as the *energy* to thrust the economy forward, to speed up production and generate rapid economic growth. We who live in the advanced nations would be able to have only a fraction of the things we now enjoy, were it not for the powerful motivating and controlling forces of the market process. So what now? Is that all over and done with? And if so, what happens next?

The Pure Market System Is No Longer Socially Acceptable

Throughout the world the modern market-oriented economies are more and more turning away from the market process. The political process—government direction and control—is making and carrying out more of society's economic choices. Governments everywhere are bypassing or overthrowing the directives of the market process.

It's happening not only in the advanced nations but in the less-developed countries, too. The less-developed countries are devising government plans and using administrative directions and controls to try to steer their economies toward their longed-for goals of economic development. Why is the powerful market process being ignored and abandoned? There are several reasons.

Many things about the way the market process works are not so acceptable anymore (some never were). Inequality is one problem—great wealth, with things being used lavishly and wasted by the rich while the poor go hungry. All modern market-oriented nations have developed programs to lessen this *inequality* generated by the market system. The modern nations produce enough so that even the poor can be adequately provided for, so governments are overthrowing the "distribution choice" of the market process and shifting more of the output to the poor.

Another problem, to some people, is the emphasis on *selfishness* as the *motive force* which makes the market process work. Some people don't like the idea of giving rewards to those who do selfish things. Selfishness has proven to be a very powerful and highly efficient force for driving the economic system (and also for achieving the survival of most living things). But most people don't consider selfishness to be a "human virtue."

But there is an even more basic problem than inequality or the emphasis on selfishness. An inherent flaw, perhaps? An inability of the freely operating market process to protect and work for society's best interest? Perhaps. Sometimes it is impossible for the freely operating market process to reflect and respond to some of the true wishes of the society. *That's* the problem.

The market process directs the society's resources to "flow toward the dollar"—that is, to go where, and to do what the *spenders* wish. The uses of all of the society's things are determined by the ways in which the people and businesses choose to spend their money. So what's the problem? Just that in the modern world, that arrangement can't *always* optimize the use of society's resources—can't *always* make the choices which will work toward the objectives and goals of the society.

The Free Market Process Cannot Set Goals for Society

There are many ways in which a modern society's true objectives are not reflected in the market process. Many desired objectives cannot be achieved simply by letting resources be directed into whatever the people spend their money for—and into nothing else. This arrangement would leave many important functions inadequately performed—perhaps not performed at all. What functions? Such things as education, fire and police protection, roads and streets, public welfare, national defense, health and hospitals, perhaps urban housing, perhaps others.

Most people have agreed for a long time that the *political process* must direct some resources into these "public" functions—that the market process acting alone can't look out for the society's best interests in these areas. But now, suddenly (almost overnight!), this *kind* of problem is exploding all over the landscape! Now there are *many cases* where the free market process can't look out for the society's best interests anymore.

What's the problem? Economists call it "externalities." It's the "spill-over effect" that happens almost every time anybody does *anything* these days.

The Problem of Externalities—the "Spill-Over Effect"

The free market process just can't control the spill-over effects—the things that happen outside the market—things like air and water pollution that don't influence the *costs* and *prices* of things. The market process would force the producer to use cheap fuel, dirty the air, and sell the product at a low price. But the *true social objectives* would require more expensive fuel, cleaner air, and a higher-priced product.

Before there were such great increases in population and industrialization, there wasn't much of a problem of externalities. But now all modern societies face the *urgent* and *unavoidable* task of bringing our heavily populated, heavily industrialized modern world into ecological balance with our natural environment. And how can the free market process do that? That's the problem. It can't.

So the society must cope with these problems some other way. And what other way is there? The political process? Government plans, regulations, controls, charges, penalties, subsidies, and such? Yes. That's the only way.

Many social choices can no longer be decided on the basis of how the people choose to spend their money. The free market process cannot direct all the choices in the society's best interests, so the political process must get involved. Governments must overthrow some of the choice-making power of the market process, must define the essential objectives, and must arrange for energy and other resources to be used to achieve the chosen objectives. Governments *must* do it. There's just no other way.

So has the market process had its day in the sun? Has it "done its thing" in ripping out the social control mechanisms that kept societies stable (and alive) for thousands of years? In its brief moment on stage it has blasted mankind off on this bewildering journey. Many people now realize that we must alter the course of our journey. So must we push the free market process off-stage after such a short (but brilliant!) performance? Not entirely. But to some extent, yes. Or at least so it seems.

THE MARKET PROCESS: FROM MASTER TO SERVANT OF SOCIAL CHOICE?

Throughout the last century and up to the depression of the 1930s the forces of the free market process really were in charge. The market process really was in "master control" over the society's resources. Private individuals and businesses, responding to market forces, determined for the economy *what* was going to happen and *where, when, how,* and *how much.* The free forces of the market process really did provide the avenue of social choice. But since World War I (in Europe) and especially since the depression of the 1930s (in the U.S.), the choice-making power of the free market process more and more has been modified, restrained, and pushed aside.

It isn't that markets and market forces have been abolished. Incentives and rewards still operate. Prices are still exerting their powerful force in conserving things and motivating the production of things. The drive to get ahead and the attractiveness of profits still motivate people and businesses. So what is the nature of this change that's occurring?

It is partly a tempering of the market forces themselves. Taxes on wages and profits change the "incentive force" somewhat; welfare payments and payments to unemployed people reduce somewhat the discomfort of being unproductive. And there are other ways the market forces have been lessened. But that isn't the big issue. Much more important—especially for the continuing long-run evolution of the world's economic systems—is this:

> The market process for a fleeting moment in history was the powerful, disruptive *master* of social choice. Now it is being broken to harness—forced into the role of *servant* to carry out the deliberate (we hope, *rational*) resource-use choices of the society—choices made by (and in view of objectives and goals chosen by) the local, state, and national governments—that is, by the *political processes* of the society.

How is it possible for the role of the market process to be changed from master to servant? After you read the next two subsections you will understand.

Society's Economic Problem: The Production and Distribution Questions

Each society faces its economic problem—of dealing with scarcity, of deciding what to do with each of its scarce resources: What to use and what to save? What to do and what to make? Who will get to have how much of what? Those are the choices which, somehow, the society must make. That's the society's *economic problem.*

Usually economists break down the economic problem into (1) the *production* question (deciding what things to produce, in what quantities; using how much of which inputs and what production techniques, and so on), and (2) the *distribution* question (deciding how big a share of the output each person will get).

How does a society get the answers to these questions? Through its economic system, of course. That's the purpose of the economic system —to work out the answers to these questions and to carry out the choices. Each economic system uses some combination of (1) the social process (following the traditional ways of answering the questions), (2) the political process (government decisions), and (3) the market process (letting resources flow to meet the demands of the people). These breakdowns:

- of the *economic problem* into "production" and "distribution" questions, and
- of the *economic-problem-solving techniques* into "social," "political," and "market" processes,

are helpful. But there's another way these questions can be broken down.

To understand what's happening right now in the rapid evolution of the world's economic systems—for example, to understand the shifting role of the market process from master to servant of social choice—we need a new breakdown. We need a breakdown between (1) economic *decision-making* (*choosing* the objectives and goals), and (2) the *implementation* of economic decisions (*directing resources* to achieve the chosen objectives and goals).

Society's Economic Problem: The Decision-Making and Implementation Questions

Solving a society's economic problem involves not one but *two* functions: (1) *making* the choices, and (2) *carrying out* the choices. Why is it so important to separate these two functions? Just this: One process (for example, the political process) may be used to *make* the decision, while another process (for example, the market process) may be used to *carry out* the decision. And that's important.

Now do you begin to see what has been happening to the role of the market process? Of course! Its *decision-making* function more and more is being stripped away; its *implementation* function is being used more and more to carry out *political process decisions!* Is that how the market process has been shifting from the role of *master* of social choice, to the role of *servant?* Of course. The market process has been becoming more of a "servant" to the society's will—as that "will" is expressed by the society's political processes.

Just as the market process can both *make* and *carry out* the economic choices for society, so can the political process perform both functions. The Soviet Union, the People's Republic of China and other Communist (that is, neo-Marxian socialist) countries rely very much on their political processes to perform both functions—to *make,* and to *carry out* the choices. Generally the plans are implemented by administrators who direct resources into the uses necessary to carry out the government's plans.

However, in recent years the Communist countries have been discovering the efficiency of the market process as "servant to the political process." They are finding out how easy it is to get labor and other resources to move in the desired directions by offering wage and price incentives. At the same time the market-oriented countries are becoming more aware of the real-world limitations on the ability of the market process, acting alone, to protect the society's resources and to generate optimal levels of social well-being. So they are shifting more of the *decision-making* function to the political process.

THE CONVERGING EVOLUTION OF THE WORLD'S ECONOMIC SYSTEMS

So what's happening? The Communist countries are slowly changing their economic systems to take more advantage of the highly efficient market process as an *implementation device.* At the same time, the market-oriented countries are introducing more government planning—stripping the market process of its decision-making role, but usually depending on the market process to carry out the plans.

As the economic systems of the world evolve, it seems inevitable that more of the choices in the market-oriented economies will be made through the political process. But it's likely that the market process will continue to be used to implement the plans. Why? Because the market process is highly efficient. No resource administrator needs to work out each little detail. People and resources move automatically in response to the market-process incentives. And with the market process, people have more freedom of choice. No one needs to be ordered around. Price adjustments can be used to pull more (or fewer) resources in each direction.

Are Economic Systems Becoming More Alike?

While the market-oriented societies are learning more about how to use the political process in setting goals and objectives and designing plans, the Communist countries are learning more about how to use the market process to increase their efficiency in implementing their plans. In most of the less-developed countries too, political-process planning with market-process implementation seems to offer the most effective approach for achieving the desired development objectives.

So is everyone happy with these changes in their economic systems? No—far from it. Many people in the United States and other market-oriented countries take "capitalism" as a sort of religion and argue against any government goal-setting and planning. (Government planning is communistic!)

Many people in the Soviet Union and other neo-Marxian socialist countries take communism as a sort of religion and argue against any use of the market process to implement their plans. (Price and profit incentives are capitalistic!) But as times are changing, some people are changing their minds. Perhaps someday these narrow attitudes will pass into history. If so, the world is likely to get along better after that.

There's another kind of problem, too. First, it isn't easy for socio-economic planners to figure out exactly how to harness the market process so as to direct the economy toward the desired objectives. It takes a lot of expert economic understanding and analysis to figure out how to do that.

Second, even if the planners knew exactly what to do, the political realities of *politics* often would prevent them from carrying out their well-designed plans. Still, somehow it's being done—not always done *well,* but being done. There's more and more planning in the "free" economies, and more use of the market process in the "planned" economies.

So what does the future hold in store? Will all of the economic systems of the world soon look alike? Of course not! But it does seem that as the years go by the world's economic systems will come to look *more* alike. You can see why. Maybe as the evolution proceeds, we will discover even better ways to organize and run our economic systems. Let's hope so.

Do We Need New Social Control Mechanisms?

Back in ancient times and feudal times—and in some societies even today—a structure of "nonmarket-type" social control mechanisms held the society together, prevented things which would have been socially destructive, and made possible the *survival* of the society. But then came the erosion of the traditional societies and the emergence and growth of the powerful market process, pushing all else aside and thrusting forward the explosive development of modern society.

What now? Are we about to go full circle? Throughout most of the time that people have been on earth, the traditional social control mechanisms—the clan, the tribe, the manor, and other such social arrangements—have "kept it all together." Must *world society* now begin to develop social control mechanisms to try to achieve for all of us what the traditional social control mechanisms achieved for the traditional societies? Has the powerful market process, as *master of social choice,* had its day in the sun—now to be relegated to the role of *servant* to the socioeconomic planners? And if so, how do we expect these national and worldwide changes in economic systems to come about? And what effects will these changes have on the future lives of people?

These are interesting and critical questions. The quality and economic conditions of future life on earth—perhaps even the continued existence of human life itself—will be significantly influenced by the way these answers come out. It isn't likely that I—or even you—will be around long enough to know the answers. All we can do at this point is to hope that the decisions we make and the directions we choose will prove to have been the right ones.

Part VIII: Economic Evolution and the Modern World—Flashback, and Outlook

Current Economic Problems and Theories are Deeply Rooted in the Past: the History of Ideas and Events Can Help Us to Understand the Present and the Outlook for the Future

Chapter 19: Current Economic Issues and Rapidly Changing Society: Flashback and Outlook

Think for a moment about the broad sweep of history you've been reading about in this book: first the thousands of centuries man has been on earth; then, about 3000 B.C., the cradles of civilization emerged. Twenty-five more centuries went by, then came the city-states of ancient Greece and Rome.

Another five centuries passed before the Roman Empire began (at about the time of Christ). After five centuries of the Roman Empire, at about 500 A.D., the medieval period began. Ten more centuries passed before the discovery of America and the development of mercantilism; another three centuries passed before the American colonies became a nation and the Industrial Revolution got underway.

The Controls of Tradition

Throughout all these hundreds of centuries, throughout recorded history and before, surely you would think there *must* have been *some* people who were observing the miseries of mankind, trying to change and improve things, trying to suggest better ways. Observing, yes. Explaining, yes. But trying to change things? Generally, no.

The societies were controlled by tradition, remember? The customs and taboos of the society told people what their "lot" was—what they were supposed to do and how life was supposed to be. Mostly, people just accepted things as they were.

The Stable Society Was the Norm

People played the same role as their parents and grandparents, facing the same problems that people had always faced. There was no disruptive social upheaval except when some conquering ruler's armies came in and changed things.

Some few philosophers wrote about economic matters, about "the material conditions of mankind," and about what was good and what was bad in matters of exchange, production, and all that. But in general these philosophies and ideas were aimed toward *maintaining the stability* of society—*preventing change.*

Remember the implicit objective of *social stability* reflected in the writings of Aristotle? And then later in the writings of the Christian philosophers of the medieval period? It was not until the Industrial Revolution came along to "blow up" the traditional social structures that big changes began to occur.

THE BEGINNING OF RAPID CHANGE

During the Industrial Revolution the philosophers began to play in a much larger ball park—no longer restricted by the necessity to place high value on the traditional concepts of social stability; liberated from the bonds of traditional ideas of monarchy, nobility, class structure, and from the traditional concepts of "right" and "wrong" in production, exchange, and prices. They were free to raise some serious questions about what was happening—and about what *ought to be* happening.

Breaking Loose From the Bonds of Tradition

Suddenly this new "liberalism" erupted in the writings of Adam Smith and Thomas Jefferson and Jeremy Bentham and others. Suddenly many traditionally accepted beliefs were coming under attack. As the world was undergoing the violent change of the Industrial Revolution, economic, social, and political thinking was responding—was going through its own violent change, touched off by what was happening in the world.

The new ball game begun by the Industrial Revolution—the population expansions and migrations and the breaking loose of just about everything—began only about two hundred years ago. But it amounted to the greatest change mankind had ever seen in all of the thousands of centuries that people had been on earth. Only recently has mankind pushed aside the "normal" relationship with nature and gained tremendous power to adapt and change and control nature. With this power it has become possible to support greatly increased numbers of people on earth.

Explosive Change Destroyed the "Natural Balance"

But the explosive change in the condition of mankind, and in the relationships between mankind and earth, has upset things. All kinds of disruptive influences and chain reactions have gotten underway. But there have been no parallel developments for maintaining harmony among people, or between mankind and the environment.

What created the problem? The violently disruptive influences of (1) the Industrial Revolution, and (2) the free market system. Working together these two forces generated great savings and massive investments in new and better capital—factories, machines, equipment, mass production. Productivity increased rapidly.

Each increase in capital brought more productivity; each increase in productivity brought more profit, more savings, more investment, more capital, and even *more* productivity. The rate of economic growth was unbelievable—far surpassing anything the world had ever seen or anyone had ever before *conceived.* The farther it went, the faster it got —rapid growth, feeding on itself, fueling the fires of its own rocket engines.

Economic Growth Becomes Explosive

Any kind of cumulative, progressive change which feeds on itself, fueling the fires of its own engines, speeding faster and faster, ultimately becomes *explosive.* Sooner or later it's bound to run into some problems. That's what has happened. And here we are caught in the midst of it all, not knowing quite what's going on or what to do.

The Basic Economic Principles Have Not Changed

If you think about it you can see that many of the things being discussed when people talk about the major current problems of the American economy in the 1970s and early 1980s were discussed by Smith, Malthus, Ricardo, Mill, and others back in the period of classical economics—some two centuries ago. That's because the *most basic principles* of economics—scarcity, opportunity cost, the power of the price mechanism, and the other principles you read about back in Chapter 1 of this book—really haven't changed. But *economic conditions* have changed greatly.

EFFECTS OF THE POST-WORLD WAR II "REAL INCOME BOOM"

People in the United States have become accustomed to a long-term trend of continually increasing economic welfare. For most of the time since World War II, each year people have been getting more and better

things. The economy during most of these years was experiencing continuing economic growth.

There were new technological developments and investments in
more and better capital—and new high-technology equipment and auto-
mated production processes aided by the rapidly expanding use of computers. Output per person was increasing. Real income—that is, the
ability to buy more and better consumer goods such as cars, boats,
appliances, new homes and all kinds of things—was increasing for almost
everybody, year after year.

Everyone who had a car was thinking in a few years they would have
a bigger car or a better car—or maybe two cars. And people were
thinking the same way about houses and boats and appliances and everything else. Why not? That's the way things were going!

Income Redistribution Was Relatively Painless

The total output of the American economy was increasing and the
population was not growing very fast. So on the average there were
more and more goods for everybody. In this economic environment it
was easy to introduce programs of "income redistribution"—to tax
money away from the more productive people (who were getting more
income year after year anyway, even after taxes) and to use this money
to improve the conditions of the poor, disadvantaged and other unproductive people. It was relatively easy to divert a lot of resources and
energies to the task of improving the conditions of the less fortunate
members of the society.

The feasibility of such "income redistribution" programs was suggested by John Stuart Mill in his *Principles of Political Economy* back in the
mid-1800s. Remember? Mill had said that although the natural economic laws (as spelled out by Ricardo) do indeed control the *production
choices* in the society, nevertheless it is possible for the distribution
choices to be redirected by the society. In the period following World
War II, the American economy demonstrated that what Mill said *could*
occur, actually *did* occur.

Income Redistribution? Or Economic Growth?

For more than 100 years economists have argued about whether we
should focus on *income redistribution* (re-slicing the "economic pie" so
that the poor get a larger slice), or on *economic growth* (expanding the size
of the "economic pie" so that the poor and everyone else can have a
larger slice).

During the steady growth period after World War II there was a good bit of "re-slicing of the pie" to help the poor and disadvantaged members of the society. But the important point is this: The "pie" was expanding fast enough so that even after the re-slicing, everyone still wound up with a larger slice than before, year after year. That's why income distribution and other government programs were relatively painless during those years. But more recently—in the 1970s and early 1980s—that situation has changed.

Do Government Programs Retard Economic Growth?

The usual position of the classical economists (Smith, Ricardo, and others) was that political interference in the distribution of output in the economy would interfere with the functioning of the system—that *ultimately* it would result in more harm than good for the people—poor people included. The idea was that as we *re-slice* the "economic pie," we interfere with the *future growth* of the pie—so ultimately everyone is worse off.

As the world entered the decade of the 1980s, many people were looking back over the turbulent decade of the 1970s—at the high inflation rate and the slowdown of economic growth—and trying to figure out why. Some were suggesting that the increasing role of government in the economy was an important part of the problem.

In the early 1980s there seemed to be an increasing feeling that government involvement in the economy—in income redistribution, taxing and spending, regulating, etc.—had become a serious deterrent to business investment and economic growth. Think back. That's what classical economics was teaching some 200 years ago!

HAVE WE BEEN IGNORING BASIC ECONOMIC PRINCIPLES?

It seems that during the long growth period following World War II, many people and interest groups forgot about (or were choosing to ignore) some of the most basic principles of economics—such as scarcity, and opportunity cost—the fact that "you can't have your cake and eat it too." People argued for and exerted political pressure to try to achieve all kinds of (no doubt desirable) objectives, such as:

- cleaning up the environment,
- requiring businesses to provide their employees a clean and hazard-free work situation,
- providing equal opportunity in employment, borrowing money, housing, etc;

- guaranteeing "minimum levels of health and decency" to all citizens
- guaranteeing medical care to all citizens,
- providing government training and job opportunities at government expense for unemployed workers,
- providing equal access to all buildings and facilities for handicapped people,
- requiring that all employers pay their workers a minimum wage,
- establishing ceilings on the amount of rent which can be charged to tenants, and on the amount of interest which can be charged to borrowers,
- establishing environmental protection laws and regulations,
- requiring that automobiles be built so as to be "safe" even in high-speed accidents,
- providing low-cost college education to all who wish to be students,
- and the list goes on and on.

Social Objectives Require Social "Opportunity Costs"

The decisions to try to accomplish objectives such as these are *normative* decisions. It would be difficult to find anyone who did not agree that such objectives as these are "desirable." But we should not delude ourselves into thinking that these objectives can be achieved without some cost—opportunity cost—to the society.

The resources and manpower and money which are directed toward these desirable social objectives must come from somewhere. And when they are used to fulfill these objectives they cannot also be used to build new technology and capital to support increased productivity and growth of the economy. The laws of *positive economics* tell us this. (You can't have your cake and eat it too!)

RECENT CONCERN ABOUT OUR ECONOMIC PROBLEMS

By 1980 there was widespread concern about the condition of the American economy, and about its competitive position in the world economy. The concern was being expressed by economists and business, government, and labor leaders, and by members of the general public.

During 1980, unemployment was increasing. Many people who were losing their jobs knew that part of the problem was that foreign producers were capturing a larger share of American markets. American producers in several industries seemed incapable of producing high quality, low-cost products to meet this foreign competition. There was developing a general awareness that the productivity of the American economy was not holding its own in the world economy.

Politically-Inspired Tax Cut Proposals

In the presidential election campaign of 1980, "American productivity" was an important issue. Republican candidate Ronald Reagan called for immediate tax cuts which would reduce the tax burden on businesses and stimulate increased investment in new, more efficient capital—to stimulate the growth of productivity. Reagan's tax-cut recommendations were immediately attacked by independent candidate John Anderson as being a "tax cut for the wealthy." The Carter administration immediately announced that they also were in favor of a tax cut, but one which would be carefully designed to stimulate future productivity of the economy, and to provide tax relief where it is most needed.

You can see how, in a political democracy such as ours, it is difficult to rally the necessary public support for the kinds of policies which may be required (by the laws of positive economics) to stimulate economic growth and increasing productivity. When enough of the people are in favor of a tax cut for the "common people"—not for big businesses and wealthy people—then politicians (who want to get elected) must respond to these wishes. And this issue raises a very basic question.

ARE DEMOCRACY AND THE "FREE MARKET ECONOMY" COMPATIBLE?

Could it be that political democracy and the "free market" economy are incompatible in the long run? Suppose most of the people feel that the government can and should provide them all of the things they consider to be necessary? or desirable?—including overcoming all of the "socially undesirable" conditions which may exist in the society? Then the politicians, to be elected, must promise all these things. And if their political careers are going to last for very long, once elected they must try to deliver on most of these promises.

Government Must Allow Some Freedom to the Private Sectors

It is obvious that the "free market economy" cannot continue to function if government drains off the income and profit required to keep the private sectors of the economy going, and growing. See the problem?

If we all try to "vote ourselves" all of the things we want—better schools, public housing, highways, public transportation, recreation facilities, welfare programs, medical care, a clean and risk-free environment, and all of the other things we would like—and if we try to vote ourselves controlled prices for all products, set at levels which we consider to be "fair and reasonable" (and perhaps "necessary things" provided *free*)—then the market system ultimately will be choked off.

The market system can't continue to operate if there is a continually increasing drain of resources from the private sectors to the public sector. An adequate flow of money and resources in the private sectors is essential for the continued health and growth of the "free market system."

Much Depends on Economic Understanding of the People

You can see that the continued existence of the market system depends on the economic attitudes and ideas of the public—on their awareness of a few basic economic principles. If the majority of the electorate feels that regulations can be imposed and profits taken away from businesses *without any detrimental effect* on workers and consumers (the general public), then they may insist on government policies which will stifle the growth of the economy—policies which ultimately will lead to economic downturn and declining standards of living for everyone. Perhaps we are already seeing some of that happening.

Could it be that the question of the compatibility between political democracy and the "free market economy" depends on the degree of economic enlightenment and understanding of the people? If most people understood the most basic principles of positive economics—the principles you learned in the first chapter of this book and then found out a lot more about as you went through the book—then I think that the future of the "free market economy" would be a lot more secure.

Will the People Support Unpleasant but Necessary Policies?

In the early 1980s it appears that there is fairly widespread public awareness of the need for increased productivity in the American economy. People seem to be aware that American industry must speed up its investments in new and better capital—that this is necessary if we are going to increase our productivity and regain the ability to compete effectively against foreign producers.

But is there enough understanding on this issue to convince people to support cutbacks of their own favorite programs—and to support reduced taxes and regulations on business?—and tough anti-inflation policies by government?—and other such policies which are difficult for many people to accept? Such policies may be necessary to stimulate increased productivity in the economy. But it is by no means certain that the people will support such policies. It will be interesting to see how the public mood evolves on these issues—and how our government policymakers respond in the coming years.

Chapter 20: Conflicting Current Economic Ideas and Theories: Synthesis and Outlook

Throughout the 1970s and early 80s the economics profession was sending conflicting signals. Public policy recommendations were coming from all sides. Most of the economists on each side of each issue (and there were many sides of most issues) seemed to be *absolutely sure* that they were right—that the policies they were recommending were the best policies for the Nation—that if their recommended policies were adopted, the Nation's economy would be better off.

When Economists Disagree, How Do Policymakers Decide?

In such an environment of conflicting policy recommendations, how does the government decide what policies to adopt? In 1975, Walter Heller (who had been Chairman of President John F. Kennedy's Council of Economic Advisors) wrote an article entitled "Why Can't Those (#$"%*!¢) Economists Ever Agree?" In 1978, *Fortune* carried an article entitled, "I Don't Trust Any Economists Today!"

When economists (all brilliant and outstanding, of course!) are giving opposing public policy recommendations—and all of them are apparently *certain* that their recommendations are right—then economic advice tends to be ignored. The members of the administration and of Congress make their decisions on the basis of their "gut feelings" and their perceptions of political realities—that is, on the basis of what they think their constituents are thinking.

THE IMPORTANT AREAS OF DISAGREEMENT

Important areas of disagreement among modern-day economists include: the "short-run vs. long-run" issue; the view about how the modern-world economy operates; and the importance of changes in the size of the money supply. In this section you will be reading summary statements about each of these.

Disagreement about the "Short-run vs. Long-run" Issue

One important explanation of the disagreement among economists is the "short-run vs. long-run" issue. Does a modern-world economy (in any given week, month, year—in *any* time period) tend to approximate the long-run equilibrium conditions described in the neoclassical model? —or not? That's the issue.

Economists who focus on the short-run view think that the economy is always responding to various short-run changes—especially changes in businesses' and investors' short-run *expectations*—and to various destabilizing "shocks." They believe that government policy can (and should) constantly be adjusted to offset the destabilizing effects of these short-run changes and shocks which are occurring all the time.

Economists who take the long-run view believe that the economy tends to approximate long-run neoclassical model conditions all the time, and that the best way to overcome any short-run instability is to let the "natural market forces" take care of it. They believe these market forces will move the economy (approximately) to the long-run equilibrium position described in the model. And they believe that any attempt by government to correct (temporary) short-run instability will only increase the instability of the economy and worsen the instability problem.

Disagreement about How a Modern-World Economy Operates

Another source of disagreement—one which is related to but somewhat different than the "long-run vs. short-run" issue—stems from differing views on "how a modern, real-world economy actually operates." On one side (the monetarist side) economists believe that the forces of the price mechanism and competition are in control—that these forces are sufficiently powerful (even in the real world of inflexible prices and monopoly power) to bring about the socially desirable conditions described in the neoclassical model. So they believe that the neoclassical model can be used as a guide in understanding the economy and in predicting how the economy will perform under various circumstances.

The opposite (post-Keynesian) view is that the existence of inflexible prices and of non-pure-competitive conditions in most markets seriously reduces the usefulness of the neoclassical model in understanding and predicting the performance—especially the *macroeconomic* performance —of the economy. The post-Keynesians believe that real-world conditions are *strikingly different* from the conditions which the neoclassical model "assumes," and that a real-world economy always operates in response to various forces *other than* those which are described in the model. The post-Keynesians therefore hold that we must look at and understand the effects of and learn how to influence these *other forces.* For example, the post-Keynesians believe that we should look *directly* at the influences of big business, big labor, and big government if we want to understand what's going on in the real-world economy.

This basic disagreement—this "difference of belief" about the relative strength of the basic forces which control a real-world economic system—underlies much of the disagreement among present-day economists. And it explains why there is so much disagreement on economic policy recommendations. Those economists who take the monetarist view (and their fellow travelers) make policy recommendations which often are the *exact opposite* of the recommendations offered by the post-Keynesians and their "fellow travelers."

Disagreement on the Role of the Money Supply

How important is *the size of the money supply* (or *change* in the size of the money supply) in influencing the economy?—in influencing total spending, production, employment, output, incomes, prices, and other macroeconomic variables? The monetarists believe that the *rate of change* in the size of the money supply is the *critical variable.* But post-Keynesians don't agree.

Post-Keynesians believe that other forces (in addition to changes in the size of the money supply) play an important short-run role. They think some other variables—especially changes in short-run expectations, interest rates, consumption and savings rates, investment spending, and in the government's taxing and spending policies—exert strong *causal influences.* Post-Keynesians believe that "change in the size of the money supply" is not the *only* causal variable—and that sometimes it is *not a causal variable at all*— that sometimes "money supply change" is a *responsive* variable, responding to economic changes *caused by* changes in other variables (such as those mentioned in the previous sentence).

The Ascendancy of Milton Friedman and the Monetarists

During the late 1970s and early 80s, inflation roared on. It did not seem to respond to any of the government's anti-inflation policies. An increasing number of economists seemed to come around to the monetarist view that the inflation problem was not going to respond to *any kind* of short-run government policy—that the only way to deal with it would be to take a long-run view—to restrict the rate of expansion of the money supply, to "suffer as much as necessary" in the short run, and to wait for the long-run effects of tight money to "wear down the inflationary bias" and bring inflation under control. (Not *all* economists moved to this position, of course. But an increasing number seemed to.)

This long-run approach is what the monetarists had been recommending all along. Several of the policy changes in the late 1970s and early 80s reflected this approach. From the perspective of mid-year 1980, it appears that the "monetarist prescription" will be having a significant influence on the public during the early 1980s. But the extent of this influence is likely to be considerably affected by what happens in the economy—by the economic conditions which evolve as the policymakers try to maintain the *slow and steady growth of the money supply* and wait for the *natural forces of the market* to bring inflation under control.

CHANGING ECONOMIC CONDITIONS REQUIRE CHANGING ECONOMIC THEORIES

The "Supply-Side" Problem

During the 1970s and early 80s the productivity and growth of the economy slowed down. Our competitive position worsened both in domestic and worldwide markets. Soon economists were placing new emphasis on "supply-side" economics, and working to develop policy recommendations to deal with the "supply-side" problem.

In this new situation, post-Keynesian economics—which focuses primarily on "demand-side" problems—became less relevant. The neoclassical model became more relevant. As you know, the neoclassical model explains how the production choices in the society are made—such as the choice between "production of goods for present consumption" and "production of new technology and capital for economic growth." The model focuses on the factors which influence these choices. So you can see why the neoclassical model became more relevant, and post-Keynesian theories, less relevant.

By the early 1980s many economists were busily working on theories to explain the supply-side problem and to provide public-policy guidance on this issue. Most of the supply-side theories and policy recommendations are deeply rooted in neoclassical economic theory.

Our New "International Awareness"

The changing international position of the United States is now having an influence on the theoretical emphasis in economics, and on public policy. It has now become clear that the United States is inextricably tied into the world economy, and that our economic policies must recognize this fact.

In the past our economic theories and policies often implicitly have assumed that the U.S. economy was "an economic island"—that our economic relationships with the rest of the world could be "assumed away" and ignored. But it has become clear that this approach is no longer viable. So now economists are trying to make the necessary adjustments in their theories and policy recommendations to reflect our changed international position.

THE NEW "RATIONAL EXPECTATIONS" THEORY

The theory of "rational expectations" is an important new development in economic theory. It emphasizes the importance of "rational expectations" concerning long-run economic conditions, as an important influence on how people and businesses make their economic decisions. This theory reflects neoclassical theory. It supports the monetarist position because it arrives at the same conclusion as the monetarists—that government stabilization policies will not work.

The "rational expectations" theory says that stabilization policies *cannot work* because the "rational expectations" of businesses and individuals cause them to behave in a *different way* than the stabilization policymakers *expect them* to behave. When this happens the stabilization policies are doomed to failure.

In the early 1980s economists are in wide disagreement about the accuracy and usefulness of the "rational expectations" theory. Some economists are absolutely sure it is right, and applicable. Others are absolutely sure that it is wrong—except perhaps in the "model world" which to them is not relevant to the real world of the 1980s. Perhaps the next few years will shed more light on this controversial new theory.

THE CHALLENGE OF THE "RADICAL" ECONOMISTS

Conflict in economics during the 1970s and early 80s was not limited to the disagreement between the monetarists and the post-Keynesians. During this period there was some increasing interest in what is called "radical economics." Membership in the new "Union of Radical Political Economists" was growing during the 1970s. These so-called "radical economists" were offering various theories and policy recommendations calling for basic changes in the American economic system.

Radical economics includes theories and philosophies which range all the way from neo-Marxian socialist ideas, to the ideas of such economists as Galbraith—who says: "Left to themselves, economic forces do not work out for the best—except perhaps for the powerful." Remember?

To the radical economists, the debate between the monetarists and the post-Keynesians is mostly irrelevant. Most radical economists think that the emphasis should be on changing the system in ways which will result in greater "social justice" and "social efficiency," and increased harmony within the society.

The "radical economics" group has grown in recent years but it still includes only a small minority of American economists. Its members are constantly offering theoretical explanations and policy recommendations for changing the economy. It doesn't appear likely that their recommendations will have very much influence on public policy over the next few years. But it's possible that changing conditions in the economy—for example, a significant worsening of economic conditions—could cause a lot more people to listen to what the radical economists have to say. If emergency conditions develop, it isn't unlikely that some of their recommendations would be adopted.

THE INFLUENCE OF THE CHANGING PUBLIC MOOD

Another change influencing economic policy in recent years has been the "changing public mood"—you might call it a "backlash" against the increasing role of government in the economy. For example, the voters in California passed "Proposition 13" limiting the amount of property taxes which could be levied on California residents. There has been a popular movement supporting an amendment to the U.S. Constitution which would require the government to "balance the budget." And public sentiment supporting spending for "Great Society" programs seems to be waning.

One reason for this "new national mood" may be that the "economic pie" has not been expanding very much in recent years—that taxes to support "Great Society" programs now are actually *reducing* standards of living of the taxpayers. Another possible explanation is that more people are now learning that taxes on business do not come from an "inexhaustible fountain" of cash-flow—that our low-productivity and declining competitive position in the world economy may be resulting (at least partly) from high taxes on American businesses.

Perhaps the more difficult economic times of the late 1970s and early 80s have been generating a "rebirth of awareness" about some basic economic principles—for example, the truth of the fact that "We can't have our cake and eat it too." Perhaps more people are becoming more willing to "take the bitter with the sweet" as economic problems arise and as the economy goes through its ups and downs. As the recession of the early 1980s worsens we may find out if this is true or not.

What about the Future?

What will happen in the next few years? Will conflicting economic ideas and theories move toward a synthesis? Or will economists continue to disagree about how the economy operates?—and about what kinds of public policies should be adopted? No one knows, of course. But from the perspective of mid-1980 it does not appear that these conflicting issues are going to be resolved anytime soon.

It seems likely that public policy recommendations will continue to conflict with each other, and that government leaders will continue to make most of their economic policy decisions primarily on the basis of their "gut feelings"—and their view of the political realities of the moment. People in government always seem to call on economists who will offer the kinds of advice they want to hear—and that isn't likely to change anytime soon.

The One Area Where Most Economists Agree

There is one economic principle that most economists seem to agree on—that is, *the great power of the price mechanism in influencing specific resource-use choices.* Economists agree that an *artificially high price* for any product or service (if you wait awhile) will *discourage consumption* and *stimulate production* and (ultimately) result in *surpluses* of that product or service. An *artificially low price* for any product or service (if you wait awhile) will *encourage consumption* and *discourage production* and (ultimately) result in *shortages* of that product or service.

This basic principle of the great *resource-directing power* of prices is a principle about which the great majority of economists speak with one voice. So the advice which (almost all) economists offer about the effects of "rigging" specific prices (either artifically "too high" or "too low") is clear. Yet government policy continues to respond to political realities and to pass legislation to artificially fix prices to try to achieve social objectives. We have had minimum wage laws, rent ceilings, agricultural price supports, "usury ceilings" on how much interest banks (and others) can charge their borrowers, ceilings on how much interest banks (and others) can pay on deposits, price-fixing in transportation and communications, and several other cases of "government price-fixing."

In each case, prices which have been set artificially low have generated shortages; prices set artificially high have generated surpluses. Yet "artificial price-fixing" by government continues, regardless of the advice economists may offer. This "government price-fixing" experience seems to indicate that the advice of economists isn't likely to be accepted by government decisionmakers unless the advice is more or less in harmony with the current ideas and mood of the people.

One final point: It is very important that you understand the kinds of conflict now going on among economists—including conflict among the government's economic advisors. The conflict is deep-seated and very serious. It is likely to have a significant impact on the government's economic policies and therefore on economic conditions in the Nation over the coming years. If you have gained an awareness and understanding of the nature and seriousness of this conflict, then one important objective of this book has been achieved.

A LOOK BACK, AND A LOOK AHEAD

If you think back for a moment you will realize that conflict and disagreement about economic matters is not new. Conflicting economic ideas have existed ever since society began emerging from the medieval period, and even before that. As the rate of change began to speed up, more conflicting ideas and theories arose.

As you know, there were many conflicting economic ideas throughout the periods of mercantilism and the industrial revolution, and these conflicts have continued on into modern times. Do you believe that history repeats itself? If so, you will find it difficult to believe that the present conflicts and disagreements among economists are likely to be resolved soon.

The Theorist-Explainers and the Activist-Changers

Think back over the past two-hundred years of explosive change. Think of the people—the philosophers and protestors and activists you have been reading about in this book. I suppose we could think of these people as falling into two groups: those who were most concerned with trying to *understand* and *explain* what was happening, and those who were most concerned with trying to *change* things. The classical and neoclassical economists were the "theorist-explainers;" the utopian socialists and communist revolutionaries were the "activist-changers."

There were a few, like Marx, who managed to play both roles. But not many. Generally, those who were trying to *explain* things (the theorist-explainers) thought those who were trying to change things were wasting their time. The natural economic forces would trip them up at every turn; their attempts to change things would only make matters worse. But those who were trying to *change* things (the activist-changers) condemned the theorist-explainers as being unproductive and irrelevant —unwilling to get involved in direct social action to try to improve things.

Is the situation much different, today? We still have the theorists trying to explain things and the activists working for change. Each blames the other for indulging in irrelevant or unproductive or ill-conceived and misdirected pursuits. The theorists accuse the activists of doing naive things—things which could never work within the "natural laws" of economics. The activists accuse the theorists of being irrelevant, out of touch with the real problems of the world, playing little games in their ivory towers.

The world has changed drastically over the last two centuries. But the people haven't changed all that much. Perhaps it's good that each generation seems to produce some theorists and some activists. Perhaps each group helps to keep the other on its toes.

Almost Everything Has Changed, Just Since You Were Born!

For a moment, think about all the changes that have been happening in your lifetime—changes in production methods, outputs, real income; changes in attitudes toward poverty, education, nationalism, wage rates, profits, war; toward the issues of urbanization, pollution, land uses; toward the economic, social, and political rights of racial minorities, of women, of young people; and all the new technology—computers, transistors, solid state electronics, polio prevention, space travel; attitudes toward dress, personal appearance, family relationships, student-professor relationships, work and leisure, wealth, home ownership, alcohol, marijuana, marriage, sex, criminal punishment; the role of government—you name it. Generation gap? Confusion? Frustration? Bewilderment? My God! How could it be otherwise?

People who are still thinking by the standards and conditions of the 1930s, the '40s, the '50s,—the '60s, even!—are already far behind the times—out of touch. No wonder it's tough to reach agreement on anything anymore! No wonder it's a real struggle to get a "representative" candidate for the U.S. presidency. No wonder it's tough on students who have to go through school and college under the surveillance and tutelage of so many different people—many people whose minds (unfortunately) were "programmed and locked in" during various different time periods in the past.

How Do We Learn to Cope with Change?

It seems miraculous that any of you who are students today manage to make it without having your personalities completely destroyed! But maybe, after all, this is the best way for education to help you to learn to adapt—to cope in a world of explosive change. Maybe this is the best way to ensure that your mind will learn to keep growing to meet the new challenges which are destined to confront you throughout your lifetime. Perhaps the frustrating college experience you're going through will help to ensure that throughout your life you won't be left back here in "the dark ages" of the 1980s.

The world today has plenty of brilliant and well-educated people whose ideas are mostly irrelevant simply because they haven't developed the built-in mental flexibility and adaptability needed to enable them to catch up and keep up with this explosively changing world. They're just left in the wake as time speeds on by.

There will always be many people who can't (or who don't want to) keep up. Maybe that's good—a stabilizing influence perhaps. But such people will always be a little bewildered. And they will be frustrated each time their lives are touched by each new manifestation of "the new tomorrow"—like when the government decides to raise taxes, or subsidize medical care, or to nationalize the railroads—or when junior decides to let his hair grow or daughter decides to move into the coed dorm.

Society Is Doing the Split Between Past and Future—Which Foot Do You Want to Be?

Perhaps it's good that society in each decade has one foot firmly planted on the known ground of the past while the other foot moves, seeking to find some better place to stand on the uncertain ground of the future. It's up to each of us—you, me, everyone—to decide, on each issue: Which role do I want to play? Which foot do I want to be?

There's no easy way to decide. No easy answer. Maybe the historical perspective and the understanding of current issues and ideas that you've gained from this book will sometimes help you to make the right decision. I hope so.

Index

basic problem of, 72, 167–169
economy, 182
Big corporations, nationalizing, 132
Bolshevik Revolution, 79
Boulding, Kenneth, 186
Bourgeoisie, 68
Bretton Woods, 98
British Isles, 26
Brook Farm, 61
Buddha, 20
Budget:
　amendment to balance, 215
　deficits, 135–136
　federal, 164
　government, 106, 149
Business:
　basic problem of big, 72, 167–169
　big, 70, 174, 211
　cycles, 93
　failed, 84
　nationalization of, 172
　taxes, 215
Byzantine Empire, 29

C

Calvin, John, 31
Calvinism, 31
Cambridge University, 75
Capital, 12, 203, 208, 213
Capitalism, 13, 39, 66, 73, 192, 199:
　accepted values of, 79
　dissenters of, 79
Capitalist, 12:
　entrepreneurs, 40
　exploitation of labor, 67–68
　industrialists, 36, 38
　system, 188
Carnegie, Andrew, 70
Carter, Jimmy, 141–142, 147, 149, 161,
　177, 180:
　administration, 141–142, 147, 159,
　　175, 181–182, 207
　energy policy, 179–180
　voluntary restraints, 141, 147
　wage-price guidelines, 144
Catholic Church:
　medieval, 31
　Roman, 27
Ceilings:
　rent, 216
　usury, 216
Central America, 31
Central planning, 188

Change:
　attitudes, 218
　economic, 70
　explosive, 203
　interest rate, 115
　international position, 213
　public mood, 214
　short-run, 128, 211
Chicago school, of economic thought,
　111–113, 170
China, 20, 28, 32:
　People's Republic of, 198
Christ, birth of, 20
Christianity, 22
Christian philosophers, 202
Christian writers, medieval, 23
Chrysler, 176
Church, Roman Catholic, 27
Cities:
　emerging, 31
　growing, 28–29
　Italian trading, 26
City-states, 201:
　Greek and Roman, 20
Civilization:
　cradles, 19–20, 201
　early, of Greece and Rome, 23–24
　far east, early, 20
Classical economics, 47–50, 52, 133,
　162
Classical economists, 56–57, 62, 66, 69,
　74–75, 94, 167, 205, 217
Class structure, 202
Clayton Act, 71–72
Colonies, 34
Command, 13, 19–21, 24:
　political process of, 9–11
　role of, 21
Commission, Interstate Commerce, 71
Communes, 61
Communist countries, 190, 198–199
Communist Manifesto, 38
Communist revolutionaries, 63, 217
Communities, utopian, 63
Company:
　American Tobacco, 71
　Standard Oil, 71
Competition, 14, 46–47, 53, 70–72, 75,
　94, 130–133, 167–169, 172, 175–
　176, 211:
　foreign, 207
　pure, 14–15
Competitive position, 206, 213–215
Compliance costs, 175
Computers, 204

Short-run, 115:
   changes, 128, 211
   fluctuations, 115, 119
   instability, 211
   vs. long-run issue, 210
Single Tax, 78
Slaves, 24–25
Smith, Adam, 42–51, 70, 94–96, 111,
   167, 172–173, 202–203, 205:
   "invisible hand," 47–50
   Wealth of Nations, 42–43, 52, 133
Social choice, 196
Social contract arrangements, 132
Social control mechanisms, 195, 200
Social efficiency, 214
Socialists:
   neo-Marxian, 214
   Utopian, 60–63, 69, 217
Social justice, 214
Social objectives, 206
Social process, of tradition, 9
Social Security Act, 90–91
Social stability, 202
Social thought, 202
Social welfare legislation, 90–91
Societies:
   affluent, 172
   ancient, 19–20
Solar energy, development of, 180
South America, 31
Soviet Union, 198–199
Spaceship earth, 186
Spanish Conquistadores, 31
Special drawing rights, 98
Specialization, 49
Spending, 111–113:
   flow, 102, 109
   government, 164
   injections, 106
   investment, 212
   policies, taxing and, 212
   sectors, 99–100
   stream, 100
   total, 102
Spill-over effect, 195
Spinning jenny, 36
Spiral:
   inflationary, 139
   wage-price, 138
Stabilization, economic, 110, 113, 119
Stabilization policies, 115, 122–124,
   130, 152, 161, 163, 214:
   Keynesian, 126
Stable Money Association, 111
Stagflation, 117

Standard of living, 187
Standard Oil Company, 71
Standby motor fuel rationing plan, 179
State, role of, 191
Stock exchange, New York, 158
Stock market, 82–83, 138
Stock prices, 137
Strategic Petroleum Reserve, 179–180
Strip mining, 132
Structure, class, 202
Substitutes, money, 144
Substitution, 17
Supply, 130:
   aggregate, 129
   excess, 101
   money, 112–115, 120, 123, 126, 130,
      136–137, 143–146, 149, 151–152,
      164, 210, 213
   oil, 177
   role of money, 212
Supply-side economics, 128–130, 133,
   144, 163, 175–176
Supply-side problem, 148, 175, 213
Surpluses, 95, 99, 101–102, 112, 118,
   130
Surplus value, 67–68
Synfuels, 180
Synthesis, post-Keynesian, 108–109
Synthetic Fuels Corporation, 180
System:
   American economic, 214
   economic, 189–200, 212
   market, 189, 193, 203, 208

T

"Tableau Economique," 45
Talmud, 22
Tax-based Incomes Policy (TIP), 147
Tax cut:
   Kennedy, 110, 136
   proposals, 207
Taxes, 111, 113, 131, 137, 164:
   business, 215
   oil import, 181
   reduced, 208
   single, 78
   windfall profits, 181
Taxing policies, spending and, 212
Tax withdrawals, 106
Technological progress, 103
Technology, 131–132, 213:
   developments in, 204
Technostructure, 171–172